The Way of Peace

Exploring Nonviolence
for the 21st Century

Pax Christi USA

The Way of Peace

Exploring Nonviolence
for the 21st Century

Shannon McManimon

Based on the original text by Mary Lou Kownacki, OSB and Gerard Vanderhaar

Published by Pax Christi USA

The Way of Peace:
Exploring Nonviolence for the 21st Century

Editor and author, 2003 version: Shannon McManimon
Layout and design: Judy Allison
Printed by: Royal Printing, Erie, PA
Item No. 533-054

This book is based on the original *Way of Peace: A Guide to Nonviolence*
edited and authored by Gerard Vanderhaar and Mary Lou Kownacki, OSB,
published by Pax Christi USA 1987.

Copyright 2003, published by Pax Christi USA
532 W. 8th Street
Erie, Pa 16502
814-453-4955
814-452-4784 (fax)
info@paxchristiusa.org
www.paxchristiusa.org

ISBN: 0-9743804-1-5

Dedication

**To
Nancy Small
for her
leadership and witness**

Introduction

"Violence is the ethos of our times. It is the spirituality of the modern world. It has been accorded the status of a religion, demanding from its devotees an absolute obedience to death." (Walter Wink, *Engaging the Powers)*

Anyone who has been paying attention knows that ours is a world filled with violence. This violence takes many forms: poverty, abuse, environmental destruction, war, hatred. We just ended the most blood-filled century in history. Could it be that our world *has* accorded violence the status of a religion? After all, our world tells and shows us to meet violence with violence, to fight fire with fire. Violence is glorified over and over again, in the media, in our national budgets, in our methods of dealing with personal problems.

Is there a better way? Can we end the glorification of violence? Can we challenge—and change—its status and begin to live in obedience to a different way of being in the world? What might this way—which many people have called "nonviolence"—look like?

This book, attempting to answer some of these questions, is an introductory guide to the spirit and practice of nonviolence, the way of peace. It draws on the developing tradition of nonviolence in recent decades as practiced by Mohandas Gandhi and Martin Luther King, Jr. and Dorothy Day and Cesar Chavez and Lech Walesa and countless women and men in widely scattered parts of the world. All of these people experimented with another method for constructive social change, of peacemaking in the face of conflict, of an alternate way of living their personal lives.

This book is for all those who are searching for another way, for those who are intrigued about nonviolence. Pax Christi USA intends it for classroom use, for parish study, for peace groups, for people of any age, but hopes that it will be especially helpful for young people in their teens and twenties. The ten parts of the book cover a wide range of material: recognizing violence in all its forms, spirituality (especially Catholic teachings and teachers), methods and nonviolent tactics, and examples of nonviolent people and campaigns around the world. It provides many definitions and characteristics of nonviolence and looks at personal and communal ways of living nonviolently, both in our daily lives and in movements for justice and peace. It calls us to recognize and discard the illusions that peace is simply the absence of physical violence and that nonviolence is inactive and ineffective.

Hopefully exploration of this book will lead to personal reflection on many themes but will also stimulate some lively conversation. Many exercises and discussion questions are included in this book, although it is not essential to complete each one to begin to understand nonviolence. While it is primarily study-based, the book contains elements of the tri-fold Pax Christi model: prayer, study, and action. In our violence-filled world, it challenges us to take initiatives for peace and to heed the words of Pope John Paul II in 1982 that "peace must be constructed patiently and with unshakable faith."

Coming from the national Catholic peace movement, this book speaks from a uniquely Catholic perspective, but others are, of course, encouraged to use it as well. It is a reminder that Catholics are called to explore nonviolence. The U.S. Catholic bishops, in their 1983 peace pastoral, *The Challenge of Peace*, wrote, "Peacemaking is not an optional commitment. It is a requirement of our faith. We are called to be peacemakers, not by some movement of the moment, but by our Lord Jesus. The content and context of our peacemaking is not set by some political agenda or ideological program, but by the teachings of his Church." (summary and conclusion) They encouraged us to find out more: "Nonviolent means of resistance to evil deserve much more study and consideration than they have thus far received." (*The Challenge of Peace*)

For Catholics or Christians, as people of faith, we must always ask what it means to be disciples of Jesus. How did Jesus respond to the violence of his time and how would he respond to the violence of ours?

The answers that we find point toward nonviolence. Jesus taught a different way and form of action and spirituality than that of his culture: "You have heard it said, 'Love your neighbor–but hate your enemy.' But I tell you, love your enemies and pray for your persecutors." (Matthew 5:43-44; see the whole of chapters 5 and 6). Today's arms race, global economic injustice, and hatred of others definitely don't encourage us to love our enemies. But Jesus continues to call us to a different response to the violence of our lives and world: to work nonviolently for peace founded in justice.

Not everyone will agree with all the contents of this book. Some parts might seem impractical or idealistic. But we believe it is solidly rooted in the gospel. It is also solidly rooted in the lives of people who have practiced nonviolence.

The intriguing tradition of nonviolence, of creating a world with peace based in justice rather than one entrenched in violence, is still in the making. It will most likely never be finished. We invite you to join the journey.

Citations:

National Council of Catholic Bishops. *The Challenge of Peace: God's Promise and Our Response. A Pastoral Letter on War and Peace.* May 3, 1983.

Wink, Walter. *Engaging the Powers: Discernment and Resistance in a World of Domination.* Minneapolis: Fortress Press, 1992.

Exploring Nonviolence

Table of Contents

Exploring Nonviolence

for the 21st Century

Part Six: Cultivating Peace in Our Daily Lives

Part Seven: Nonviolent Witnesses

Part Eight: Nonviolence in Action: Campaigns in the United States

Exploring Nonviolence

for the 21st Century

Imagine a New World

Part One

Nonviolence:
A Way to Imagine a New World

All around the world, people are dedicating their lives to nonviolence, in the hope of bringing about a new world. It is through their imaginations and their work that this new world will be born. Without the creativity and vision of countless people, prominent and unknown, men and women, younger and older, of all races, ethnicities, abilities, and sexual orientations, this dream would be just that–a dream. But because they dare to dream, dare to work for a vision they may never realize, the world is changed daily.

Recognizing the power of nonviolence and its hope for the survival of our planet, the United Nations (UN) declared 2000 the "International Year for the Culture of Peace" and the first decade of the 21st century the "Decade for a Culture of Peace and Nonviolence for the Children of the World."

It is in the same spirit that this book is re-released. May the spirit of nonviolence, already expressed by so many people–past and present–further fill our world and birth it anew for the children of today and tomorrow.

Can we imagine a more peaceful and just world?

Opening Prayer

Prayer space may contain images from nature or of people who inspire us.

Reader 1:
Loving Creator,
> Be with all of us who are beginning and continuing the way of peace.

Reader 2:
Thank you
> For the women and men who have gone before us, inspire us, and beckon us to join them
> For the beauty of creation
> For your grace and inspiration in our lives
> *Please add other prayers of thanksgiving.*

Reader 3:
Help us
> To create a place where all are loved, cherished, valued, and respected
> To begin to imagine a new world
> To live your way of peace
> *Please add other prayers.*

After a few moments of silence, Reader 1:
With the prophet Isaiah, help us to imagine a vision of your peaceful kindom, where

"The wolf shall live with the lamb,
the leopard shall lie down with the kid,
the calf and the lion and the fatling together,
and a little child shall lead them.
The cow and the bear shall graze,
their young shall lie down together;
and the lion shall eat straw like the ox.
The nursing child shall play over the hole of the asp,
and the weaned child shall put a hand on the adder's den.
They will not hurt or destroy on all my holy mountain;
for the earth will be full of the knowledge of God
as the waters cover the sea." (Isaiah 11:6-9)

We ask this in your name.

All: Amen.

Note: Prayers throughout this book are generally formatted for groups and readers indicated for different sections. Obviously, however, individuals can use the prayers as well. In some cases, it is indicated that you can add your own responses, petitions, or prayers of thanksgiving. Please also use whatever makes your space more prayerful, such as candles, an open Bible, images, or sacred objects. (Sometimes suggestions or examples precede the prayer.) It is usually helpful to take a few moments of silence before and after each prayer, to reverence the sacred time.

A Brief Overview of Practitioners and Movements of Nonviolence

While nonviolence may be receiving more attention lately, especially with the UN endorsements, it is not new. Nonviolence and its tactics have been used for thousands of years to respond to every level of violence: to assert human dignity, in refusing to go to war or to kill, to counter oppression, for protecting the earth, to demonstrate God's love.

Nonviolence has often been in response to God's call. In approximately 1350 BC, Hebrew midwives committed the first recorded act of nonviolent resistance: in honor of life and God, they refused to carry out the Pharaoh's order to kill all Hebrew baby boys (Exodus 1:15-22). Later, Jesus and the first Christians nonviolently refused to worship the emperor and to serve in war. Other Christians, such as St. Benedict and St. Francis, espoused nonviolence. Peace churches such as the Mennonites, Quakers (Religious Society of Friends), and Brethren furthered concepts of nonviolence.

While nonviolence has often been a religious conviction, it has been a secular one as well. It has also expanded beyond a refusal to kill. In the 20th century, people all around the world saw nonviolence as relevant to organized movements for social change. People have employed nonviolent tactics for social, political, humanitarian, philosophical, and economic reasons, as well as religious.

It was in the 20th century that the word nonviolence itself first appeared. Earlier terms used by labor organizers, slavery abolitionists, and others included "nonresistance," "passive resistance," "moral force," and "nonviolent resistance."

Hundreds of examples of pragmatic and philosophically-based nonviolence exist; following is an extremely brief history of some of the significant nonviolent acts, names, and movements. As you will see, we are not the first social change activists to explore nonviolence. (Many other books document these movements; see the resources section to learn more. Parts Eight and Nine also chronicle many of these movements and provide more details.)

In the United States

Nonviolence has a long history on and many ties to the North American continent. Indigenous people practiced nonviolence in what we now call the United States long before Europeans colonized it. Stephen Zunes, Lester Kurtz, and Sarah Beth Asher report estimates that over half of the North American population of European ancestry is directly descended from people who fled Europe to resist the violence of military conscription. Furthermore, the colonists used some tactics of nonviolence in their attempts to end British rule.

In the 19th century, this work, often in the form of education, letter-writing, and publishing, expanded. Organizations such as the New England Non-Resistance Society and the League of Universal Brotherhood and individuals such as the abolitionist William Lloyd Garrison worked for peace and social change. The abolition movement widely used nonviolence to advocate an end to slavery. The Underground Railroad, most often associated with Harriet Tubman, is an example. Abolitionists such as Sojourner Truth felt that violence would not help in their struggle because it would not end hatred; instead, people needed to undergo a moral change. In 1846, Henry David Thoreau, a famous author, spent a night in jail for refusing to pay taxes to support the Mexican War. Toward the end of the century, the women's and labor movements used nonviolent principles.

In the early 20th century, international war became a primary focus. With the start of World War I, groups such as the Women's Peace Party, the American Union Against Militarism, the People's Council of America, the Fellowship of Reconciliation (FOR), the American Friends Service Committee (AFSC), the Women's International League for Peace and Freedom (WILPF), and the Anti-Enlistment League (and the War Resisters' League after the war) advocated alternatives to violence (one being conscientious objection). While this focus continued throughout the century, the mostly religious stand against war broadened extensively to include other areas of injustice and to seek to establish a constructive philosophy for action and justice. In 1932, the WILPF, in support of the World Disarmament Conference, organized a Peace Caravan that stopped in 125 cities from Hollywood, CA, to Washington, DC. During World War II, many men (and women, although they were not drafted) objected to the war, refused to cooperate, and undertook strikes and boycotts. In prison, many of these men extended their witness to include not only war, but other issues, such as the racial injustice and segregation of the prison system.

In the mid-20th century, people of color used nonviolence–boycotts, mass demonstrations, marches, sit-ins, and freedom rides–to obtain civil rights, such as voting, school opportunities, and access to public facilities. James Farmer, Ella Baker, Bayard Rustin, Martin Luther King, Jr., and thousands of others were active in groups such as the Congress of Racial Equality (CORE), the Southern Christian Leadership Conference (SCLC), and the Student Nonviolent Coordinating Committee (SNCC). Opposition to the U.S. war in Vietnam also provoked an outpouring of nonviolence. Farm workers, through the union United Farm Workers of America, used strikes and boycotts of grapes and lettuce as well as other tactics to gain labor rights. Beginning in the 1970s, the anti-nuclear and environmental movements gained strength. For instance, people sailed ships into nuclear test zones to protest these weapons. Greenpeace actions incorporated new elements of direct action to save the environment. In June of 1982, 750,000 people gathered in New York City to demonstrate for disarmament. The Sanctuary movement in the 1980s used nonviolence to protect people fleeing wars in Central America and other campaigns such as the Pledge of Resistance also vowed to work against U.S. violence in Central America. The last decade of the century saw massive nonviolent grassroots efforts to end the sanctions on Iraq, to close the U.S. Army School of the Americas, to stop police brutality, to end corporate greed and domination, to gain rights for people living with HIV and AIDS, and to end hate violence. This new century has seen nonviolence play a significant role in the anti-globalization movement and in

Sojourner Truth

the response to the attacks of September 11, 2001, by groups like September 11th Families for Peaceful Tomorrows, family members of victims of those attacks who have spoken out eloquently against military solutions to terrorism.

Devere Allen, Jeannette Rankin, Jessie Wallace Hughan, Evan and Norman Thomas, AJ Muste, Dorothy Day, Jane Addams, Barbara Deming, and others wrote, lived, and taught about nonviolence. Countless groups dedicated to nonviolence, such as the Peacemakers, the Committee for Nonviolent Action, Vietnam Veterans Against the War (VVAW), and Veterans for Peace (VFP), have existed, many of which are still around today. The struggles of people of color, women, people with disabilities, and

"The peace movement knows that there is something fundamentally evil about this society . . . one comes to know the seriousness of the situation and to realize it's not going to be changed just by demonstrations. It's a question of risking one's life. It's a question of living one's life in drastically different ways." **–Dorothy Day, 1975**

lesbians, gay men, bisexual and trans-gendered persons have helped to clarify dominance and have led to new movements and alliances. People have come to the realization that nonviolence can apply to all aspects of life and that nonviolence is a lifestyle that requires commitment and courage but one which can be profoundly transformational.

All Around the World

In other parts of the world, people have thought, written, and acted on nonviolence. For example, the writings of the Russian author, Leo Tolstoy, have been very influential. In the latter half of the 19th century, nonviolent resistance to war and occupation occurred in Hungary, France, and Finland.

In the 20th century, nonviolence was often used in response to invasion or domination, both from within and outside a country. India's movement (1930s and 1940s) to be free of British colonial rule, with the leadership of people such as Mohandas Gandhi, Vinoba Bhave, and Abdul Ghaffar Khan, took nonviolence to a new level. Nonviolent resistance to Nazi occupation occurred in World War II (1940s) in such countries as Bulgaria, Denmark, Finland, and Nor-

way. In El Salvador (1944), nationwide strikes forced a military dictator to flee the country. In South Africa (1980s), Blacks and sympathetic whites, with the leadership of young people such as Mkhuseli Jack and "elders" such as Desmond Tutu, used largely nonviolent tactics to overcome the brutal system of apartheid (race-based discrimination). The people of Central and South America, in the grip of cruel dictatorships, utilized nonviolent means to resist these governments and to demand an end to war (1970s and 1980s). In the late 1980s and early 1990s, nonviolent movements led to the fall of unjust governments in the Philippines, many republics of the former Soviet Union, Haiti, and elsewhere. The struggle continues today in Burma/Myanmar (Aung San Suu Kyi is a principle figure) and other countries.

Often, the struggle for a more just form of government goes hand in hand with the struggle for human rights. This was certainly the case in Central and South America, where the people demanded not only an end to war, but also to human rights violations and to an unfair distribution of land, resources, and power. For instance, *Las Madres de la Plaza de Mayo* (Mothers of the May Plaza) in Argentina demonstrated every week (even though public demonstrations were forbidden), filed petitions, marched, and held prayer services, demanding to know what had happened to the people who had been disappeared. In El Salvador, Archbishop Oscar Romero preached nonviolence and love and was assassinated for these ideals. In Poland (1980s), Lech Walesa and the Solidarity trade union movement gained labor rights and eventually a new government.

These movements continue today. At the end of the century, thousands of families in Brazil, Honduras, and elsewhere are part of a movement to reclaim land from the rich and the powerful so that they may feed their families. In Mexico, *Las Abejas* (the Bees) continue to work nonviolently for social change, even after paramilitaries massacred 45 of their members at a peace prayer service in Acteal in December 1997. They ask simply for their basic rights: a life with peace, justice, and dignity for their children and the right to live without fear. In other countries, such as El Salvador and Colombia (home of the *Movimiento de* los *Niños* and *las Niñas por la Paz*–the Children's Movement for Peace), young people have vocally renounced violence and are reviving traditions of nonviolence and culture to affect change. Around the world, people are creating "Zones of Peace," striving to break free of violence and oppression. Peace education efforts are underway.

The anti-nuclear movement continues to have a presence around the world as well. Women in England, opposed to the hosting of nuclear weapons in their country, began holding a vigil outside of Greenham Commons in 1981. Mordechai Vanunu gained prominence because he publicly exposed Israel's secret nuclear weapons program, was kidnapped by the Israeli government, and has been imprisoned since speaking out in 1985, spending most of this time in solitary confinement.

Today with the rapid expansion of communication, people are more aware than ever of the struggles of others around the world for peace and justice. Thus people in Australia are able to support the nonviolent struggles of activists in Nigeria and Thailand. U.S. activists support the people of East Timor and Tibet. In fact in many struggles, the inspiration to start or to continue nonviolent resistance has come from the example and stories of other struggles around the world.

Gandhi

"AS USUAL, morning came, as it has for the last two thousand years. The sunlight blended with the *tzotzil* candles recently lit anew. Far from being uprooted, faith has been pruned and is reborn in the illuminated hands of the faithful.

They had been massacred and injured. There were fifty orphans, hundreds of tormented people, thousands dispossessed to this day, millions who were outraged and affronted. Twilight came on, and–as they shared the bread and ate the tortilla, served the wine and enjoyed the coffee–[brother- and sisterhood] flourished.

The miracle of living is being celebrated with burning flames in hearts of peace who build justice, who join together in their respect of human rights, who are the ferment of social transformation."

–Pedro Arriaga Alarcón, priest with *Las Abejas* (*The Bees*), Chiapas, Mexico, 1998.

Questions:

What has led you to explore nonviolence at this point in your life?

Do you know of other groups working to create a nonviolent world? What are they trying to accomplish?

Imagine a New World

Our Voices

Today it is evident that violence exists in our world (Its forms will be explored further in Part Two). In the face of overwhelming and catastrophic violence, what good can we possibly do?

First we must acknowledge that all of us are in some ways part of and cooperate with systems of violence. We must ask forgiveness and repentance for this. Then we must work to change both ourselves and those systems. Each of us has contributions to make in bringing about a new world filled with nonviolence, love, and justice. Hopefully, this book will give us direction or ideas about how to do this.

We do not know where this path will lead us. Martin Luther King, Jr., for instance, today known as a great teacher and leader, never imagined himself leading a movement. Yet nothing matters more than learning to live more gently. As writer and teacher of nonviolence Colman McCarthy stated, "The earth is too small a star and we too brief a visitor upon it for anything to matter more than the struggle for peace." Every action, every word, every step that we take in this direction helps.

"Nothing could be worse than fear that one has given up too soon and left one effort unexpended which might have saved the world."

–Jane Addams, Nobel Peace Price 1931

"TELL ME the weight of a snowflake," a coal-mouse asked a wild dove.

"Nothing more than nothing," was the answer.

"In that case, I must tell you a marvelous story," the coal-mouse said.

"I sat on the branch of a fir, close to its trunk, when it began to snow–not heavily, not in a raging blizzard–no, just like in a dream, without a sound and without any violence. Since I did not have anything better to do, I counted the snowflakes settling on the twigs and needles of my branch. Their number was exactly 3,741,952. When the 3,741,953rd dropped onto the branch–nothing more than nothing as you say–the branch broke off."

Having said that, the coal-mouse flew away.

The dove, since Noah's time an authority on the matter, thought about the story for awhile and finally said to herself, "Perhaps there is only one person's voice lacking for peace to come to the world."

–Kurt Kauter

Questions:

As you continue your study and reflections on nonviolence, think about how your life, words, and actions, which may seem like "nothing more than nothing," make a positive difference or negatively impact other people and the earth.

Do you agree with Colman McCarthy's statement? Why or why not?

Criticism of Nonviolence

Many people don't understand or believe in nonviolence or in the power of our united efforts. One of the most frequent criticisms used to dismiss nonviolence is that it doesn't work. This criticism is true–sometimes. Four factors are important to point out: 1) violence doesn't always work, either; 2) even when nonviolence doesn't "work," it (hopefully) doesn't lead to further unwanted suffering (although those who practice nonviolence are willing to undertake personal suffering so that the suffering of others may be relieved); 3) sometimes the results may not come for a long time–perhaps decades; 4) nonviolence has only very rarely had the dedication and commitment of thousands of people, unlike military strategies.

The third and fourth points have received increasing attention. Historian Theodore Roszak wrote,–"People try nonviolence for a week and when it doesn't 'work' they go back to violence, which hasn't worked for centuries."

Nonviolence, like anything else, isn't easy. Nonviolence requires discipline, preparation, commitment, analysis, training, and knowledge. It requires a burning commitment and a desire for change, as well as a realization that change can be a very long process. It usually works best when practiced in community, when many people together are dedicated to the philosophy and practice of nonviolence.

Question:

What criticisms of nonviolence do you have?

Creative Responses

Nonviolence begins with an attitude and a vision. Although we may not be quite able to envision a whole new world, we can attempt to bring it about each day. Practitioners of nonviolence are not looking to modify systems of violence–to make war more just, for instance–but to transform the world, to create a new system. This will take great creativity on our part.

This is one of the most exciting aspects of nonviolence: it allows for–even demands–creativity. In time, nonviolence is still relatively unexplored, allowing for new ideas and action. Through creative action, we can demonstrate that nonviolence does work.

Sometimes though, we do not focus in the right direction. Michael Nagler, chair of the Peace and Conflict Studies Program at the University of California-Berkeley and a teacher, author and researcher of nonviolence for over 25 years, spoke of the nonviolent journey in this way: "I am constantly reminded of a cartoon that showed a prisoner staring wistfully through the bars of his cell at the flowers and trees and sunshine and people outside, not realizing that the cell had no back wall. We could walk out of the violence trap if we only realized that it is possible to do so, if we could learn to turn around." It takes looking at the world in new and creative ways and then acting on those possibilities.

Nonviolence requires a further form of

Following in the footsteps of nonviolent visionaries, we can work together to create new systems, to live with joy, and to bring God's love and reconciliation into the world.

dedication and creativity. People often talk about using nonviolence in conflict situations. However, as people of nonviolence, we cannot live solely "in opposition." While it may seem that there is so much violence, hate, and misuse of power in the world that we could spend our whole lives, day in and day out, protesting systems of domination, we must also voice a new way. In addition to responding differently to conflict, to working on negotiating, to using strategies of nonviolence, and possibly to committing civil disobedience (all themes explored in later chapters), we must also act positively, by living out a vision of God's Just Kindom. People concerned about the environment, for instance, should not only protest corporate waste and practices that harm the earth, but they should also buy locally, reduce consumption, and plant trees.

Through our words, actions, behavior, and lifestyle, we can demonstrate a new way of being in the world. Following in the footsteps of nonviolent visionaries, we can work together to create new systems, to live with joy, and to bring God's love and reconciliation into the world. By living positively, our lives themselves are an answer to those who deny the power of nonviolence. Throughout the remaining chapters, keep this thought in mind, especially as you read examples of people who are attempting to live positively.

PERHAPS ONE of the people who most explored the connections between creativity (in the form of art), faith, and ideas of justice was Fritz Eichenberg, a frequent contributor to *The Catholic Worker*. In a 1952 pamphlet, Eichenberg wrote, "We must recapture what we have lost; we must fight for our faith, fight our way back to God. We must become creative again, whole again, and aware of our responsibility as architects of a new moral order. . .We have to mend our ways and try to bring order into chaos, piece the fragments together, become whole again, holy again. We must go back to creative work and significant play, we must drop all empty substitutes. . . ." Eichenberg and many others believe that it is not enough to live nonviolently and gently, that we must also create. This can take many forms. For Eichenberg it was art. Fyodor Dostoyevsky went even further and said, "The world will be saved by beauty." What gifts of creativity can you share with the world?

1001 Uses for a [Disarmed] Submarine

The U.S. military is one of the world's greatest sources of violence. While it supposedly exists for our protection, in actuality it is very destructive for our country and our world in many ways. First and most obviously, the military exists to fight wars, the greatest outward expression of violence. Even when not at war, the military is responsible for much environmental damage. The military is also harmful for young people when it tracks them into certain types of jobs, forces them to learn to kill, and denies them rights that other U.S. citizens have. The energy and creative power that get channeled into the military are enormous: two-thirds of scientists and engineers in the U.S. work for defense contractors or on defense contracts in science and industry. (Center for Defense Information, 1998)

The military budget consumes enormous financial resources. Rather than building human potential and taking care of human needs such as education, jobs, housing, and health care, the United States spends hundreds of billions of dollars each year on the military–adding up to trillions of dollars in a decade. This is, in itself, violence. For the amount of money that it costs for 6500 of the U.S.'s nuclear weapons (about 1/3 of the current total), we could hire 425,000 teachers for our young people. (Business Leaders for Sensible Priorities)

Submarines are a great expenditure for the military. Currently, the U.S. has 18 Trident submarines which each carry 24 missiles. This fleet thus carries 50 % of the US's strategic warheads. The nuclear weapons aboard these submarines are each 100 Kilotons (the bomb dropped on Hiroshima was 12.5 Kilotons). (Center for Defense Information) There is enough nuclear power aboard these ships to destroy our planet. For the cost ($2.3 billion) of another type of submarine, the Seawolf, we could send millions of children to Head Start. (Business Leaders for Sensible Priorities) The U.S. is planning to build more of these submarines, despite the fact that they were designed to fight a now-defunct Soviet submarine and despite the fact that the U.S. already has the most lethal submarines in the world.

In order to address this tremendous violence, we need to use our creativity. We must be able first to devise other, non-military solutions to the world's problems. And we must, in the words of Isaiah (2:4), turn swords into plowshares and spears into pruning hooks, turning from harm to construction.

Here are some potential uses (humorous, of course) of a decommissioned submarine:

(Drawings by Bill Livermore)

INNER-CITY REC CENTER

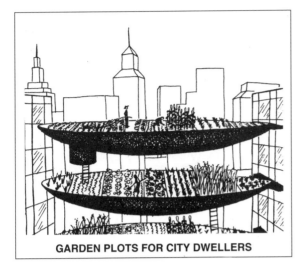

GARDEN PLOTS FOR CITY DWELLERS

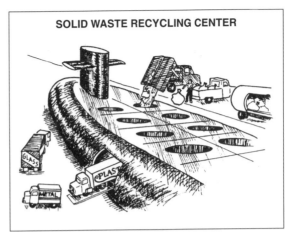

SOLID WASTE RECYCLING CENTER

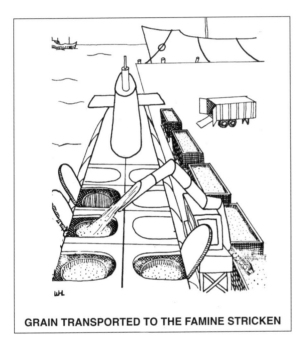

GRAIN TRANSPORTED TO THE FAMINE STRICKEN

ECUMENICAL PEACE CATHEDRAL

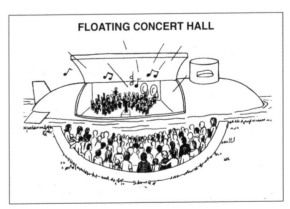

FLOATING CONCERT HALL

Questions:

Draw and/or write a description of another use of a disarmed submarine, missile, or bomber.

Do you think that it is possible to create something good out of something whose main purpose is destruction?

A New World:
The Dream and Hope of Nonviolence

Sometimes it is easy to get stuck in the ways and violence of today's world. We have a hard time imagining that things could be different, that weapons of war and hatred can be turned into tools of creation and equality. But to bring about a new world, we must be creative in imagining how our lives and society should be. Through our dreams and hopes of a better world, we begin its creation.

What is the dream and hope of nonviolence? What are your dreams and hopes for our world and for the children of the world?

While each person's hopes and dreams may differ, there are probably some common themes. As nonviolent people, we should hope to create a future in which all people are treated with respect and dignity and in which we care for the earth that nurtures us.

In Robert Muller's dream, humans recognize the unity and equality of all peoples, work for peaceful solutions to problems, respect the environment, protect human rights, constantly better ourselves, and as Christians, love and honor God.

The New Genesis   by Robert Muller

And God saw that all nations of the Earth, black and white, poor and rich, from North and South, from East and West, and of all creeds were sending their emissaries to a tall glass house on the shores of the River of the Rising Sun, on the island of Manhattan, to study together, to think together and to care together for the world and all its people. And God said: that is good. And it was the first day of the New Age of the Earth.

And God saw that soldiers of peace were separating the combatants of quarrelling nations, that differences were being resolved by negotiation and reason instead of arms, and that the leaders of nations were seeing each other, talking to each other and joining their hearts, minds, souls and strength for the benefit of all humanity. And God said: that is good. And it was the second day of the Planet of Peace.

And God saw that humans were loving the whole Creation, the stars and the sun, the day and the night, the air and the oceans, the earth and the waters, the fishes and the fowl, the flowers and the herbs, and all their human brothers and sisters. And God said: that is good. And it was the third day of the Happy Planet.

And God saw that humans were suppressing hunger, disease, ignorance and suffering all over the globe, providing each human person with a decent, conscious and happy life, and reducing the greed, the power and the wealth of the few. And God said: that is good. And it was the fourth day of the Planet of Justice.

And God saw that humans were living in harmony with their planet and in peace with one another, wisely managing their resources, avoiding waste, curbing excesses, replacing hatred with love, greed with contentment, arrogance with humility, division with cooperation, and mistrust with understanding. And God said: that is good. And it was the fifth day of the Golden Planet.

And God saw that people were destroying their arms, bombs, missiles, warships and warplanes, dismantling their bases and disbanding their armies, keeping only policemen of peace to protect the good from the bad and the normal from the mad. And God said: that is good. And it was the sixth day of the Planet of Reason.

And God saw humans restore God and the human person as the Alpha and Omega, reducing institutions, beliefs, politics, governments and all human entities to mere servants of God and the people. And God saw them adopt as their supreme law: "You shall love the Lord your God with all your heart, all your soul, all your mind and all your strength. You shall love your neighbor as yourself. There is no greater commandment than these." And God said: that is good. And it was the seventh day of the Planet of God.

Question:

Imagine what God saw and did on the eighth day. Write and draw it.

Closing Prayer

All:

God, Creator of all life, we gather before you now in awe. You have created a world filled with blessings. We ask that you help us to treat that world and its people with respect. Remind us continually of the beauty that surrounds us. Walk with us as we learn about and follow the paths of peace. Help us to reach out to each other in love.

Reader:

"Because of our faith in Christ and in humankind, we must apply our humble efforts to the construction of a more just and humane world. And I want to declare emphatically: Such a world is possible. To create this new society, we must present outstretched, friendly hands, without hatred, without rancor–even as we show great determination, never wavering in the defense of truth and justice. Because we know that seeds are not sown with clenched fists. To sow we must open our hands."

Adolfo Pérez Esquivel, Nobel Peace Prize recipient, 1980

Silence for reflection

Response *(by all)*: **Help us to sow the seeds of justice and peace.**

Side 1: In a world crying out for love but still filled with too much hatred and violence,
Response.
Side 2: In a country that speaks of equality but often fails to live up to that promise,
Response.
Side 1: In our communities in which some people are considered worth less than others,
Response
Side 2: In our churches where we often neglect Jesus' teachings of compassion,
Response.
Side 1: In our families when words or deeds hurt each other,
Response.
Side 2: In ourselves, when we are tempted by the world to desire more and to neglect what really matters,
Response.

All join hands.

Reader:

Jesus, we gather with you, hoping and dreaming, with hands held open to each other as we journey. We pray that you help us to follow in your footsteps and in the footsteps of those who have gone before us, determined to create a new world based on your justice. Walk with us each step of the way, opening our hands to sow seeds for a better tomorrow. In your name, we pray,

All: Amen.

Part One: Reflections

1. Why are you using this book? What do you hope to gain?

2. Practitioners and movements of nonviolence imagine a new world. Can you imagine a peaceful, just, nonviolent world? If not, why not? What prevents you from doing so?

3. What kind of world would you like to see? Make a list of words that would describe it or draw a picture that reveals this vision. Do you know of a song, poem, or quote that captures this hope and dream?

4. Think of three actions that you could take that might help a new world become real or at least more possible.

5. What do you already know about or have questions, concerns, or difficulties about regarding nonviolence?

Suggestions for Action

- Read about a nonviolent struggle for justice and peace (some suggested resources below). Share your knowledge.

- Learn about, join, and/or start a group working to bring peace, whether locally, regionally, nationally, or internationally. For instance, Pax Christi USA has information on starting campus and local groups. Other organizations do as well.

- Begin to dream and hope a new vision for the world. Dreaming and hoping may not seem like much of an action, but if we cannot dream it, it will not be.

- When you hear someone advocating violence as a solution, think of other ways of resolving the situation. If you are comfortable, share these ideas by talking with people in your community, writing letters to national or world leaders, or in other ways.

A Sampling of Sources and Resources

On the History of Nonviolence:

Ackerman, Peter and Jack DuVall. A Force More Powerful: A Century of Nonviolent Conflict. New York: St. Martin's Press, 2000. (Profiles 6 movements (India's independence from Great Britain; resistance to the Nazis in Denmark in World War II; Civil Rights Movement in Nashville, Tennessee; the Solidarity movement in Poland; ending apartheid in South Africa; and the overthrow of a dictatorship in Chile). The 3-hour video by Steve York premiered on PBS, September 2000.)

Cooney, Robert and Helen Michalowski, eds. The Power of the People: Active Nonviolence in the United States. Philadelphia: New Society Publishers, 1987. (Pictorial encyclopedia of nonviolent struggles in the United States, roots, peace churches, organizations.)

Laffin, Arthur J. and Anne Montgomery, eds. Swords Into Plowshares: Nonviolent Direct Action for Disarmament, Peace, Social Justice. Marion, SD: Fortkamp Publishing/Rose Hill Books, 1996.

Lynd, Staughton and Alice Lynd, eds. Nonviolence in America: A Documentary History. Maryknoll, NY: Orbis Books, 1995. (Documents from and brief background on nonviolent leaders and movements from the 17th through the 20th centuries.)

McAllister, Pam. You Can't Kill the Spirit. Philadelphia: New Society Publishers, 1988. (Women and nonviolence.)

O'Gorman, Angie, ed. The Universe Bends Toward Justice: Reader on Christian Nonviolence in the U.S. Philadelphia: New Society Publishers, 1990.

Zunes, Stephen, Lester R. Kurtz, and Sarah Beth Asher, eds. *Nonviolent Social Movements: A Geographical Perspective*. Malden, MA: Blackwell Publishers, 1999. (Mostly covers movements other than in the United States; includes a general overview, the Middle East, Europe, Asia, Africa, Latin America, and an overview of nonviolence in the U.S.)

On Weapons Expenditures:
Business Leaders for Sensible Priorities: 1350 Broadway, Suite 2210; New York, NY 10018; phone: 212/563-9245; e-mail: TheFolks@Businessleaders.org; http://www.businessleaders.org; http://www.moveourmoney.com

Center for Defense Information: 1779 Massachusetts Avenue, NW, 6th Floor; Washington, DC 20036; phone: 202/332-0600; e-mail: info@cdi.org; http://www.cdi.org

Miscellaneous other resources of interest:
Easwaran, Sri Eknath. Nonviolent Soldier of Islam: Badshah Khan, A Man to Match His Mountains. Tomales, CA: Nilgiri Press, 1999. (On Abdul Ghaffar Khan of India and the nonviolent army "Servants of God.")

Ellsberg, Robert. Fritz Eichenberg: Works of Mercy. Maryknoll, NY: Orbis Books, 1992.

Pax Christi USA Peacemaker Pamphlet Series features small paperbacks that tell the stories of ten holy and heroic figures, for young and old readers alike. These books are long enough to give readers a thorough portrait of the lives and messages of these revered individuals, but short enough to be readable. A discussion guide comes with each set of 10. An excellent educational resource. Pax Christi USA, 532 W.8th St., Erie, PA 16502; phone: 814-453-4955 x231; e-mail: sales@paxchristiusa.org; www.paxchristiusa.org

Pax Christi USA Words of Peace–Pocket-sized books of 50 to 70 pages each, our Words of Peace series features selected writings on peace from some of the world's more prominent peacemakers. Pax Christi USA, 532 W.8th St., Erie, PA 16502; phone: 814-453-4955 x231; e-mail: sales@paxchristiusa.org; www.paxchristiusa.org

Woodcrest Bruderhof Website, section on Chiapas, contains information on Las Abejas: http://www.revolutioncenter.org

Credits

Nagler quote reprinted from *America Without Violence: Why Violence Persists and How You Can Stop It* by Michael Nagler, by permission of Island Press. Copyright 1982 by Michael N. Nagler.

Cartoons reprinted with permission from Ground Zero, published by Ground Zero Center for Nonviolent Action, 16159 Clear Creek Road NW, Poulsbo, WA 98370.

Kauter story reprinted with permission from *New Fables Thus Spoke*, "The Caribou," by Kurt Kauter.

Excerpts from *The New Genesis* by Robert Muller. Copyright 1982 by Robert Muller. Reprinted by permission of Doubleday & Company, Inc.

Reality of Violence

Part Two

The Reality of Violence

Nonviolence must be grounded in a vision based on both a hope for the future and the reality of the present. Such a worldview does not exist in a vacuum but is rather a response to our violence-filled world.

No one can disagree that we live in a violent world. Its reality is too obvious. It is evident at all levels of our experience: personal/interpersonal, national, international, and institutional. We see violence abroad and we see violence in our own country. And when we look within ourselves, we find that same demon not far beneath the surface in our own hearts.

While some of these forms of violence are easily recognized, others are more difficult to understand or identify. It is important that we learn to recognize violence in all its forms, to unmask it, and to name it for what it is.

The Reality of Violence

- *Types of Violence (Personal/Interpersonal; National; International; Institutional)*
- *Acts of Violence*
- *Interpersonal Violence*
    - *Child Abuse and Neglect*
    - *Media*
    - *Guns*
    - *Respecting Life*
- *Violence Nationally*
    - *The Death Penalty*
- *International Violence*
    - *Victims: Rwanda, Romani People*
    - *Interdependency on the World*
    - *Sweatshop and Child Labor*
    - *Nuclear Weapons*
- *Institutional Violence*
    - *Poverty*
    - *Patterns of Wealth and Distribution*
    - *Military Spending*
    - *Violence Against Those with Less Power, Such As Women, People of Color, the Environment*
- *Reflections*
- *Suggestions for Action*
- *A Sampling of Sources and Resources*
- *Credits*

Opening Prayer

A bowl of water and a piece of bread may be placed in the center of the prayer space.

Reader 1:

Oh God, you invite all the people of the world into abundant life with you. Yet too often we do not recognize that though you desire this for all your children, our actions and beliefs sometimes prevent it. Guide us to recognize all the forms that violence takes in our world. Help us to recognize how violence keeps us from you and from the greatness of your love. We know that you hear the cries of those affected by violence, those whom the world rejects, uses, and discards. Help us also to hear their cries and to live our lives in response to these cries.

Reader 2:

A reading from the prophet Isaiah (55:1-5a)

"Everyone who thirsts, come to the waters;
and you that have no money, come, buy and eat!
Come, buy wine and milk without money and without price.
Why do you spend your money for that which is not bread,
and your labor for that which does not satisfy?
Listen carefully to me,
and eat what is good, and delight yourselves in rich food.
Incline your ear, and come to me;
listen, so that you may live.
I will make with you an everlasting covenant. . . ."

Reader 1:

Teach us to listen for your voice, God, especially as it comes to us through those who are poor and cast out and those most affected by violence.

Reader 2:

Remind us of your covenant, that all are invited to share in your abundant life.

Reader 1:

Invite us to the waters.

Reader 2:

Invite all to join in the feast of your love.

All:

We pray in your name and in the name of your beloved child, Jesus, Amen.

Types of Violence

There are many types of violence. Often it is difficult to separate these types of violence from each other. This chapter will introduce and give examples of the following types of violence:

Personal/interpersonal: The way we interact with and treat ourselves and others around us. In addition to being violent towards others by lashing out verbally or physically, we can be violent to ourselves, by not taking care of our bodies or by thinking or believing that we are worthless. Such actions keep us from recognizing that God is within each of us. They deny the human worth and dignity inherent in each person.

National: Policies, practices, and actions that occur on a large scale in nations throughout the world can be violent. (This chapter gives an example from the United States.)

International: The most obvious example of international violence is war and preparations for war. (This chapter gives examples of violence in other countries, shows ways violence crosses borders, and gives a weapons example.)

Institutional: This type of violence is the violence that is rooted in and carried out by the practices and policies of our nations and world through institutions such as governments, corporations, schools, churches, and courts. It makes assumptions about the value of people, saying that some people are worth more than others because of their social, economic, or physical characteristics. Institutional violence dehumanizes by reducing persons to objects. It condemns some people to death at an early age, denies others the right to adequate housing, harms the earth that gives us life, and indulges First World consumerism. Institutional violence destroys self-worth and dignity and denies humans the ability to make decisions about their own lives. It is dangerous because these consequences are not necessarily intentional or conscious. It is also dangerous because often these types of violence are surrounded by silence and not named as violence–they are seen as just the way things are or "should be."

Examples include: racism (discrimination based on race), ageism (discrimination against people because of their age–usually the young and the elderly are affected), ableism (discrimination against people based on perceived physical differences or difficulties, such as against people who are blind or use a wheelchair), and classism (discrimination based on social and economic standing).

Forms of Violence

Some forms of violence may fit easily into one of these categories; others do not. On September 11, 2001, 19 men hijacked planes and crashed them into buildings. (Another plane crashed in central Pennsylvania.) These acts of violence, in which no "traditional" weapons–guns, bullets, or military equipment–were used, killed about 3,000 people. They were carried out mostly on civilians who happened to work or be in buildings that are symbols of U.S. military and economic power.

As the men left behind no note, no one was able to say exactly what motivated these acts. Horrendous violence, in this case, was easy to identify but not easy to understand or classify. It did lead to more violence, the U.S. bombing of Afghanistan. Did any of these multiple forms of violence make our world more safe or just?

Questions:

The acts of September 11th have been labeled terrorism.
What is your definition of terrorism?
Does it fit one of these types of violence?

Senators OK Money for "Bunker Busting" Nukes

South, North Korea Trade Shots on Border

One soldier killed, six injured in series of attacks on troops

Police seek Gang-Slaying Witnesses

Suspect arrested in assault on girl in store

Fighting Intensifies in Liberia

Seven killed in Kashmir pilgrimage explosion

Violent strike in Belfast

NAACP presents lawsuit against gun industry

Death penalty sought in Kentucky dorm fire

Father charged with murder of New Hampshire kids

Weekend inmate raped at prison

Bar fight leaves one dead, one injured

Monk killed during stand-off at monastery

Slayer faces trial in 2 apparently racial killings

Watch the national and local news for a few days.
Write a list of headlines that reflect the news.

Acts of Violence

Here are twenty-three possible acts of violence. Check the ones that fit that description for you. State the reasons for your choices.

1. a mother slaps her child

2. an alliance of countries bombs civilians in war time

3. a man rapes and beats a woman

4. security police torture prisoners to extract "vital information"

5. a woman shoots and kills her husband after fifteen years of beatings and abuse

6. two students gossip about another student

7. people, companies, and restaurants throw out 96 billion pounds of food per year in the U.S.

8. governments worldwide spent approximately $780 billion on defense and weapons compared with $80 billion on education in one year in the late 1990s

9. advertising continually uses women as sex objects to sell everything from microwave dinners to Cadillacs

10. a young person becomes addicted to alcohol

11. the defense "sacks" a quarterback and his leg is broken

12. a teacher ridicules a student publicly for a poor assignment

13. a father yells at his child for being too noisy

14. a butcher kills a cow

15. in 1999, the average CEO at a large company made 475 times the average factory worker (up from 42 times in 1980 and 85 times in 1990)

16. a dealer makes a cocaine sale at a high school

17. students in Mexico riot after months of protesting drastic increases in education costs

18. a teenage gang burns a building in the inner city

19. a person straps a bomb to him/herself and blows up a building

20. 12% of the US population lives below the federal poverty line

21. three dozen US states send people to death row to await execution

22. a multinational corporation relocates its factories to a country where wages are lower

23. New York City banks denied home mortgages twice as often to Blacks as to whites of the same income (findings of a 2000 study)

QUESTIONS:

Did you consider all of these examples violent?
Does it surprise you that some people do?
Do you think that they are all the same type of violence?
Reflect on how these examples relate to your life.

Interpersonal Violence

Child Abuse and Neglect

Life on the Street is a Dead End

Anne ran away from home because her mother wouldn't believe Anne's reports that her mother's boyfriend repeatedly tried to abuse her sexually. After taking a bus to Los Angeles, she was taken in by a nicely dressed woman for free. Treated very well until her fourth day, Anne was then expected to begin work as a prostitute. Anne later ran away once again.

The police picked up Tony as he sat on a street curb, saying he didn't want to go home. At 2 a.m., he was brought to Covenant House. Ten years old, Tony had been delivering drugs for his mother, a dealer. He tripped the metal detector and remembered that he was carrying a semi-automatic weapon with 19 bullets.

Covenant House offers hope to the 50,000 kids who come through the doors each year–a chance for a future and a belief in themselves. Covenant House shelters approximately 1400-1500 young people per year, nearly half a million since the doors opened.

- In 1998, 903,000 children were found to have been abused (physically and/or sexually) or neglected. (U.S. Department of Health and Human Services)

- More than 1000 children die in the U.S. each year from maltreatment. (U.S. Department of Health and Human Services)

- Covenant House states that 300,000 kids live on the streets. (December 1998)

Child abuse is an example of interpersonal violence–one person acting violently toward another person. Most likely, all of us witness examples of interpersonal violence daily–people yelling at each other, ridiculing each other, or abusing their own bodies. The media also brings us multitudes of examples of this form of violence.

Media

There has been a lot of debate about the effects of the media on our actions, especially on the actions of children. While hundreds of studies have found negative effects, we cannot seem to part with the violence and commercialism of our televisions. Could it be that we cannot admit these effects because the average U.S. child will spend more time in front of the television than in school by adulthood? TV can have negative effects on us both in the amount of violence we witness and the amount of time we spend watching.

- By the end of elementary school, the average U.S. child will have seen 8000 murders and 100,000 other acts of violence on television. (American Psychological Association)

- Cartoons have 20-25 violent acts per hour, versus 3-5 per hour on prime time. Cartoons usually fail to address the effects of violence. (American Academy of Pediatrics)

- The average U.S. child aged 2 - 11 spends 1197 minutes (nearly 20 hours) per week watching television and 38.5 minutes per week in meaningful conversation with a parent. (*New York Times*, December 30, 1997)

- By the time today's children reach age 70, they will have spent 7 to 10 years in front of the television. (American Academy of Pediatrics)

Questions:

Studies have shown that young children often cannot distinguish between media and real life. What effects do you think viewing the level of violence on TV has on children?

Children are often called "our hope for the future." Do these statistics demonstrate that our society treats them as such? What changes might be necessary?

Can how we choose to spend our time be in itself violent or nonviolent?

What connection, if any, do you think that there is between child abuse and media violence?

What are some other examples of interpersonal violence?

In what ways are we violent towards ourselves?

Guns

In 1996, handguns murdered

2 people in New Zealand.	106 people in Canada.
15 people in Japan.	213 people in Germany.
30 people in Great Britain.	9390 people in the United States.

* Center to Prevent Handgun Violence/Hand Gun Control

Gun violence is a prime example of interpersonal violence. Rather than attempting to solve problems with nonviolence–words, mediation, or other methods–people resort to the taking or injury of another's life.

• There are approximately 192 million privately owned firearms in the U.S., 65 million of which are handguns. (Center for the Prevention of Handgun Violence/Handgun Control)

• A 1998 study found that there is a gun in 43% of households with children. (Handgun Control)

• In 1998, firearms killed 30,708 people in the United States–a significant drop from previous years. (National Center for Health Statistics)

• The rate of firearm deaths for children ages 0-14 is 12 times higher in the U.S. than in 25 other industrialized nations combined. (Center for Disease Control and Prevention)

• In the 1990s, the number of children who died from gunfire was between 10 and 16 per day (averaged each year). (Children's Defense Fund)

Questions:

Do you or someone in your household own a gun? Do you think many people in your neighborhood own guns? Does this make you feel safer or less safe? Why?

You may have heard the saying, "Guns don't kill people; people kill people." How do the above statistics reflect this position? Why do you think we in the U.S. have such a problem with gun violence?

Respecting Life

Catholic social teaching promotes the concept of a "consistent life ethic." This idea is very important to nonviolence as well. It means that we respect life at all times, from "the womb to the tomb." As evidenced by our epidemic of gun violence, we, as a society, do not do this.

What are some other ways that this plays out? Often, it means that the most vulnerable in our society–the very young, the poor, the ill, the elderly–are accorded little respect. To attempt to live a life of nonviolence, we must respect all life.

For many Catholics, the idea of a consistent life ethic has meant examining many structures in our society–and discovering that our society does not hold this value.

Violence Nationally

The Death Penalty

Lack of respect for life in our country is demonstrated by the U.S.'s use of the death penalty. The death penalty (also known as capital punishment) has the support of the majority of people in the United States. It may seem, on the surface, to be a way to prevent crime and to combat violence. However, studies show that this is not the case and that the system is inherently flawed and biased against people who are poor and people of color.

On a more basic level, it is violent. The Reverend Jimmy Oreech, a United Methodist minister, said, "The death penalty is also clear evidence that we have lost our struggle with violence, that we have been seduced by violence." Using or threatening to use the death penalty says that violence is a solution to violence, rather than addressing the causes of violence (or what would lead someone to take another person's life).

Many religions, including the Catholic Church, have spoken out against the death penalty, as have people working to reform the criminal justice system and other activists. In 1974, the Catholic bishops declared their opposition to the death penalty "out of a commitment to the value and dignity of human life." They wrote that we are to encourage respect for life, preserve human dignity, and demonstrate Christ's message of love and salvation. Many people see the death penalty as what people who commit terrible crimes of violence deserve. Yet the bishops wrote, "We do not believe more deaths are the response to the question."

One glaring example of how the death penalty violates human dignity is the execution of minors, sometimes too young when sentenced to comprehend their crimes fully. Amnesty International reports that there are only six countries in the world known to have executed juvenile offenders in the 1990s: Iran, Nigeria, Pakistan, Saudi Arabia, Yemen and the U.S. The U.S. has executed more people who committed crimes while under age 18 than the other five countries *combined* and is the only country to have done so since 1997. As of January 2000, some 70 juveniles were on death row. Like the majority of the 4000 people on death row, they were mostly men of color and most of their victims were white.

Why
do we kill people
who kill people
to show that
killing people is wrong
?

Questions:

What is your opinion on the death penalty?

Why do you think that so many people believe that it is the answer to violent crime?

What questions does the death penalty raise about violence?

A Prayer to Abolish the Death Penalty

God of Compassion,

You let your rain fall on the just and the unjust.

Expand and deepen our hearts

so that we may love as You love,

even those among us

who have caused the greatest pain by taking life.

For there is in our land a great cry for vengeance

as we fill up death rows and kill the killers

in the name of justice, in the name of peace.

Jesus, our brother,

you suffered execution at the hands of the state

but you did not let hatred overcome you.

Help us to reach out to victims of violence

so that our enduring love may help them heal.

Holy Spirit of God,

You strengthen us in the struggle for justice.

Help us to work tirelessly

for the abolition of state-sanctioned death

and to renew our society in its very heart

so that violence will be no more.

Amen.

Helen Prejean, CSJ

International Violence

Victims

Rwanda

The Rwandan killings of 1994 are the first genocide officially recognized by the United Nations since the end of World War II. In just three months, ethnic Hutus killed 800,000 ethnic Tutsis–over one-third (300,000) were children. Later, after the Tutsi-led forces declared victory in the country, between 1 and 2 million Hutus fled the country. Approximately 114,000 children were lost or separated from their families.

This genocide does not exist in a vacuum, however. Other forms of violence preceded it. Rwanda, heavily dependent upon coffee exports, had extreme difficulties when the coffee market crashed. The country turned to the International Monetary Fund (IMF) for assistance. (When countries make deals with the IMF, they usually have to restructure their economies and take other measures that often end up hurting the people.) The aid Rwanda received went largely toward the purchase of weapons. With privatization, famine, and the use of loan money for arms, the people fell into desperate situations. Rwandans of different ethnic backgrounds also belonged to different social classes; this class system had been used to divide the people.

A comprehensive study of the genocide, *Rwanda: Death, Despair, and Defiance*, published by African Rights in 1995, tells the story of a 13-year-old girl who survived, "I tried to get up but it was in vain. I was very weak from my injuries and there were so many bodies everywhere that you could hardly move. A few children, perhaps because they are unaware of the dangers, stood up. I called one of the children to help me. She was a girl of about nine. She replied that she couldn't help me because they had cut off her arms. I struggled and managed to sit up. But what I could not do was stand up.

Finally I saw a young woman I knew, a neighbor. I called out to her. At first she does not answer. I insisted and she finally responded. When I looked closely, I saw that she too had had her arms cut off. By now I don't know if what I am feeling and seeing is real life or a nightmare. I asked her if it was real life or a nightmare. She confirmed that it was real."

Romani people

The Roma (more commonly known as Gypsies) are one of, if not the, world's most hated minorities. Roma, a nomadic people who live constantly with discrimination and negative stereotypes, reside primarily in Central and Eastern Europe. While official estimates state that there may be as few as 2.3 million Roma in Europe, the Minority Rights Group estimates that there may be as many as 8.6 million. The following is just one of many examples of the horrible violence directed at the Romani people.

"In central Slovakia, in July 1995, Romani teen-ager Mario Goral was attacked by a group of skinheads in Ziar nad Hronom. Following an evening roaming the city and beating, threatening, and cursing Roma, as well as throwing Molotov cocktails at a pub frequented by Roma, skinheads captured Goral, doused him with gasoline and polystyrene, and set him on fire. The mixture coats the victim's skin and makes extinguishing the flames more difficult and the burns deeper. Goral died ten days later."

–Petrova, Dimitrina. "Get Out, You Stinking Gypsy: Dawn police raids, random beatings, mob violence, and other staples of Romani life." *Transitions*, Vol. 4, No. 4, September 1997. (Petrova is from the European Roma Rights Center.)

Question:

After reading these accounts, how do you feel?.

Reality of Violence

Interdependency on the World

"Before you finish breakfast this morning, you've depended on more than half the world. This is the way our universe is structured . . . we aren't going to have peace on earth until we recognize this basic fact of the interrelated structure of all reality."

–Martin Luther King, Jr.

(Television): Assembled in **China**. Workers, mostly young women, assembling televisions, work 7 days a week for over 16 hours per day in the busy season. With overtime wages, they make 29 cents an hour.

(Pencil): Graphite from **Madagascar**. 72% of the population lives on $1 or less per day.

(Cement): Cement from **Kenya**. Only 30% of the people living in rural Kenya have access to safe water.

(Power): Electricity from coal mined in **West Virginia**. 88% of the state's schools are in need of significant repair; 20% of its adults cannot read; over 17% of its people have no health insurance; nearly 28% of its children live in poverty.

(Food): Bananas and pineapples from **Guinea**, where only 36% of people (and only 22% of women) can read and write. Only half of the country's young people are in school; slightly over one-third of the girls attend school.

(Coffee): Coffee from the **Democratic Republic of Congo**, where the infant mortality rate is over 10%. The DRC struggles under foreign debts of over $14 billion, well over 20 % of its Gross National Product.

(Food): Fruit from **Guatemala**. Children here often fare poorly: only 50% reach the fifth grade. In rural areas, 57% of those under age 5 have stunted growth. 75% of Guatemalans live in poverty, without access to adequate nutrition.

(Sugar and newsprint): Among **Bangladesh**'s exports are sugar and newsprint. This country, in which half of the children have low birth weights, must import food grains.

(Rubber): Rubber is among **Cameroon**'s many exports but the country must import foodstuffs and used clothing. Cameroon, like many countries, has been forced by international pressures both to export to and borrow from wealthy countries. It has been forced to change its economy in ways that have harmed, not helped, the people of the country. In 1996-1997, 4% of Cameroon's spending went toward basic social services while 36% went towards paying for debts owed to wealthy countries.

(Toys): **Haiti** manufactures many toys, but its own children and people struggle to survive. Less than one-quarter of the population has access to safe sanitation; flush toilets and sewage systems are almost nonexistent. Only 3% of the children in rural areas complete school. Over one-third of the country–2.4 million people–resides in urban slums.

(Furniture): Teak furniture from **Honduras**, which has extensive forest and mineral resources. It is, however, one of the poorest and least developed countries in Latin America, made worse by the devastation of Hurricane Mitch in 1998. Widespread slash-and-burn agriculture contributes to the destruction of its forests.

(Clothes): Manufactured in **Lesotho**. As in much of Sub-Saharan Africa, AIDS is ripping Lesotho apart: 25% of the women and 10% of the men ages 15-24 are HIV positive. (Rates of infection in the U.S. are 0.2% and 0.5%, respectively.)

(Lamp): Tungsten filament from **Bolivia**. A child born in the U.S. will consume and pollute more in her or his lifetime than 40 children born in developing countries.

Sweatshop and Child Labor

The examples from the previous page—such as food we eat and materials for building and products—show our dependency on products and services from around the world. In order to produce these goods, many children and adults slave away under abusive conditions—brutal, demanding work for next to no pay:

- The International Labor Organization, the UN specialized agency which seeks the promotion of internationally recognized human and labor rights, estimates that 250 million children between the ages of 5 and 14 are working in developing countries. (UNICEF 2000)

- Press for Change's Jeff Ballinger (also a Harvard University professor) pointed out in the early 1990s that an Indonesian Nike factory worker would have to make Nike shoes for over 44,000 years in order to earn what Michael Jordan got from the shoemaker in 1991 for advertisements. In 1994, Ballinger stated that merely 1 % of Nike's annual ad budget would raise 12,000 young Indonesian women making Nike shoes above the poverty line.

- This problem has truly become global: New York City has approximately 1500 garment sweatshops which illegally employ about 7000 children, some as young as 8. In one, a 15-year old immigrant worked at a table sewing pleats into cheap white chiffon skirts for $1 an hour. The temperature in the room was 8 degrees Fahrenheit. (Walker, Brooks, and Wrightsman)

"MY NAME is Wendy Diaz. I am from Honduras. I'm 15 years old. I started working at Global Fashion when I was 13 years old. At Global Fashion there are about 100 minors like me–13, 14, 15 years old, some even 12. On the Kathie Lee pants we were forced to work, almost every day, from 8 a.m. to 9 p.m. On Saturday we worked til 5 p.m. Sometimes they kept us all night long, working until 6:30 a.m.

"The treatment at Global Fashion is very bad. The supervisors insult us and yell at us to work faster. The plant is very hot, like an oven. They keep the bathroom locked, and you need permission to use it only twice a day. We are not allowed to talk at work; if they see us talking, they punish us. Everyone in the plant is very young; the majority are 16-17 years old.

"I'm an orphan. I live in a one-room home with 11 people. I have to work to help three small brothers. Right now we are making clothes for Eddie Bauer and J. Crew. There are still a lot of minors in the factory."

(Testimony given at a press conference with Congress-person George Miller, May 29, 1996)

Questions:

Does any of this information surprise you?
How does it relate to Martin Luther King's quote?

Had you considered the potential violence that even an ordinary act (such as eating) has because of the "interrelatedness of all reality?"

We see from where we stand.

–Haitian Proverb

Nuclear Weapons

Nuclear weapons are perhaps the greatest form of violence humans have ever created. Their use, threats to use them, and their very existence are massively violent.

This is a chart of the nuclear world.

The single dot in the center represents the total of all the bombs dropped by the Allies in World War II: 3 megatons.

The rest of the dots represent the world's current nuclear weapons, an equivalent of 3600 World War IIs: 10,800 megatons.

Humans have only used nuclear (atomic) weapons twice: August 6 and 9, 1945, by the United States against Japan. The devastation they caused was enormous. Yet it is nothing compared with the capabilities of today's existing weapons.

• The bomb dropped on Hiroshima, Japan, was the equivalent of 12-15 kilotons of the explosive TNT; the one on Nagasaki, the equivalent of 20-22 kilotons. Nuclear weapons have been tested with loads the equivalent of 58 *mega*tons.

• The National Resources Defense Council estimates that at the end of 1997, Britain, China, France, Russia, and the U.S. had 36,000 nuclear weapons. Eight more countries have the capability of developing weapons and four more have attempted to do so.

• The U.S. maintained 13,750 nuclear warheads in 1997. (Department of Defense 1997)

• An estimated $8 trillion ($8,000,000,000,000) has been spent on nuclear weapons since 1945. (World Military and Social Expenditures 1996)

• Laurentian Shield Resources for Nonviolence coordinates a campaign to oppose ELF, the command center in Wisconsin which sends messages to start a nuclear war. In the 1990s, it made the following observation: "Years in which some alien power would have had to begin dropping Hiroshima-sized bombs on earth, one per day, in order to finish the entire arsenal now at the command of ELF by the end of the millennium: 1644."

Iwao Nakamura, 11ᵗʰ grade boy (5ᵗʰ grade in Hiroshima, August 6, 1945)

"TODAY, AS I begin to write an account of my experiences after five years and several months have passed, the wretched scenes of that time float up before my eyes like phantoms. And as these phantoms appear, I can actually hear the pathetic groans, the screams.

"In an instant it became dark as night, Hiroshima on that day. Flames shooting up from wrecked houses as if to illuminate this darkness. Amidst this, children aimlessly wandering about, groaning with pain, their burned faces twitching and bloated like balloons. An old man, skin flaking off like the skin of a potato, trying to get away on weak, unsteady legs, praying as he went. A man frantically calling out the names of his wife and children, both hands to his forehead from which blood trickled down. Just the memory of it makes my blood run cold. This is the real face of war. To those who knew nothing of the pitiful tragedies of Hiroshima's people, the scene would seem like a world of monsters, like Hades itself. A devil called war swept away the precious lives of several hundred thousand citizens of Hiroshima."

(From Arata Osada)

Question:

When is enough enough?

Institutional Violence

The manifestation of violence which is perhaps most difficult to understand is institutional violence. This violence is not so easily seen or witnessed. It is the type of violence set up by our systems, the violence that denies the human dignity of billions of people the world over.

Our world is filled with resources and wonder. We produce enough food, for instance, to provide everyone with enough. Yet our systems are set up in such a way that millions–indeed, billions–spend every day in poverty, lacking the necessities of life.

- Of the 4.4 billion people in developing countries, nearly three-fifths lack basic sanitation, almost one-third have no access to clean water, one-fourth do not have adequate housing, one-fifth have no access to modern health services, and one-fifth of children do not attend school to grade 5. (United Nations Development Program, Human Development Report 1999)

- Despite technological advances, more than 20,000 people die from hunger daily because of poverty. This is not due to a lack of food but to a lack of economic access to food. (Dr. Monkombu Sambasivan Swaminathan, January 2000)

Poverty is one form that institutional violence takes. Despite the U.S.'s belief in "pulling yourself up by the bootstraps," it is often very difficult–if not impossible–to escape the structures of poverty. In the U.S., lack of affordable housing, child care, accessible transportation, health care, and drug rehabilitation are all major factors contributing to poverty.

- Around the world, 1.3 billion people live on less than $1 per day. (United Nations Development Program, Human Development Report, 1997)

- The total U.S. commitment to key domestic social programs (meeting such needs as health, housing, education, and job training) was $26.7 billion less in 1998 than in 1980. (National Priorities Project, 2000)

Why are some people denied basic human dignity? More and more people are coming to realize that our economic systems are largely responsible. Wealth is becoming increasingly concentrated in the hands of a few. People living in rich, industrialized countries are encouraged to consume ever-increasing amounts. Out-of-control consumption provides luxuries for some while leaving less for necessities for the majority of the world's people.

- In 1999, the combined wealth of the three richest people in the U.S.–Bill Gates, Warren Buffet, and Paul Allen–was $156 billion, well above the combined Gross National Products of the poorest 43 nations on Earth. (United Nations Development Program, July 1999)

- A worker making $24,000 in 1994 would have made $138,000 in 1999 if her or his pay increased at the same rate as that of a CEO (Chief Executive Officer). (*Business Week*, April 19, 1999)

- Of the world's 100 largest economies, 49 are nations and 51 are corporations. (*Field Guide to the Global Economy,* The New Press, 1999)

- "In defining research agendas, money talks louder than need–cosmetic drugs and slow-ripening tomatoes come higher on the list than a vaccine against malaria or drought-resistant crops for marginal lands." (United Nations Development Program, Human Development Report 1999)

Massive, unnecessary (by any standards), and wasteful spending on militaries is also a major form of institutional violence. Military spending, besides preparing to kill each other, especially harms the poor since it robs from social programs. This money, instead of being spent on uplifting human dignity, is used to develop more and "better" ways of killing each other. The U.S., while by far the largest spender, is not the only culprit.

- In 1999, the Pentagon spent nearly $33 million an hour. (Budget from Center for Defense Information)
- The U.S. spent more on military research in the past seven years than on health research in the past century. (Former U.S. Senator Paul Simon, 1997)

- Despite a decline in the past five years, world military expenditures in 1995 amounted to more than $1.4 million per minute. (World Military and Social Expenditures 1995)

- In 1992, world military spending was $815 billion—the combined income of 49% of the world's people. (United Nations Development Program, Human Development Report, 1994)

Certain groups or areas are definitely major victims of institutional violence, among them indigenous peoples, women, people of color, and the environment. Such groups are afforded less respect and often used.

- Seventy percent of the world's poor are women, as are two-thirds of the people who are illiterate. (United Nations Development Program, Human Development Report 1995)

- The poverty rate among Blacks, 26.1%, is 2.5 times greater than the rate for whites. The poverty rate for Latinos is 25.6%. (Shared Capitalism Institute, May 2000)

- Environmental toxins and waste are more highly concentrated in communities of color. More than three dozen American Indian reservations have been targeted for landfills, incinerators, and other waste facilities. (Grassroots groups defeated the majority of these.) About 60% of all African-Americans live in communities with abandoned toxic waste sites. (Environmental Justice Resource Center, Clark Atlanta University)

- Wild species are becoming extinct 50-100 times faster than the natural rate. (United Nations Development Program, Human Development Report 1998)

- Over 42 billion pounds of agricultural petrochemicals are applied each year on US food crops. Often, less than 1% of the pesticides reach the target pest, while the rest goes into the ecosystem. (Earth Day Network)

The god of PEACE is never glorified by human violence.
MERTON

"TRUE PEACE and security does not lie in superior firepower but in a world where every person is enabled to develop their full human potential. The well being of our nation's people holds the key to our future peace and security. We could offer all who hunger the bread they need if we were willing to drop our stones. If we eliminated even one of the F-22 fighter planes planned for production this year, we could build 31 new elementary schools. If we chose to eliminate just three new attack submarines, we could build 90,000 affordable apartment units. The United Nations Development Program estimates that the basic health and nutrition needs of the world's poorest people could be met for an addition $13 billion per year, about 5 % of this year's US military budget."

—*Bread Not Stones*, A Statement by Bishop Members of Pax Christi USA, 2000

"A nation that continues year after year to spend more money on military defense than on programs of social uplift is approaching spiritual death."

—Martin Luther King, Jr.

Questions:

How do systems perpetuate violence? What role does poverty play?

How do you respond to someone who is without a home?

"YOU SAY you want to know what it's like to be poor? Well, you've come to the right person. But you won't enjoy my definition ...I'm dirty. I'm smelly. And I have no proper underwear beneath this rotting dress. I don't know about you, but the stench of my teeth makes me half sick. They're decaying and they need to be fixed. That takes money.

"Listen to me without pity . . . Listen with understanding, if you can. What is poverty? Poverty is getting up every morning from a dirty and illness-stained mattress—a hard, lumpy mattress. Sheets? They have long since been used for diapers, for there are no real diapers here either.

"That smell? That other smell? You know what it is—that, plus sour milk and spoiled food. Sometimes it's mixed with the stench of onions cooked too often. Onions are cheap. We're like dogs in that we live in a world of smells and we've learned to identify most of them without searching them out . . ."

—A mother from the southern Tennessee hills

"LET US recognize that as with individuals, so with social structures: they can be outwardly orderly yet inwardly violent. And if violence means violating human integrity, then without hesitation we must call violent any social structure that condemns human beings to hopelessness and helplessness, to less than human existence. Further, it is clear that people concerned with non-violence must show not only compassion for the victims of violence but also a determination to change the structures of society that make them objects of compassion."

—**William Sloane Coffin**

Closing Prayer

Reader 1:

God, we ask forgiveness for the times and ways in which we participate in violence. Help us to recognize violence in the many forms it takes and faces it wears. Guide us to name violence, to refuse to let silence or lack of open, physical violence be taken as a sign of peace. Walk with us on our journey into nonviolence and into your covenant of true peace.

Take a few minutes to reflect silently on the violence we see and participate in and to ask for God's forgiveness. How might we change? After a few minutes,

Reader 1 can start the following prayer and all others can join in (divided into two sides).

"Say No To Peace"

(source unknown)

Side 1: **Say "no" to peace**
if what they mean by peace
is the quiet misery of hunger,
the frozen stillness of fear,
the silence of broken spirits,
the unborn hopes of the oppressed.

Side 2: **Tell them that peace**
is the shouting of children at play,
the babble of tongues set free,
the thunder of dancing feet,
and a father's voice singing.

Side 1: **Say "no" to peace**
if what they mean by peace
is a rampart of gleaming missiles,
the arming of distant wars,
money at ease in its castle
and grateful poor at the gate.

Side 2: **Tell them that peace**
is the hauling down of flags,
the forging of guns into ploughs,
the giving of fields to the landless,
and hunger a fading dream.

All: **Amen.**

Part Two: Reflections

1. After reading these pages on violence, do you feel:

angry   enlightened   overwhelmed
    desiring to change   numb
    depressed   (other)
Why?

2. Which of the preceding examples of violence surprises you? Which of the preceding examples of violence confuses you? Do any seem like they are not examples of violence? Did any challenge your definition of violence?

3. Are there any forms of violence that you find noticeably missing? List them.

4. What are some of the differences and similarities between the types of violence?

5. What do you think it will take to alter the state of violence in the world?
    more money   more personal conversion
    more prayer   more alternatives
    more people involved in change
Add your suggestions:

6. This chapter demonstrates that our world is filled with countless forms of violence that affect us all. Saint Paul, in the letter to the Romans (12:2), wrote, "Don't conform yourselves to this age, but be transformed by the renewal of your minds, so that you can judge what God's will is—what is good, pleasing, and perfect." How can we refuse to be conformed to the violence of our world? What can we do to discern the will of God? Listen for God's response as you pray.

7. Wendell Berry has written, "In the face of all annihilating weapons, the natural next step may be the use of no weapons. It may be that the only possible effective defense against the nuclear weapon is no weapon at all. It may be that the presence of nuclear weapons in the world serves notice that the command to love

one another is an absolute practical necessity, such as we never dreamed it to be before, and that our choice is not to win or lose, but to love our enemies or die." After reading about the violence in our world, do you agree with Berry?

Why or why not?

8. What areas of violence in your life need to be transformed?

Suggestions for Action

• Be conscious of how you use your words as weapons against other people or yourself. Try to eliminate this form of interpersonal violence as much as possible.

• Refuse to watch or support violent television programming, especially during "prime time" and other hours when many children watch.

• In response to the increasing use of the death penalty in the United States, many citizens have taken a "Declaration of Life." This signed document states that capital punishment is wrong and states that the signer, if murdered, wishes that the perpetrator not be subject to the death penalty. Consider signing the document–see appendix A for the text.

• When you buy new clothing or other products, check the labels. Try to buy sweat-free (groups below have more specific suggestions, companies that use sweatshops, etc.)

• Limit your consumption. Explore these ideas in a group; Pax Christi USA offers a consumerism issue packet entitled "Through the Eye of a Needle."

• Organize to provide a physical presence for people who may be targets of violence. For instance, after the September 11th attacks, groups and individuals organized to accompany Arab-American and Muslim people who had received threats or felt unsafe.

• Do something about the issue or form of violence that most concerns you. Contact any of the groups below for resources or more action ideas. One idea is always to write your elected representatives. The local phone book usually lists various offices. You can write to your Congresspeople: Senator _____; U.S. Senate; Washington, DC 20510; Representative _____; House of Representatives; Washington, DC, 20515. To find out who your Congresspeople are, visit http://www.senate.gov and http://www.house.gov/writerep. The President's address is: The White House; 1600 Pennsylvania Avenue NW; Washington, DC 20500.

A Sampling of Sources and Resources:

See Appendix B for more statistics on various types of violence.

Miscellaneous resources:
The Public Education Network maintains an extensive website of facts on weapons, consumption, discrimination, education, the environment, government, health, the media, poverty, and transportation: http://www.penpress.org

The National Priorities Project offers tools and resources on federal budget and policy priorities, looking to promote social and economic justice. 17 New South Street, Suite 302; Northampton, MA 01060; phone: 413/584-9556; http://www.natprior.org

The Resource Center of the Americas provides information to promote justice, democracy, and human rights. Topics include labor, economics, immigration, indigenous rights, and the environment. 3019 Minnehaha Avenue South; Minneapolis, MN 55406; phone: 612/276-0788; e-mail: membership@americas.org; http://www.americas.org

Consumerism Issue Packet: Through the Eye of a Needle–a five-week process focused on five aspects of consumerism: affluenza, overconsumption, sweatshops, the environment and simple living. Suitable for use by small groups as well as individuals, each session contains prayers, reflection questions and action suggestions. The process encourages participants to examine potential purchases in light of a purchasing check-list. Great for introducing social justice issues to your parish or small group. Pax Christi USA, 532 W.8ᵗʰ St., Erie, PA 16502; phone: 814-453-4955 x231; e:mail: sales@paxchristiusa.org; www.paxchristiusa.org

Child Abuse and Neglect:
Covenant House: to be placed on the mailing list: 346 W. 17th Street; New York, NY 10011; Attention: Donation Mail; phone: 800/388-3888; e-mail: dcmail@covcorp.org; http://www.convenanthouse.org. Over 20 locations worldwide.

National Clearinghouse on Child Abuse and Neglect: http://www.calib.com/nccanch/

Media
The Center for Media Literacy is a national advocacy organization that provides educational materials and training programs to foster critical thinking about the media. 4727 Wilshire Boulevard, #403; Los Angeles, CA 90010 ; phone: 800/226-9494 or 323/931-4177; e-mail: cml@medialit.org; http://www.medialit.org

Paper: "Television, Violence, and Children" by Carla Kalin, University of Oregon: http://www.interact.oregon.edu/MediaLit/FA/MLArticleFolder/kalin.html

Guns:
The Center to Prevent Handgun Violence and Handgun Control: 1225 Eye Street, NW, Suite 1100; Washington, DC 20005; CPHV: phone: 202/289-7319; http://www.cphv.org and HGC: phone: 202/898-0792; http://www.handguncontrol.org

The Violence Prevention Center does research, education, and advocacy against firearms violence. 1140 19th Street NW, Suite 600; Washington, DC 20036; http://www.vpc.org

Respecting Life:
Consistent Life (Formerly the Seamless Garment Network): P.O. Box 792; Garner, NC 27529; www.consistent-life.org

Death Penalty:
"Abolishing the Death Penalty: Breaking the Cycle of Violence," a prayer-study-action resource packet from Pax Christi USA; www.paxchristiusa.org or 814-453-4955, ext. 231.

Citizens United for Alternatives to the Death Penalty (CUADP): www.cuadp.org, 1-800-973-6548

National Coalition to Abolish the Death Penalty: 1436 U Street NW, Suite 104; Washington, DC 20009; phone: 202/387-3890; e-mail: info@ncadp.org; http://www.ncadp.org

Prejean, Helen, CSJ. "A Prayer to Abolish the Death Penalty" with action suggestions. Erie, PA: Pax Christi USA.

Religious Organizing Against the Death Penalty: c/o AFSC Criminal Justice Program:1501 Cherry Street; Philadelphia, PA 19102; phone: 215/241-7130; http://www.deathpenaltyreligious.org; also published "Sermons, Homilies & Reflections on the Death Penalty"

Around the World (Victims section):
African Rights works for justice in Africa from an African perspective: 11 Marshalsea Road; London SE1 1EP; UK; e-mail: afrights@gn.apc.org; http://www.peacelink.it/afrights/homepage.html

European Roma Rights Center. H. 1386 Budapest 62; PO Box 906/93; Hungary; http://errc.org

Sweatshop and Child Labor:
Walker, Nancy E., Catherine M. Brooks, and Lawrence S. Wrightsman. *Children's Rights in the United States: In Search of a National Policy. SAGE Publications, Thousand Oaks, CA, 1999.*

Video on globalization and the global economy, "Global Village or Global Pillage?"
http://www.villageorpillage.org

The National Interfaith Committee for Worker Justice has produced a report entitled, "Cross Border Blues: A Call for Justice for Maquiladora Workers in Tehuacán." It is available online at http://www.uniteunion.org/sweatshops/guess/mexico/mexico1.html; 1020 W. Bryn Mawr Avenue, 4th floor; Chicago, IL 60660; phone: 773/728-8400; e-mail: info@nicwj.org; http://www.nicwj.org

The UNITE! Union has a Web page with lots of information and links about sweatshops: http://www.uniteunion.org/sweatshops/sweatshop.html

The newest student-led anti-sweatshop campaign is the Workers Rights Consortium: http://www.workersrights.org

Zoned for Slavery: the Child Behind the Label, a 23-minute educational video on Central America's maquiladora export assembly; National Labor Committee: 275 Seventh Avenue, 15th Floor; New York, NY 10001; phone: 212/242-3002; e-mail: nlc@nlcnet.org; http://www.nlcnet.org

Nuclear Weapons:
The Nuclear Age Peace Foundation answers frequently asked questions about nuclear weapons, provides steps for disarmament, offers links, and more: PMB 121, 1187 Coast Village Road, Suite 1; Santa Barbara, CA 93108-2794; phone: 805/965-3443; e-mail: wagingpeace@napf.org; http://www.wagingpeace.org

Laurentian Shield Resources for Nonviolence: 12833 E. Highway 13; Maple, WI 54854; phone: 715/364-8533

Osada, Arata, ed. Children of Hiroshima. Tokyo, Japan: Publishing Committee for Children of Hiroshima, 1980.

Poverty, Wealth Distribution, and Other Forms of Institutional Violence:
Bread for the World works for policies that would eliminate hunger: 50 F Street, NW, Suite 500; Washington, DC 20001; phone: 202/639-9400 or 800/82-BREAD; e-mail: bread@bread.org; http://www.bread.org

Jubilee USA Network works to cancel the debt of deeply impoverished countries. Jubilee USA Network: 222 East Capitol Street; Washington, DC 20003-1036; phone: 202/783-3566; e-mail: Coord@j2000usa.org; http://www.j2000usa.org

United For a Fair Economy works for a more fair distribution of wealth in the United States: 37 Temple Place, 2nd Floor; Boston, MA 02111; phone: 617/423-2148; e-mail: info@ufenet.org; http://www.unitedforafaireconomy.org

United Nations Children's Fund (UNICEF): http://www.unicef.org (See especially their publications Progress of Nations and State of the World's Children, done each year.)

Anderson, Sarah and John Cavanagh with Thea Lee. The Field Guide to the Global Economy. New York: New Press, 1999. (Published in conjunction with the Institute for Policy Studies, Washington, DC.)

"Toward a Globalization of Solidarity: A Pax Christi USA Prayer, Study and Action Packet on Globalization;" www.paxchristiusa.org or 814-453-4955, ext. 231.

United Nations Development Program, Human Development Reports (http://www.undp.org):

- 2003: Millennium Development Goals
- 2002: Deepening Democracy in a Fragmented World
- 2001: Making New Technologies Work
     for Human Development
- 2000: Human Rights and Human Development
- 1999: Globalization with a Human Face

- 1998: Consumption for Human Development
- 1997: Human Development to Eradicate Poverty
- 1996: Economic Growth and Human Development
- 1995: Gender and Human Development
- 1994: New Dimensions of Human Security
- 1993: People's Participation

Environment:

Environmental Working Group: 1718 Connecticut Avenue, NW, Suite 600; Washington, DC 20009; phone: 202/667-6982; e-mail: info@ewg.org; http://www.ewg.org (also has offices in Oakland, CA and Seattle, WA)

Worldwatch Institute: 1776 Massachusetts Avenue, NW; Washington, DC 20036-1904; phone: 202/452-1999; e-mail: worldwatch@worldwatch.org; http://www.worldwatch.org (See also groups and resources in Part Six.)

Racism:

Activesolidarity.net is a web resource for anti-racism and movement building. http://activesolidarity.net

ColorLines magazine is about race, culture, and organizing: PMB 319; 4096 Piedmont Avenue; Oakland, CA 94611; phone: 510/653-3415; e-mail: colorlines@arc.org; http://www.colorlines.com

Crossroads Ministry is an interfaith ministry for racial justice that provides education, training, and organizing to dismantle racism and build multicultural diversity. 425 South Central Park Avenue; Chicago, IL 60624; phone: 773/638-0166; e-mail: crossroadschicago@sbcglobal.net

The People's Institute for Survival and Beyond helps people and groups develop more analytical, anti-racist, culturally-rooted and effecive community organizing. 7166 Crowder Boulevard, Suite 100; New Orleans, LA 70127; phone: 504/241-7472; http://www.thepeoplesinstitute.org

The Prison Activist Resource Center is committed to exposing and challenging the institutionalized racism of prisons and the criminal prosecution system. PO Box 339; Berkeley, CA 94701; phone: 510/893-4648; e-mail: parc@prisonactivist.org; http://www.prisonactivist.org

WhitePrivilege.com is an online resource for antiracism activism and education. http://whiteprivilege.com

Women of Color Resource Center is a social justice organization that promotes the political, economic, social, and cultural well-being of U.S. women and girls of color. 1611 Telegraph Avenue #303; Oakland, CA 94612; phone: 510/444-2700; e-mail: info@coloredgirls.org; http://www.coloredgirls.org

Credits

Part Three

The Method of Nonviolence

The violence of our world seems overwhelming at times. We could probably give in to it. We could be paralyzed into inaction. We could get stuck in feeling guilty about the ways we are or have been violent or have not recognized different forms of violence. We could say that violence cannot end and that more violence is the answer to problems. But there is another way–nonviolence. Nonviolence provides a moral basis as well as strategies and tactics for dealing with conflicts and choices in life. It give us ways of taking positive steps for change.

Unfortunately, the practical side of nonviolence is sometimes ignored. Nonviolence, like anything else, takes training, knowledge, and commitment. We must learn to respond and to live in a different manner than our society teaches us, to live positively and to use good communication skills rather than resorting to violence.

It also requires a translation into our daily lives. How do we choose to spend our money? How do we deal with relationship difficulties? What prejudices or assumptions do we bring to interactions with others– especially those from different backgrounds? What do we as individuals and as a country do to keep us safe from terrorism and other forms of violence? These are some of the choices that nonviolence asks us to confront. The answers we discover will most likely challenge us and may even call us to enter into a nonviolent struggle to address injustice or violence. What might such a journey involve?

The Method of Nonviolence
• *Opening Prayer*
• *Definitions of Nonviolence and Where We Use It*
• *A Different Response*
• *Positive Action and Communication*
–Understanding
–Focusing
–Negotiating
• *People Power: Community*
• *Nonviolent Campaigns*
• *Nonviolent Actions*
–101 Ways to Foster Nonviolence in Your Life
• *Civil Disobedience*
• *Closing Prayer*
• *Reflections*
• *Suggestions for Action*
• *A Sampling of Sources and Resources*
• *Credits*

Opening Prayer

In silence, take time to reflect on why you have decided to take the journey of nonviolence. What do you hope to learn today? How is God helping you on your journey? What gifts and perspectives do you need most (such as patience, courage, honesty, or an ability to dialogue)?

The United Farm Workers Prayer —Cesar Chavez

Reader 1: Show me the suffering of the most miserable;
so I will know my people's plight.

Reader 2: Free me to pray for others;
for You are present in every person.

Reader 3: Help me take responsibility for my own life;
so that I can be free at last.

Reader 4: Grant me courage to serve others;
for in service there is true life.

Reader 1: Give me honesty and patience;
so that the Spirit will be alive among us.

Reader 2: Let the Spirit flourish and grow;
so that we will never tire of the struggle.

Reader 3: Let us remember those who have died for justice;
for they have given us life.

Reader 4: Help us love even those who hate us;
so we can change the world.

All: Amen.

Definitions of Nonviolence and Where We Use It

What is nonviolence? Definitions may perhaps be as numerous as the number of people who attempt to live or act nonviolently. One of the difficulties with the word "nonviolence" is that it defines itself as what it is not. But it is important to define nonviolence in terms of what it is. For a working definition, we can say that nonviolence is positive action for true good for all of God's creation, motivated by love, using only means that help and do not harm. It is a positive force–persuasion rather than coercion (intimidation). Nonviolence seeks solutions that are beneficial to all parties and which unite them. Nonviolence is most frequently used in reference to human relationships, but it is critical that it also take into consideration effects on and relationships with the non-human world.

How does it play out in a person's life? Someone who tries to live life every day in a spirit of nonviolence, who tries to take positive action for true good, will find constant challenges in everyday life and relationships. Challenges will also arise from the consideration of the vast number of ways even the simplest action impacts the environment, others, and our community and world.

To understand how nonviolence can play out in our lives, it may help to envision ourselves at the center of several concentric circles. First, we encounter violence within ourselves: our desires, self-image, attitudes (some created by our surroundings and culture).

The next challenge comes from our most immediate circle, the people around us–family, friends, people at work or school, neighbors–people with whom we come into contact and occasionally disagree over one matter or another. Someone we know may attack us–physically, verbally, emotionally.

Another concentric circle surrounding us is the larger community in which we live, the society of which we are a part. We are challenged by injustices in that society, systems that oppress some of our sisters and brothers, keep them in poverty, discriminate against them because of their race.

Nonviolence is positive action for true good for all of God's creation, motivated by love, using only means that help and do not harm.

The largest of the concentric circles surrounding us is the world community, organized presently in the form of nation-states. International conflicts can easily erupt into the organized violence of war in which we, as citizens, have a stake. Increasingly, the more prominent global relationships are economic, occurring through trade and transnational corporations.

We may be pressured to become involved in some of these conflicts–in the family, for instance, or if we are approached by the military with promises of money for college, adventure, and travel. Other conflicts we may choose to enter because of our compassion with those who are suffering, with those who are victims.

How have other people defined nonviolence and what terms have they used or created?

Brazilian definition of *firmeza permanenta* (relentless persistence): it is active and shows creativity, courage, and commitment.

Dom Helder Camara (Brazilian archbishop): "What we call nonviolence is simply living out the Gospel. It includes a commitment to respect the sacredness of each person and the determination to overcome all domination."

Shelley Douglass (U.S. peace activist): "The point of nonviolence, after all, is to search for the right and loving thing to do and do it, remaining centered in the truth."

Mohandas Gandhi (Indian activist): *Satyagraha* (truth-force; sometimes translated as soul-force) is a firm grasping after the truth.

Staughton and Alice Lynd (authors and activists): "Nonviolence is breaking through to the deepest level of human communication by creative means. It is a way of being, as well as of doing."

Michael Nagler (professor of nonviolence): "Nonviolence is a positive force generated by self-sacrifice in the cause of Truth."

Wally Nelson (conscientious objector, civil rights activist, and war tax resister): "Nonviolence is the constant awareness of the dignity and humanity of oneself and others; it seeks truth and justice; it renounces violence both in method and in attitude; it is a courageous acceptance of active love and goodwill as the instrument with which to overcome evil and transform both oneself and others."

Questions:

Which of these definitions speaks to you? At this point, how would you define nonviolence?

In what areas of your life do you find it most difficult to live nonviolently?

Have you had any experiences in your life that have convinced you that nonviolent ways of handling conflict are better than violent ones?

Have you had any experiences in which nonviolent ways of resolving conflict have been successful? Unsuccessful?

Are you aware of any instance in which nonviolent methods have been successful in your immediate circle? In your local community? On the national or international level?

A Different Response

In each of the circles of our lives, we face difficult or violent situations. Each time, we can choose to respond violently or nonviolently. Although each situation has its own complexities that must be taken into consideration and dealt with spontaneously, with improvisation, certain basic themes are common to a nonviolent approach to any conflict involving any of the circles.

First we must discover and name the aggressive behavior. Analysis and knowledge are crucial, especially when dealing with violence in one of the larger circles. Then we can resolve not to react in the same manner, not to give in to compulsive competition, the winning through intimidation that quickly emerges in most conflicts, or threats. Nonviolence asks that we don't allow ourselves to be provoked by these tactics. When we encounter someone who vents anger on us, tries to cheat or humiliate us, or uses physical violence against us, we have to be prepared to respond in a different way.

Daniel Berrigan has written that peacemakers refuse to play enemy to someone who names them enemy. The first thing a nonviolent person does when confronted with hostility is to hold up, not play the game, not get caught up in defensiveness and counter-hostility. Rather, with all the calmness that can be gathered, side-step the aggressiveness, let it go on past, suffer the hurt. Then move in with a different approach, always showing respect and compassion for the "adversary."

But what of the situations in which we are in conflict with someone we love, rather than an "enemy?" Our interpersonal relationships may be the ones in which our nonviolence is most tested. We have so much invested in them. It is often difficult to step back or to try not to respond violently when we feel attacked in some way.

When we have a disagreement with a parent, sibling, or friend, we cannot just "let it go." In fact, that may be even more harmful in the long run. Conflict under the surface or hurts that grow into grudges can result in permanent damage or an end to relationships.

In situations of conflict with someone in a close personal relationship, verbal violence is often the result. While certainly less physically dangerous than other forms of violence, it is still hurtful and can easily lead to other forms of violence over time. How can we choose "a different response?"

Generations of people have come up with ways in which to deal with these situations, although they may not have called them "nonviolent." Someone may have told you to "count to 10" before responding in anger. In the 1990s, "WWJD" bracelets, signs, and bumper stickers appeared, counseling people to ask themselves "what would Jesus do?" before responding to a situation. While it may be difficult, we need to find a way such as this that works for us personally. We must resolve the conflict, not just ignore it. But we must do so in a way that allows both sides to express their feelings and work together toward a solution. In personal relationships, it may help to remember–at the first sign of conflict–the love that we have for the person. It may help to remember the love that God has for all of us. If we focus on love or on the good qualities of the other person, we may more easily let go of our anger. Taking deep breaths, calming down our bodies, is still good advice. These first steps help us to identify the aggressive behavior and to begin to change the situation of conflict.

PEACEMAKER: DAN Berrigan is a Jesuit priest, poet, teacher, resister, hospice worker, and advocate of nonviolence. He has written dozens of books and hundreds of essays and has participated in numerous acts of nonviolent direct action, including Plowshares. Berrigan first gained public attention in 1968 (during the Vietnam War) when he and others poured homemade napalm over draft files in Catonsville, Maryland.

Question:

What methods can you think of that might help you to respond nonviolently to those who are close to you?

Positive Action and Communication

The second theme is what we do positively after we control our impulse to do something negative. Now the nonviolent action begins. President Abraham Lincoln once remarked, "I destroy my enemies when I make them my friends." The nonviolent approach to conflicts– all conflicts–is to try to turn enemies into friends or to remember that the person we are in conflict with is already our friend. The goal of nonviolent action is not to repress or defeat, but to convert. If the change from enemy to friend takes place, the person is no longer someone to be overcome, but a cooperator in finding a peaceful solution. Often, this is a long process. Sometimes we may not even be around to see the results.

At all times, we must show respect and compassion for a person who is our adversary or with whom we disagree. Christians are instructed to love one another as God loves us. When we are nonviolent and attempt not only to not label another as "enemy" but also to love our adversary, we are participating in the divine love of God.

When we are in a situation of conflict, it is easy to demonize the other person(s). For instance, suppose a certain business owner, through intimidation and demeaning remarks, has prevented people of color from receiving fair treatment in the store or restaurant. It may seem easier to dismiss this person as a bigot– to call her or him names. But nonviolence requires that we treat the shopowner with the respect deserved by all members of the human community. It does not mean ignoring the violence; we may respectfully–and vocally–label behavior as racist and attempt to change the conditions in the business. If we do so, we consider the possible consequences of action (e.g., might it get people of color fired from their jobs?) In engaging the violence, we also separate the individual from the role or actions she or he plays or takes, indentifying racism as the enemy to be overcome–even if the shopkeeper doesn't agree! In this way we redefine the situation as you and me against the problem. With this mindset, it will be easier to engage in effective communication.

How to change an adversary into a friend or a difficult situation into a positive one is the big question. We suggest that it involves three phases: understanding, focusing, and negotiating.

---

*If we could read
the secret history of our enemies,
we should find in each (person's) life
sorrow and suffering enough
to disarm all hostility.*

–Henry Wadsworth Longfellow

Question: Have you ever had the experience of making an enemy a friend? Describe how that happened.

Understanding

Helen Keller said, "I do not want the peace which passeth understanding; I want the understanding which bringeth peace." In any conflict, our first responsibility is to find out what's going on with the other person or group. As we react, we should be alert to the reasons for the difficulty. Why is a friend upset today? Is it something we have done or is s/he not feeling well or having trouble at work or school and using me as a convenient target? Why is the U.S. about to go to war in some distant land? What have they done to us to deserve such a response? What might we have done to provoke their actions? What's going on in their minds? Why are they acting this way? The answers are not always clear or easy, but the search for understanding should go on as long as the conflict lasts. Responses will be different according to the answers we find. Listening closely to the other person(s), rather than focusing solely on our own hurt or anger, can help us to remember that they are hurting or angry too.

When facing issues of national or institutional violence, answers may not be readily apparent. We may have to study, to search out answers. Often, this involves looking for alternative sources of information; what we find in the mainstream media may very well reflect the viewpoint of the aggressor and not the victims of violence and thus not give the full picture.

The Swiss theologian Karl Barth once said that the proper way to do theology in these times is with the Bible in one hand and the daily newspaper in the other. The nonviolent person will want to keep up with current events, always looking at them with peace eyes. The men and women at the controls of the political, economic, and military machinery of the nuclear age are well aware of what is going on in the world and are adjusting their operations accordingly. Peacemakers, who seek nonviolent ways of resolving conflicts and building more humane structures, should have sufficient insight into the shifting day-to-day world scene and be ready to understand and demonstrate how nonviolent action can be more effective than violence.

The effects of study and awareness are multiplied by sharing ideas with other people. Discussions, exchanging viewpoints, and learning what others consider important help to focus and clarify what we are dealing with privately.

A nonviolent person also needs to know and understand nonviolent techniques. It's helpful to know the principles on which these techniques rest, as well as some historical examples. This calls for study, for time spent seriously investigating the realities that confront us and the ways of dealing with them peacefully. The study will be energized by our nonviolent experiences, and these in turn will become more and more rewarding as they include the results of the study.

Nonviolent people's knowledge should be sufficiently extensive and accurate not just for effectiveness, but also to ensure that we will be taken seriously, not dismissed as blowing in the wind or floating on naive idealism.

Focusing

Second, we focus the conflict. We do this by concentrating on resolving the present problem, rather than dwelling on past offenses. We keep our attention on the specific issues that divide us now, rather than roaming over the broad background of the past.

Martin Luther King, Jr., called it forgiving. He said that forgiveness meant coming to reconciliation now. Jesus forgave sinners now, when they were repentant. He didn't dredge up the past or call attention to it in any way. Looking to the future, he said, "Go on your way–but from now on, don't sin any more." (John 8:11b)

Forgiveness, or focusing, is not the same as forgetting. We have to remember past problems so that we won't allow the same conditions to produce the same conflict again. We also have to recognize that the roots of the conflict may lie far in the past. But our attention should be on solving the problems now.

> "LOVE IS the only force capable of transforming an enemy into a friend. We never get rid of an enemy by meeting hate with hate; we get rid of an enemy by getting rid of enmity. By its very nature, hate destroys and tears down; by its very nature, love creates and builds up. Love transforms with redemptive power." —Martin Luther King, Jr.

Question:

Recall a conflict situation with which you were not satisfied. What did "they" say and do? How did you respond? Go back and replay the situation. What more "disarming" approach could you have used?

Conflict at Home

Home may be where you experience many of your conflicts. Disagreements between parents and children, over money, and other aspects of family life can be managed successfully. Even the youngest members of the family can learn how.

To help their children find nonviolent ways of resolving differences, James and Kathy McGinnis of St. Louis teach them a three-step process: *Express your wants clearly. *Listen to other people's wants. *Come up with alternatives.

Jim McGinnis recalls one dispute between his five-year-old and his three-year-old over who would ride the tricycle. One was on the trike and the other was blocking its movement.

He asked the children if they were happy with the situation. They weren't, and he asked what they could each do to change that.

"We could take turns," said the five-year-old, adding, "For ten minutes each." When McGinnis said he'd be willing to tell them when the time was up, the three-year-old volunteered to let her older brother go first.

–from Christopher News Notes

Negotiating

President Woodrow Wilson said, "If you come at me with your fists doubled, I think I can promise you that mine will double. . . . But if you come to me and say, 'Let us sit down and take counsel together' . . . we will find that we are not so far apart after all."

Negotiation is a give and take exchange with the other side, the goal being to reach an outcome with which both can live. Negotiation can start quickly, with the first interchanges of the conflict. It can begin by the first faint acknowledgement of a common interest. When President Jimmy Carter invited Anwar Sadat (the Muslim President of Egypt) and Menachem Begin (the Jewish Prime Minister of Israel) to discuss territory settlements, the atmosphere was at first tense and filled with mistrust. There was a long history of Arab-Israeli distrust as well as personal incompatibility between the men. Eventually, one of the men took out a picture of his grandchildren. The other then told about his grandchildren. From there the negotiations proceeded, each side making changes as the situation demanded.

President Carter worked hard to create an atmosphere of informality. As a result of these little steps, the men signed two documents: "A Framework for Peace in the Middle East" and "A Framework for the Conclusion of the Peace Treaty Between Egypt and Israel."

In nonviolent negotiation we avoid ultimatums. People respond poorly to ultimatums. We should always try to give the other side a way out. They should be given options to respond to, not demands to which they must conform. People who feel that their backs are pushed against the wall usually become defensive and look for a way to strike back. We listen carefully so that we can jointly discover a solution.

In negotiating we don't want to say anything hurtful or humiliating. We don't want to appear morally superior when this will be taken as a sign of counter-hostility. We should take care to avoid self-righteousness and the kind of moral pressure that humiliates the other side. We recognize their weaknesses, embarrassment, and fears, as we acknowledge our own.

The process of understanding, focusing, and negotiating does not happen in three neatly separable stages. Every interaction with the other side is part of the negotiation. Throughout the whole process, we're always searching for more understanding of motives and interests. From the beginning we keep our efforts focused on resolving the present conflict and building future cooperation. The process can't always be put into practice fully, but it is the blueprint for a nonviolent approach to conflicts.

When communicating, here are some things to keep in mind:
- Make your objectives reasonable.

- Maintain eye contact.

- Don't use abrupt gestures (as they may be interpreted as violent).

- Sometimes it may be necessary to state things that may seem obvious to you.

- Listen carefully.

Questions:

Understanding, focusing, negotiating–what are the pitfalls you foresee in trying to use these methods in resolving conflicts? Which do you think you are best at? Which would you find most difficult? What can you do to develop these techniques?

From your experience, would you add any other steps to the process?

Think of your most recent conflict with someone close to you. Did you use any of these steps? If not, how might the situation have been resolved differently?

People Power: Community

In order to practice nonviolence, whether in our daily lives or in a larger struggle against a deeply-rooted institutional injustice, we should have community. Community affirms us, loves us, and gives us strength. It is helpful in discernment and making decisions as well as in moving forward. Often, the forces of violence seem so large that they threaten to overwhelm us. Having a group of people to whom we can turn is vital for sustaining for the long haul. Being in community is also an important aspect of being Christian; God calls us to be in relationship with others.

Community takes many forms. Many people struggling to live a life of Christian nonviolence choose to live in "intentional communities," sharing the basic necessities of life. Others have community through their church or with neighbors. The community of some extends to people all over the country and the world who share values of love and justice.

Having community also helps us to live positively. We may get bogged down by all of the injustice in the world or feel that we are always in opposition to something. But living a life committed to nonviolence is also a commitment to live positively, to make healthy choices for ourselves, our friends and neighbors, and our world. We can choose to make each decision, every day, out of love, working to create a better world. The slogan "reduce, reuse, and recycle" is an example of a positive choice: we make the best use of those material things that we already have. Choosing to smile at someone who appears to be having a bad day is another example of a way to live positively in the world. Community can guide us through this journey, give us advice, and gently remind us of places where we can improve. It also makes us responsible to someone and something larger than ourselves.

A community is never there for itself.
It belongs to something greater
—to the poor, to humanity,
to the Church, to the universe . . .
The community—those with whom we live—
is only a starting point, to enable our hearts
to open to this universal dimension.
Community has no sense
unless it is seen with its roots,
its branches and its fruit.

—Jean Vanier

What ways can you introduce nonviolence into your faith community's spiritual life?

Some examples:

• Meet with your faith community's liturgy commission. See if people are open to introducing nonviolence in homilies, songs, and petitions.

• Make a packet or resource listing available to the community.

• Conduct special prayer services in which you pray for victims of violence and ask for courage and strength to be nonviolent.

• Prepare bulletin inserts using resources from Pax Christi USA.

Questions:

Do you have a sense of community in your life? What are these places?

How can you foster community?

Nonviolent Campaigns

Sometimes, violence is readily apparent, close to the surface, such as a drive-by shooting or when someone yells at us. At other times, deadly violence hides behind economic policies that crush the poor. How we respond to the first (examples within our personal circles) may differ from how we respond to the second (examples within larger circles). While we use the strategies outlined above in all situations, sometimes we may join with others in a campaign.

Campaigns are made up of people who are concerned about an issue, whether it be racism, nuclear weapons, environmental pollution, or loss of community land. The people may not agree on everything but have decided to work together to address a problem. Several concepts are worth noting in this process:

• Consensus: This is a cooperative process for decision-making that is based on hearing and valuing everyone's voice, opinion, and fears. Rather than making decisions through voting, working from the consensus model means taking the time to allow everyone to discuss and to come to agreement on the issue. The group does not move forward until everyone accepts and understands the outcome, put together from the viewpoints of all people. By using this model, no one feels as if she or he "won" or "lost." Everyone is valued and decisions are well thought-out. It requires good listening skills and takes a long time.

• Affinity Groups: These are a special type of group that has been used very effectively in mass actions. They are self-sufficient support systems of a small number of people who act together and form the basic decision-making body in mass actions. Sometimes the people have known each other for a long time; sometimes they have not. Affinity groups are a way of forming community and reducing or eliminating feelings of isolation. They have been used with great success in protests against nuclear weapons and unjust global economic structures.

Training is essential for nonviolent campaigns and also to address criticisms of nonviolence strategically. Recently, nonviolence has been used as a tactic to mobilize tens of thousands of people–in Seattle against the World Trade Organization and in Washington, DC against the International Monetary Fund and World Bank. Organizers, utilizing nonviolence largely as a tactic, have recognized the importance of training. Using the Internet and mass meetings, people have learned what to expect, how to conduct themselves nonviolently, how to defend each other nonviolently, and how to achieve their goals.

Some situations of injustice will require a long-term strategy and campaign. The *Handbook for Nonviolent Action* suggests the following steps:

- investigation/research
- negotiation/arbitration
- public forums
- picketing, leafleting
- demonstrations
- strikes/boycotts
- civil disobedience

Information gathering and analysis should look at policies, consequences, the various actors, and the power relations involved. It is necessary to form goals, find participants, organize, prepare, and determine reactions. Dialogue is important, as is attempting to look for public support. This type of process will be further described in the next several sections.

(See also Appendix C for the steps of effective nonviolent peacemaking action as outlined by a researcher of nonviolence.)

Constructive Action:

Gandhi and the campaign to free India specifically emphasized constructive programs. They not only resisted the British occupation of their country (see Part Nine), but began to establish a new society. For instance, they set up small cottage industries to make cloth (rather than importing it). Other campaigns have started their own schools, papers, infrastructure (such as transport), businesses, and gardens and food sources.

Some groups that do training:

Center for Third World Organizing: 1218 East 21st Street; Oakland, CA 94606; phone: 510/533-7583; e-mail: training@ctwo.org; http://www.ctwo.org

Fellowship of Reconciliation, Peacemaker Training Institute: PO Box 271; Nyack, New York 10960; phone:845/358-4601; e-mail: pti@forusa.org; http://www.forusa.org

JustAct: 333 Valencia Street, Suite 325; San Francisco 94103; phone: 415/431-4204; e-mail: info@justact.org; http://justact.org

Midwest Academy: 28 East Jackson Boulevard, #605; Chicago, Illinois 60604; phone: 312/427-2304; e-mail: mwacademy1@aol.com; http://www.midwestacademy.com

United States Students Association: 1413 K Street NW, 9th floor; Washington, DC 20005; phone: 202/347-8772; e-mail: grow@usstudents.org; http://www.essential.org/ussa/

Pax Christi USA also does retreats for young people, centered around different issues relating to nonviolence.

Request a copy of the National Youth and Militarism Program of the American Friends Service Committee's brochure "Leadership Training Programs for Young People." 1501 Cherry Street; Philadelphia, PA 19102; phone: 215/241-7176; e-mail: youthmil@afsc.org; http://www.afsc.org/youthmil

Nonviolent Actions

A nonviolent strategy should have two aims. The first is to make people conscious of the real power they already have within themselves. The moment people decide to assume responsibility for their lives, they begin to feel a kind of personal power: "No matter what others do, I am in control of myself. I have at my center a core that cannot be touched unless I let it be." Nonviolent action aims to reinforce this conviction and bolster this spirit. ("I am somebody. Together we can make a difference.")

Once people realize they have this power, they look at things differently. They see that all human events–political processes, economic activities–can be affected by it. A fundamental principle underlying nonviolence is that government at any level, political or social, is effective only if the people agree to it. A system of taxation depends largely on people willingly paying. Even a dictatorship depends on people being willing to go along with it. The practices of corporations can happen only when people encourage them, implement them, buy the products, and do not speak out.

Some people may be physically forced (coerced); others may be intimidated into going along. But if people refuse to cooperate, if they courageously stand up to intimidation, the economic and political system of any institution will not work. People only have power over us if we allow them to have it.

Nonviolence, then, seeks to change power relations. We take responsibility for injustice and refuse to cooperate with it. When we nonviolently deny our cooperation to people or systems, we reverse the power struggle.

So the first aim of any nonviolent strategy is for people to find the strength to do something different from the established ways or status quo. Individuals are important, but nonviolent campaigns usually take teamwork.

The second aim is to speak directly to the minds and hearts of those on the other side of the conflict. They must be reached. Gandhi showed how it could be done in India by getting to the British authorities finally. King reached the conscience–or at least the practical judgment–of civic officials in the United States.

Peace researcher Gene Sharp has identified 198 different nonviolent actions that can be used to speak to the minds and hearts of those on the other side of a conflict and to those undecided. He grouped them into three principle categories. These different strategies can be used to reach the goals of the nonviolent campaign.

1. PROTEST AND PERSUASION:

Any show of disapproval or approval of a course of action, from telling a person that what he or she is doing should be stopped, to letter-writing campaigns, petitions, vigils, marches, and rallies, can communicate with the other side. The purpose of actions like this is to bring a conflict to light and to expose it, in the hopes that those responsible for the problem will see the truth and change. Often these acts–such as slogans, banners, or skits–are symbolic. Other times, they are educational: leaflets or teach-ins. Songs have often been used as a form of protest, in labor movements, among slaves, to pass messages in and out of prison, at rallies and vigils. These methods can be used to influence different groups (lawmakers, corporate boards) or the public.

If the social climate is tolerant, these methods are relatively easy to carry out. But when the views expressed are unpopular or go against the majority's convictions, even the mildest action may require great courage and can have a significant impact.

An example of protest and persuasion tactics is demonstrations against the School of the Americas (SOA). The SOA is a training ground for soldiers from Latin American countries. It is located at Fort Benning, Georgia, and paid for with millions of U.S. tax dollars. Graduates of the school have been responsible for some of the worst human rights violations in Latin America, including massacres of hundreds of unarmed civilians and assassinations of religious leaders, union leaders, and human rights workers. In the mid 1990s, several hundred–and then several thousand–people started going to Fort Benning each year to voice their opposition to this school which had conducted training in techniques of torture, blackmail, and other violations. They used leaflets, banners, signs, songs, etc. They carried symbolic coffins representing thousands of killed and disappeared in Central and South America.

2. NONCOOPERATION:

A second level of nonviolent action is a refusal to allow some functions of a society to operate by not cooperating with the system. Strikes and boycotts are examples. In the face of injustice, people may choose to stop assisting certain activities. Refusing to pay federal taxes (a vast portion of which support the bloated military, an important aspect of preparing for war) or to register for the draft, disobeying unjust laws, closing one's place of business, providing support for those violating unjust laws—these kinds of noncooperation can get in the way of the normal functioning of a society. Noncooperation can be social, political, or economic.

All these initiatives can carry the risk of personal loss or injury. Willingness to accept the loss is a key element in their effectiveness.

Protests against clothing made in sweatshops are an example. Thousands of people have boycotted companies such as the Gap, Disney, and Wal-Mart due to conditions in their factories. Many people, mostly women and children, work for extremely low wages in terrible working conditions to make clothes for which people in the U.S. pay large sums of money. Another is boycotting certain companies, such as Shell Oil and Exxon, which are responsible for business practices that pollute and destroy the environment.

3. INTERVENTION:

A significant step beyond withdrawing cooperation is taken when people directly insert themselves into a social process in a way that brings it to a temporary halt or establishes a new social process or pattern. Sit-ins, blocking entrances, occupying offices, sitting down on railroad tracks–all these actions confront authorities with persons putting themselves in vulnerable positions in an effort to stop important activities. Their purpose is to draw attention to the unjust system and to show the oppressor the strength of the nonviolent movement.

Intervention poses a more direct and immediate challenge to the status quo. It can lead to quicker success or it can bring on sharper repression for a while, as the dynamics of nonviolence continue working for a constructive change.

In 1999 and 2000, there were dramatic examples of this in the streets of Seattle and Washington, DC, directed against world financial institutions (the World Trade Organization, World Bank, and International Monetary Fund). Thousands of people formed human barricades to try to prevent these undemocratic bodies from meeting. People demanded that their voices be heard, that the human needs of people take priority over the profits of corporations.

Question:

Complete the following chart that helps to line up the concrete benefits and risks, both personally and to a "cause," that might result from doing any of the actions that Sharp mentions.

Check off any of these you have participated in.
Circle any you might consider doing in the near future.

	BENEFITS	RISKS
PROTEST AND PERSUASION		
• letter writing		
• petition campaign		
• vigil or rally		
• march		
• street theater		
NON-COOPERATION		
• refusing to pay part or all of federal taxes (war tax resistance)		
• refusing to register for the draft		
• refusing to obey an unjust law		
• boycotting a place of business		
INTERVENTION		
• sit-ins		
• blocking entrances		
• sitting down on railroad tracks or in a corporate office		

What questions come to mind about making such choices?

Do a role-playing exercise using strategies of nonviolence. How would you respond?

Here are some possible situations:

• A group is leafleting outside a clothing store about the use of sweatshop and child labor and is confronted by a hostile shopper.

• You have a meeting with your school administrators to discuss why they won't institute recycling on campus.

• Your employer has issued a memo saying that any employee's political activities, such as civil disobedience actions that could cast the agency in a bad light, are prohibited.

• The bus on which a Christian Peacemaker Team group is traveling in Palestine has been stopped by a group of five armed men, who order three Palestinians off the bus.

One way to role-play these situations is to have people in the group take turns being different parties in the conflict. Rotate positions. This helps people think through all sides of the situation. It also leads to an understanding of the people involved and the power dynamics.

Before stepping into each role, you might want to take a few minutes to think about the conversation, the situation, the arguments each side will use, the emotions that will come up. After you have finished, discuss what it felt like to be in each position. How effective were the people attempting to use nonviolence? What more information was needed?

101 Ways to Foster Nonviolence in Your Life

Educate yourself on injustice and nonviolence.

Be aware of God's embrace.

Question the status quo.

Spend time with a child.

Be conscious of your privileges–on the basis of place of birth, skin color, gender, wealth, etc.

Shout "Yes!" to life.

Use gender-inclusive language.

Seek justice and reconciliation, not victory.

Serve someone in need.

Use cars less–walk, bike, use public transit, or at least carpool.

Listen.

Get training in nonviolence.

Take responsibility for ending injustice.

Buy locally-made, produced, or grown products.

Value art, song, dance, poetry.

Avoid stereotypes.

Ask for forgiveness.

Challenge someone who says something offensive, be it a comment or a joke.

Say thank you–and mean it.

Learn another language or study another culture.

Plant flowers or trees.

Spend time in prayer or quiet reflection.

Refuse to have enemies.

Consider war tax resistance.

Speak for the voiceless.

Turn off the television.

Seek to understand.

Create something beautiful.

Share.

Write letters to the editor about important issues.

Resist materialism.

Stop needing to be "number one."

Recognize that everyone has a "piece of the truth."

Compromise.

Forgive someone who has hurt you or a loved one; let them know.

Make a connection with someone who is different from you.

Ask God to help you on your nonviolence journey.

Spend quality time building relationships.

Speak truth to power.

Offer solutions.

Live with compassion for all life around you.

Praise God.

Let go of fear.

Don't buy war toys.

Celebrate diversity.

Reach out to someone who is hurting.

Conserve energy and water.

Celebrate the beauty of life and creation.

Let elected representatives know which policies you approve and disapprove of.

Affirm and support your friends and family.

Stop rumors.

Smile.

Bring your own (reusable) bags to the store.

Sign a petition.

Research a nonviolent social movement.

Eat less meat or none at all (for the environment, in solidarity with the poor, in respect of animals).

Reclaim your power as a child of God.

Oppose all wars.

Spend time outdoors.

Check the labels on the clothing you buy; be conscious of who might have made them, under what conditions.

Let go of your defenses.

Encourage your faith community to study nonviolence.

Reduce, reuse, recycle, restore.

Follow your conscience.

Don't buy into advertising–literally or figuratively.

Respect all human rights of all people: civil, political, social, economic, cultural.

Treat your body well.

Talk to someone about why violence is bad.

Get a job that supports people, human needs, or the environment–not corporate greed.

Ask your school to teach nonviolent conflict resolution.

Put others first.

Speak out against violence in the media and "entertainment."

Laugh.

Really try to understand the viewpoint of someone with whom you disagree.

Attend a demonstration for peace.

Relax your body posture.

Support organizations that work for peace and justice.

Try using consensus decision-making.

Read about someone who has tried to live nonviolently.

Remember that each day is a blessing and a gift.

Accept your own worth.

Watch a video about justice or peace with friends and discuss.

Recognize and name the divine in every person you encounter.

Refuse to be silent in the face of what really matters.

Question assumptions.

Truly concentrate on what someone is saying to you.

Don't hold grudges.

Write to someone in prison.

Slow down.

Be more aware.

Express your feelings before you reach the stage of anger and hostility.

Start a study circle on nonviolence or a related topic.

Cultivate awe.

Become aware of your own biases.

Seek out and create community.

Be open to transformation.

Cultivate a spirit of calm and inward quiet.

Spend time with someone you love.

Imagine a world without violence and hatred.

Give of yourself.

Choose nonviolence always.

Civil Disobedience

Civil disobedience, far from being a new idea, is a part of our history and religious tradition. The Hebrew Scriptures tell how women saved the baby Moses in defiance of government law; in the Christian Scriptures the book of Acts is filled with stories of how the disciples were jailed for obeying God, rather than human law. St. Thomas More preferred execution as a traitor to betraying his conscience by denying his faith. In the religious tradition, some people prefer to call this witness "divine obedience," that is, doing what God commands us to do by working for justice.

In our own time, civil disobedience has become part of U.S. tradition. During the American Revolution, the colonists violated unjust British laws peacefully as a means of protest–the Boston Tea Party is a famous example. Before the Civil War, the abolitionists and the Underground Railroad broke the law to force an end to slavery as well as to save those slaves who had been able to escape their masters. The Civil Rights Movement and the anti-Vietnam/U.S. War campaign used sit-ins and illegal marches to protest unjust laws and an unjust war. The labor unions have, time and again, used strikes and boycotts to redress grievances. American Indians, due to violations of their treaty rights, committed civil disobedience by fishing; through nonviolent strategies and court actions, they got their rights back. Other examples include the Sanctuary movement (to protect victims of human rights abuses in Central and South America), the anti-nuclear weapons movement, and the movement to end the sanctions on Iraq.

Civil disobedience depends on the idea of importance of conscience: conscience must be obeyed first, then the law. A person's conscience can lead one to see a law, regulation, or practice as unjust and to refuse to obey it. Civil disobedience seeks to change the unjust law and to act on public opinion to do what it cannot do alone.

Civil disobedience is not the first step to be taken in confronting injustice; it should be preceded by letter-writing, petitions, vigils, rallies, and acts of legal noncooperation where they are applicable. When these methods have failed to bring about the needed change, then people may want to resist the injustice openly.

Sometimes individuals may commit civil disobedience in an effort to inform the public, to bring about change, or to stand for a moral principle. These efforts are invaluable. Civil disobedience on a large scale can also produce change more quickly since the authorities have more difficulty enforcing a law that is being broken by many demonstrators. As one popular slogan says, "There ain't no power like the power of the people 'cuz the power of the people don't stop!"

Although civil disobedience is not inherently nonviolent, the classic instances of civil disobedience, and most successful ones, have been nonviolent. Usually this means that when engaging in an act of civil disobedience one does it "openly," in a manner that is respectful of life and the rights of others, and that the dissenter is willing to suffer the consequences–disapproval of friends and family and the penalties of the law.

To perform an act of civil disobedience is not necessarily to deny civil authority, but to disapprove of the abuse of authority. One must prayerfully decide when it has become necessary to choose obedience to God's law rather than to civil law. Civil disobedience is to be carried out in the hope that it will make the world more just and more peaceful.

> "OVER THE years, many have come to see that acts of nonviolent resistance must be creative and must always seek to clearly communicate our YES to life as well as our NO to the evil we are resisting. Many have also come to see that our resistance should not just be to a particular weapons system, law, or policy, but must also address the web of violence, greed and fear which underlies the U.S. system and which also lies in the very depths of our own hearts. In response to the violence and lies perpetrated by the state, I believe we must always seek to incarnate into our resistance and peacemaking efforts the self-emptying love of Jesus and the 'truth-force' of Gandhi."
>
> —Art Laffin, Plowshares activist and Catholic Worker

The Trouble With Our State

Dan Berrigan

The trouble with our state
was not civil disobedience
which in any case was hesitant and rare

Civil disobedience was rare as
    kidney stone
No, rarer; it was disappearing like
    immigrants' disease

You've heard of a war on cancer?
There is no war like the media
There is no war like routine
There is no war like 3 square meals
There is no war like a prevailing wind

It blows softly, whispers
Don't rock the boat
The sails obey, the ship of state rolls on.

The trouble with our state
—we only learned it afterward
when the dead resembled the living
who resembled the dead
the civil virtue shone like paint on tin
and tin citizens and tin soldiers
marched to the common whip

—our trouble
the trouble with our state
with our state of soul
our state of siege—
was
civil
obedience.

DAN BERRIGAN, in his book, *No Bars to Manhood*, writes, "We have assumed the name of peacemakers, but we have been, by and large, unwilling to pay any significant price. And because we want the peace with half a heart and half a life and will, the war, of course, continues, because the waging of war, by its nature, is total—but the waging of peace, by our own cowardice, is partial." He explains that people are willing to give up everything during war: their families, their homes, their very lives. But they are not willing to let go of normalcy to wage peace. "There are no makers of peace because the making of peace is at least as costly as the making of war—at least as exigent, at least as disruptive, at least as liable to bring disgrace and prison and death in its wake."

PEACEMAKER: At a Congressional hearing, Mother Jones was asked, "Where is your home?" She answered, "...my address is like my shoes. It travels with me. I abide where there is a fight against wrong."

Mary Harris "Mother" Jones (1830-1930) was a pioneer labor organizer. She worked with the labor movement until her death at age 100—giving speeches, talking to politicians, leading marches. She was called—"the grandmother of all agitators" and was known for her spirit.

I abide where there is a fight against wrong.

—Mother Jones

Closing Prayer

Reader 1:

A reading from the first letter of Peter (3:8-12)

All of you must be of one mind. Be sympathetic, loving, compassionate, humble. Never return evil for evil, or insult for insult, but give a blessing instead. You were called to do this, to inherit a blessing yourself. For,

> "Whoever would love life
> and see good days
> must keep the tongue from evil
> and the lips from deceitful talk.
> They must turn from evil to good,
> they must seek peace and pursue it.
> For the eyes of Our God
> are on the just,
> and the ears of Our God
> attend to their prayers.
> But the face of Our God
> is turned against evildoers."

Reader 2:

Loving, compassionate God, bless us today and all days as we try to follow the paths of your love. Hear our prayers and give us words of love and blessing.

Side 1: Help us to live every day in a spirit of nonviolence.

Side 2: Guide us to act in peace towards ourselves, our families, our friends, our communities, our cities, our nation, and our world.

Side 1: Help us to respond in love to all people with whom we come in contact.

Side 2: May we work to heal our relationships and our world.

Side 1: May we seek out community to help us along our journey of seeking and pursuing peace.

Side 2: Sometimes we will be afraid. Give us courage, God, to live and act nonviolently

All: Speak to our hearts and minds, Creator. Help us to respond to the challenge you place before us: to live nonviolently. Amen.

Part Three: Reflections

1. Many people believe that the question is not whether, but when obedience to God requires that a Christian engage in civil disobedience. The following are examples of civil disobedience approved by some Christians. Where do you draw the line?

Ask yourself about each of the following examples, "Do I approve of civil disobedience by a Christian in this instance? Why or why not?"

YES   NO

a. In a certain country, it is against the law to be a Christian or to hold any church services. A small group holds secret Bible meetings and celebrates the Eucharist.

b. A soldier about to be sent to the Gulf believes he cannot in conscience fight there. He is court-martialed and sent to prison.

c. Three people walk onto the Nevada nuclear test site, kneel down, and begin praying for disarmament. The police arrest them for trespassing.

d. A group attempts to block entrances to a large corporation to protest what transnational corporations are doing in poverty-stricken countries: making substantial profits at the expense of the poor.

e. Members of peace groups sit on railroad tracks to prevent trains that are carrying nuclear weapons from passing.

f. A group enters a factory and dismantles parts for bombs.

What other ways do you see of resolving these situations? Why do you think these people were called to act in such ways?

2. Father Domingos Barbé said that "the key elements of active nonviolent struggle are strength and gentleness." What do you think are the key qualities a nonviolent person should have?

3. If you were to use (or have used) any of the methods of nonviolent action listed in this chapter, do you feel that God would be (was) part of this decision? Why or why not?

4. In what ways can you use the communications strategies (understanding, focusing, negotiating) outlined in this chapter?

5. What methods of nonviolent action most attract you or could you see yourself doing in the near future?

Suggestions for Action

- Choose or find the definition of nonviolence that is most helpful to you. Write it out and keep it in a place where you will see it often. Pray and reflect on it.

- Be conscious of the times you respond violently with your words, expressions, or actions. Practice responding in a different way.

- Forgive an old hurt.

- Practice some of the "101 Ways to Foster Nonviolence in Your Life."

- Learn more about consensus decision-making and try it out in a group you are a part of.

- Find out what nonviolent campaigns are happening in your area; participate in a nonviolent action. Groups like Pax Christi are often part of such campaigns; contact a peace group for more information.

A Sampling of Sources and Resources

Berrigan, Daniel, S.J. No Bars to Manhood. New York: Bantam Books, 1970.

Coover, Virginia, Ellen Deacon, Charles Esser, and Christopher Moore. Resource Manual for a Living Revolution. Philadelphia, PA: New Society Publishers, 1985. (A handbook of skills and tools for social change activists–includes activities, theory, group dynamics, consciousness raising, and community living.)

Dingerson, Leigh and Sarah H. Hay. The CO/MOTION Guide to Youth-Led Social Change. Washington, DC: Alliance for Justice, 1998. (Alliance for Justice: 11 Dupont Circle NW, 2nd Floor; Washington, DC 20036; phone: 202/822-6070; e-mail: alliance@afj.org; http://www.afj.org)

Just Peace–Compiled by Mary Fritz, SSJ, edited by Robert Keeler. A collection of nine essays that move the paradigm shift further away from the debate on the "just war" theory and closer toward the question of how to build a just peace. Scholars, theologians and activists address the conditions under which violence arises, the progress in church teaching on war and nonviolence, the theology of peacemaking and guidelines for cultivating peace. Pax Christi USA, 532 W.8th St., Erie, PA 16502; phone: 814-453-4955 ext. 231; e-mail: sales@paxchristiusa.org; www.paxchristiusa.org

Kownacki, Mary Lou, OSB. The Nonviolent Moment: Spirituality for the 21st Century. Drawing deep insights–her own and those of others–into the nature of human relationships and peacemaking. She offers the reader a personal process for developing a spirituality of nonviolence tailored to face and transform the violence and suffering of our times. Each chapter concludes with reflection and action suggestions. Excellent resource for individual reflection, faith sharing groups, parish gatherings, families, classes, or religious communities. *Pax Christi USA, 532 W.8th St., Erie, PA 16502; phone: 814-453-4955 x231; e-mail: sales@paxchristiusa.org; www.paxchristiusa.org*

Laffin, Arthur J. and Anne Montgomery. *Swords Into Plowshares: Nonviolent Direct Action for Disarmament, Peace, Social Justice.* Marion, SD: Fortkamp Publishing, Rose Hill Books, 1996.

Nagler, Michael. *The Steps of Nonviolence.* Nyack, NY: the Fellowship of Reconciliation, 1999. (Short booklet.)

School of the Americas Watch. PO Box 4566; Washington, DC 20017; phone: 202/234-3440; e-mail: info@soawatch.org; http://www.soaw.org

Sharp, Gene. *The Politics of Nonviolent Action.* Boston, MA: Extending Horizons Books, 1973. (Three books: *Power and Struggle, The Methods of Nonviolent Action, The Dynamics of Nonviolent Action.*) (A major exploration of the nature of nonviolent struggle, including an examination of political power, methods of nonviolence, and the operation of nonviolence in practice.) Albert Einstein Institute (to advance the worldwide study and strategic use of nonviolent action in conflict): http://www.aeinstein.org Sharp's original 198 methods of nonviolence are available at http://www.aeinstein.org/198_methods.html

Vanier, Jean. *Community and Growth.* London: Darton, Longman and Todd Publishers, 1979.

War Resisters League. *Handbook for Nonviolent Action.* New York and Hampton, CT: War Resisters League and Donnelly/Colt Graphix, 4th printing, November 1999.

Wink, Walter. *Powers Series,* Minneapolis: Fortress Press. *Naming the Powers: The Language of Power in the New Testament,* 1984; *Unmasking the Powers: The Invisible Forces that Determine Human Existence,* 1986; *Engaging the Powers: Discernment and Resistance in a World of Domination,* 1992. Or see *The Powers that Be: Theology for a New Millennium.* New York: Galilee Doubleday, 1998 (a digest of the Powers series).

Credits

"Conflict at Home" from Christopher News Notes, No. 285, "Conflict: What's Good About It–What's Bad About It."

Part Four

The Spirit of Nonviolence

The nonviolent position is often misunderstood. Some associate it with cowardice, passivity (submissiveness or inactivity), and naivete. Yet just the opposite is true. While the characteristics and goals of a nonviolent person may not always be the ones the world values, praises, and honors, they are definitely not inactive or weak. The *Bhagavad Gita* (Hindu sacred scripture) says: "If you want to see the brave, look for those who can forgive. If you want to see the heroic, look at those who can love in return for hatred."

These are some characteristics of nonviolence, showing that it is both a method and a spirit. It is based on respect and love for people and all of creation and taking concrete steps to act in truth and justice.

How do you view nonviolence? What are its building blocks?

> ### The Spirit of Nonviolence
>
> - *Opening Prayer*
> - *Jesus' Third Way*
> - *Two Prophets of Nonviolence Show Us the Way*
> - *Active, Not Passive*
> - *Non-Harm*
> - *Truth-Seeking*
> - *Justice as Foundational*
> - *Willingness to Accept Suffering*
> - *The Nonviolent Spirit*
> - *Closing Prayer*
> - *Reflections*
> - *Suggestions for Action*
> - *A Sampling of Sources and Resources*

Opening Prayer

Reader 1:

Loving God, we gather here before you now in this place, in stillness. We come to you from many places–some of us struggling with decisions or relationships in our lives, others constantly aware of the calmness of your presence guiding us. Some of us are new to the journey of nonviolence, others have been struggling with it for a while. We ask your presence among us as we learn, share, and grow. We ask your presence as we name, silently or aloud, our prayers, hopes, dreams, and fears.

Allow time for people to voice their prayers and intentions.

Reader 1:

Loving Creator, we humbly ask you to hear our prayers. May we feel the presence of your Spirit always moving in our lives, guiding us in faith and love. Amen.

Novena of the Holy Spirit
Author Unknown

All:

Come Holy Spirit, Spirit of Wisdom, open my eyes to see all of life, events, and people with the vision of my God, who creates all and sees all that is good.

Come Holy Spirit, Spirit of Understanding, give me deep insight into the wonder and mystery of my life's journey as I walk by faith as light in the darkness.

Come Holy Spirit, Spirit of Counsel, teach me to listen closely to hear your voice, for you speak to me in so many different ways.

Come Holy Spirit, Spirit of Fortitude, pierce through and calm all my fears.
Strengthen me with a firm faith that I may live and proclaim your words with courage.

Come Holy Spirit, Spirit of Knowledge, expand my mind and heart, so that as I come together with all men and women of good will, we may learn and grow in your ways.

Come Holy Spirit, Spirit of Reverence, lead me in the praise of my God, for all creation reflects God's glory and overflowing goodness.

Come Holy Spirit, Spirit of Wonder and Awe, fill me with a sense of the greatness of my God, into whose hands I entrust my spirit, now and forever.

Amen.

Jesus' Third Way

Many people think and have been taught that humans have two choices (often described as instincts) in conflict situations: flight (to submit to the power of another, be afraid, and run) or fight (assault the other). Theologian, author, and lecturer Walter Wink has written about our third choice: Jesus' Third Way of nonviolent direct action. This way involves facing the conflict loudly and head-on but not in a way that uses violence.

When following Jesus' Third Way, we use creativity to change power relations. Wink gives three specific examples, found in Matthew 5:38-42, through which Jesus demonstrated this Third Way. These examples are turning your cheek, giving your shirt as well as your coat, and carrying a soldier's pack two miles instead of one. These Bible verses have often been interpreted to say that we should give in to others (let them abuse us) or that we must be humble or that we should try harder. But these interpretations, Wink demonstrates in his book *Engaging the Powers*, entirely miss the point. To people in first century Palestine, these responses would have thrown off power relations, upset the status quo, and shamed

oppressors. (See chapter 9 of Wink's book for more details.) In each of these instances (and others besides), Jesus' example of nonviolent direct action meant liberation, the assertion of human dignity and freedom, and the exposing of injustice.

Wink lists more of the characteristics of the Third Way, many of which are expanded upon later in this chapter (and in other places in the book):

- Find a creative alternative (such as humor) to violence
- Assert your dignity and humanity
- Do not allow yourself to be humiliated (even if you have been in the past)
- Expose the injustice of the system
- Shame the oppressor into repenting
- Recognize your own power
- Be willing to undergo the penalty of breaking unjust laws
- Seek the transformation of situations and people

This is the spirit of nonviolence. It is this spirit that we must work with and toward as we attempt to follow the way of peace.

Two Prophets of Nonviolence Show Us the Way

In the twentieth century, a Hindu lawyer from India named Mohandas (also known as Mahatma, meaning "great soul") Gandhi demonstrated Jesus' nonviolent way with new life. After experiencing racial discrimination while living in South Africa, in 1906 Gandhi began what was to be a lifetime of nonviolent struggle against oppression. His first nonviolent campaign took place against this discrimination in South Africa. He later moved back to India and, against great odds, he fashioned a massive

nonviolent movement to end colonial rule and injustices within Indian society.

Gandhi insisted that nonviolence was a new way of looking at things in one's life: a new attitude of mind and heart that changed everything a person did. Gandhi said that he was inspired as much by Jesus' teachings in the Sermon on the Mount (Matthew 5, Luke 6) as he was by his own Hindu scriptures. With the guidance of such religious teachings, he skillfully combined religious idealism with practical realism to wage a successful "war without violence" to free India from British rule. The liberation of India established forever the immense power of this gentle doctrine.

Martin Luther King, Jr. furthered and refined Gandhi's ideas, teachings, and actions as a way to address racial oppression in the United States. King saw clearly that what Gandhi had done, as he put it, was to "lift the love of Jesus above mere interaction between individuals to a powerful and effective social force on a large scale."

King grew up in Atlanta, Georgia, in a South separated by segregation. He became a minister and a leader in the U.S. Civil Rights Movement, a nonviolent mass movement to challenge racial discrimination, especially in the South. For this work and for his consistent stand for justice, he won the Nobel Peace Prize in 1964.

Under King's leadership people marched. They demonstrated; they boycotted; they went to jail. They confronted the violence of racism with the nonviolence of love. In doing so, they impressed on the U.S. consciousness the power of nonviolence, of love, and of nonviolent action.

King's experiences in the Civil Rights Movement led him to embrace nonviolence as a way of life and to make connections between racial injustice, poverty, and all forms of violence, including war. He longed to create the "beloved community" in which all people would be treated with love and dignity and have enough. Peace in this community would come not from the absence of tension but from the presence of justice.

These two twentieth century prophets of nonviolence opened up before the world a whole range of possibilities for calm, courageous, and effective action to lower the intensity of violence and to enhance the dignity of those who once had been victims. Both strongly believed that people are not permanently set against each other as enemies, but rather, even in the depths of oppression, they can engage each other in dialogue. They saw that people considered weak because others held power over them could in fact rise up nonviolently, create moral pressure, and make the oppressor recognize the injustice, leading to its correction. They recognized that we must stand against oppression and injustice, but also for love, human dignity, and relationship.

Gandhi called this method *satyagraha*, "truth-force" or clinging firmly to the truth. Martin Luther King, Jr., called it soul-force. Christians call it the love that can overcome the world.

Nobody can win a war.
Today the choice is no longer
between violence and nonviolence.
It is either nonviolence or nonexistence.

—Martin Luther King, Jr.

Question:

As you journey further into the study of nonviolence, what are some questions that you have for people of nonviolence, such as Gandhi and King?

Nonviolence is really tough. You don't practice nonviolence by attending conferences—you practice it on the picket line. And if you've been here two or three days, you know how difficult it is.

—Cesar Chavez

Active, Not Passive

When we examine more closely the dynamics of nonviolence as taught and lived by Jesus and practiced by Gandhi and King, we see right away that it is not an abstract philosophy. The spirit of nonviolence is not a spirit of passiveness in the face of evil or of inaction in the middle of conflict. It is much more than passive dissent, more than turning the other cheek, more than being unwilling to fight back.

Nonviolence is not the "easy way out" or the coward's approach to problems. In fact, Wink and Gandhi are among those who believe that one must pass through the "fight" stage in order to embrace nonviolence. This does not mean a person has to engage in violence. But the person who accepts nonviolence must be aware of his or her anger at injustice and must be willing to fight to end it. If he or she is, then violence can be renounced and nonviolence embraced.

Nonviolence, then, is not inaction, running away, or taking abuse. Jesus' Third Way is an activity, a mindset, and an approach to conflict. Nonviolence is an active refusal to submit to injustice, an active showing of love, an active process of engagement.

The point of nonviolence is not to escape conflict or to strive for a conflict-free existence. We can escape conflict only if we escape all human interactions. Nonviolence, in fact, brings conflict that already exists out into the open, revealing and naming injustice. The challenge is to wage conflict constructively and creatively, rather than the methods of violence which destroy and humiliate. Nobel Peace Prize winner Adolfo Pérez Esquivel has said, "Peace is not the absence of conflict, but rather the means to overcome conflict and generate a relation of coexistence despite differences among people."

Nonviolence is not for cowards. It calls for deep inner strength, the strength of self-control, the strength of maintaining respect for oppressors without giving in to the impulse to strike back. The nonviolent person does not simply quiet down when trouble starts, but instead stands up, faces the difficulty, tells the aggressor that what is happening is wrong, and prays for courage.

Jesus, for instance, had a lot of trouble with some of the Pharisees. Several times he called them "hypocrites," the Greek word for actors on a stage. He confronted them openly, publicly, fearlessly. He argued with them; he challenged them. Confrontation is an established technique for changing attitudes. People sometimes see things differently when they are forced to face an opposing view. Jesus showed his love for these people, hoping they would develop a more wholesome attitude. He did so actively and vocally.

The spirit of nonviolence calls for patient determination, seeking ways of reaching opponents, helping them to acknowledge the truth, working with them to change their ways, and being open to the piece of the truth that they may offer to us.

Questions:

Find examples in the scriptures of Jesus experiencing conflict. How did he handle these situations? Put yourself in the scene and participate in the event. How did you feel afterward? What do you especially need to work on?

Non-Harm

The most critical assumption underlying nonviolence is that both parties in any conflict share a common humanity. Some people's humanity may be warped by a desire for power, buried under the weight of official duties, or hidden by habits of violence or beliefs, but it is always there.

The nonviolent approach to conflict comes directly out of a respect for the sacredness of life. All people, even aggressors, enemies, or perpetrators of unjust systems, have a fundamental human dignity. The nonviolent person consciously and deliberately appreciates that dignity.

The very first consequence of this respect is to refrain from harming those persons, no matter how aggressive or intimidating they may be. Therefore, nonviolence begins with a firm resolution not to hurt one's opponents. "Bless those who persecute you; bless and do not curse," wrote Saint Paul. (Romans 12:14)

Even if we do not agree with their actions, we must always remember that they are owed respect as members of the human family. To deny this is violence. As Michael Nagler, who has studied and taught nonviolence for over 25 years, says, "Dehumanization is the beginning of all violence." The nonviolent person affirms the worth of others and respects them as fundamentally valuable even when their actions are ugly and evil. At times this is very difficult; it can be easy to put down or slander people who are acting violently or unjustly.

According to the book of Genesis, all humans are made in the image and likeness of God. We respect this God-likeness by refusing to disrespect the person possessing it. Gandhi understood the firm religious basis for non-harm: "God is the common bond that unites all human beings. To break this bond even with our greatest enemy is to tear [God's Self] to pieces. There is humanity even in the most wicked."

Respect for one's own human dignity as well as that of the opponent leads to engaging in a conflict, to trying to resolve differences, to removing injustices, and to finding constructive alternatives. The nonviolent person will enter into the conflict and take up the issues, but always with the kind of respect that will refrain from wanting to harm the opponent no matter how the opponent is behaving at the moment.

The human person is the clearest reflection of God's presence in the world: all of the church's work in pursuit of both justice and peace is designed to protect and promote the dignity of every person.

–The Challenge of Peace

Prayer

A modification of the Buddhist Karuna meditation:

"We might sit in stillness and visualize the person whom we love most in the world. We surround that person with our love and care, praying for them or holding them in our hearts. Then we invite into that caring the people next closest to us and surround them with the same love and care. We move out with our invitations, out to an ever-widening circle of people, inviting them into the same warmth of love that enveloped the most-beloved. At the end of our meditation, we invite into our love the people from whom we feel most estranged, those whom we dislike, fear, or hate. We invite them into our love and keep them there in prayer. I believe that such constant practice in love can help us to become more deeply loving people."

–Shelley Douglass, "Ending the Spiral of Violence," in *Educating for Peace and Justice*.

More and more people are coming to realize that the principle of non-harm must extend to our earth. According to the book of Genesis, God created humans to be stewards of the earth, to watch over it. Instead, we have come to view the earth as simply another tool in our exploitation process. We do not pay attention to how our actions affect the delicate balance of the earth's ecosystems. To be nonviolent, we must re-learn how to take the earth into consideration, to praise the Earth's bounty, and to respect it.

Truth-Seeking

Gandhi insisted that nonviolence be based in truth. And for him, that which is truthful is life-affirming. The test of truth is what is good for life: that which supports and nurtures life is true, that which attacks and destroys it is false. Respect for truth also leads to an attitude of what he called "good will toward all life." In fact, Gandhi believed so strongly in the importance of truth that he called it another name for God.

But it's not always clear where truth lies in human controversies. Does carrying a gun discourage a potential enemy and thus affirm the life of those who are threatened by that enemy? Or does it serve to provoke that enemy still further and help cause the very violence it is supposed to prevent? What is the truth here? Which way provides the greater support to life?

How can one be sure that one's own cause is, in fact, true? Can't there be truth on both sides? Isn't it arrogant to claim that our way and only our way is true? More than arrogance, doesn't any insistence that one has a lock on the truth lead to intolerance and fanaticism? Gandhi thought so. He said, "I am but a seeker after truth. I claim to have found a way to it. I claim to be making a ceaseless effort to find it. But I admit that I have not yet found it. To find truth completely is to realize oneself and one's destiny, that is, to become perfect. I am painfully

It's not always clear where truth lies in human controversies.

conscious of my imperfections."

Gandhi said that *satyagraha* excludes the use of violence because human beings are "not capable of knowing the absolute truth, and therefore not competent to punish." The spirit of truthseeking includes enough uncertainty that a person refrains from taking (or harming) human life in the name of any cause.

But the difficulties in achieving truth need not be paralyzing. In some situations, truth is clearly evident: slavery, child abuse, torture, concentration camps, nuclear war. These are so clearly contrary to human well-being that a conscientious person has no difficulty knowing which side to take.

In other less obvious conflicts, truth must be sought carefully and persistently. Anyone probing for truth should approach the search with humility, open to the insights of others, always ready to adjust one's perceptions with new knowledge or different perspectives. A great part of seeking after truth is listening. Jim Bristol, a Quaker pacifist, wrote that it was more important to understand others than to convince them that we are right. Aware of our tendencies toward self-righteousness, the truth-seeker is ready to accept honest criticism and change direction if a better way becomes evident. Until that happens, the part of the truth we have discovered will continue to guide the way.

Question:

"What is truth?" asked Pilate. **(John 18:38)**
What is your answer to this question?

Justice as Foundational

In seeking after truth, justice must be pursued, especially for the poorest and most vulnerable. Without true justice and reconciliation, the end of violence is not possible. As Pope Paul VI said, "If you want peace, work for justice."

As peacemakers, we must attempt to understand why people act violently. We may find injustice at the root, even if that is not how it is named. People may act violently in an attempt to draw attention to injustice (such as a military occupation) or to force change or because they see no other options. When overwhelmed, beaten down again and again, or faced with immense institutional or structural violence, they may turn to interpersonal violence or conflict on a larger scale (like war or acts of terrorism). If we try to seek peace but ignore how violence is rooted in injustices such as the growing gap between rich and poor, racism, and sexism, we cannot really hope to build a world of nonviolence.

As residents of one of the wealthiest countries in the world, we–both as a group and as individuals–often get in the way of the pursuit of justice. Part of our exploration for truth, then, must be to search out these injustices. Jim Bristol wrote, "What millions of middle-class people and other non-poor fail to recognize is that they themselves are accomplices each day in meting out inhuman, all-pervading violence upon their fellows. To be realistic, we must attack the violence of the status quo in which we all share, no matter how unwillingly." We must be aware of the ways in which we and our lifestyles contribute to injustice, and then work to change this.

Over and over, the Bible condemns injustice. Jesus clearly demonstrates that justice is key to acting and living in the spirit of nonviolence. He taught that people should actively oppose the injustices of their society and that they should try to live in new ways of just relationships. Only when people are free to live in dignity and act with respect towards all of creation, instead of living under oppression and humiliation, will we have a nonviolent world.

Question:

Do you agree with Jim Bristol's assessment?
How does it or doesn't it ring true for your life?

"ALTHOUGH ADVOCATES of nonviolence talk about the necessity of both direct action–protest–and of constructive program, we do not yet really see the union of these two aspects in a clear workable form. More important, perhaps, is the fact that most of us either do not realize, or have not accepted, the reality that disarmament and peace and the development of a 'nonviolent world' call for some startling changes in economic, social and political structures." **–Marjorie Swann**

Willingness to Accept Suffering

A person of nonviolence will face violence—be it verbal, emotional, or physical. The nonviolent person must open his or her heart and voluntarily take on the suffering of an unjust situation without violently retaliating.

This suffering, the taking on of violence, seeks to transform relationships and to stop cycles of violence rather than allowing them to continue. The certainty of facing this suffering or violence may be the most difficult aspect of nonviolence.

This does not mean that a person of nonviolence seeks out suffering, inflicts suffering on him or herself, or accepts abuse (especially in personal relationships). Rather, as nonviolent people, we are called to model

Jesus' example of suffering–suffering chosen as a way of accomplishing a greater good and transforming the world. Even when facing suffering, the nonviolent person is active, not passive. Nonviolence does not mean resigning oneself to being verbally, emotionally, or physically abused; it is not nonviolent to allow cycles of violence to continue. Instead, the Third Way, the way of nonviolence, says that people must actively counter oppression. They must creatively find ways to expose violence and to take initiative to assert their dignity and worth as human beings. In fact, telling someone to do nothing in a situation of violence or injustice is exactly the opposite of the spirit of nonviolence. Sometimes, using the techniques of the previous chapter–such as negotiation–can be helpful. At other times, one must remove oneself from the situation.

What does this mean practically? How might we suffer for standing up for nonviolence? The forms that violence against a person of nonviolence may take in responding to a person's nonviolent acts or words vary widely. Young people who seek to resolve personal conflicts at school without resorting to violence may be called "wussy" or "wimp." They may face the slurs of their peers, people talking behind their backs, or social rejection. At a demonstration against U.S. bombing in Iraq, nonviolent vigilers may be called traitors, unpatriotic, communists. These are examples of verbal violence.

When people are even more challenged by nonviolent actions or when they feel even more is at stake, they may respond with physical violence. Students participating in sit-ins in the South during the Civil Rights Movement were spit upon, showered with ketchup and mustard, and hit, as well as verbally taunted. Other people were beaten up or even killed for nonviolently standing for their beliefs. Gandhi and King were both assassinated–strong proof that some people feared the power of their nonviolent witness.

Often people of nonviolence face censorship, psychological pressures, economic sanctions or financial hardships, or arrest. They may find that people they thought were friends disagree with their nonviolent stand and may even distance themselves; this, too, is a form of suffering. Ultimately, the person completely dedicated to nonviolence must be prepared to make the final sacrifice: to give her or his life.

We are called to follow in Jesus' footsteps–all the while remembering that his path led him to the painful crucifixion of a criminal. The Austrian peace activist Hildegard Goss-Mayr has written, "The moment we attack an injustice, we must be prepared and willing to accept the sacrifices and the suffering that necessarily will result from the attack. For those whose conscience is attacked will react with violence; this violence can become a real symbol of the cross for some of those engaged in nonviolent action."

Yet the follower of Jesus can find some comfort in his words: "If you find that the world hates you, remember that it hated me before you. If you belonged to the world, the world would love you as its own . . .Remember what I told you: a subordinate is never greater than a superior–so know that they will persecute you as they persecuted me. . ." (John 15:18-19a, 20a) But through it all, "know that I am with you always, even until the end of the world." (Matthew 28:20b) We know that Jesus walks the path of nonviolence with us and that the love of humanity and the help of community can sustain us.

Nonviolent people do not suffer simply for the sake of suffering; they do so in an attempt to transform relationships and injustices. Nonviolence appeals to the essential humanity in an adversary. At some point, nonviolent action, done in courage and love, can trigger a nonviolent response in the other person or group, can fan the spark of decency that, no matter how low it may burn for a time, cannot be extinguished completely. A key to triggering this human response is the willingness of the nonviolent person to suffer without retaliation. The human truth in a confrontation is hardly ever apparent to the person or group acting violently or unjustly. But a nonviolent person steps forward as someone more willing to receive pain than to inflict it for what is believed to be right and true and just.

If, however, the adversary meets violence in return, continued aggression becomes self-justifying. But it is difficult to sustain aggression against someone who is not fighting back, someone who courageously and lovingly faces the attacker, preferring to suffer rather than continue the cycle of violence. Through this suffering, willingly accepted by the person of nonviolence, hearts and minds can be affected.

"Suffering is infinitely more powerful than the law of the jungle for converting an opponent," wrote Gandhi. "Rivers of blood may have to flow before we gain our freedom, but it must be our blood."

By no means does this mean that people of nonviolence should submit to or become victims of abuse. The turning point when using nonviolence comes not because the nonviolent person acts like a victim, bowing down and passively accepting blows and insults. It occurs because the would-be victim stands strong in the courage of conviction and is willing to take the blows in order to witness to the truth. When the person or group acting violently begins to recognize this, the aggression falters.

Question:

Have you ever suffered because of your choice to follow Jesus' teachings or example, as you understand it? If so, how did you handle this?

> "TO OUR MOST BITTER opponents we say: We shall match your capacity to inflict suffering by our capacity to endure suffering. We shall meet your physical force with soul force. Do to us what you will, and we shall continue to love you. . .Throw us in jail and we shall still love you. Send your hooded perpetrators of violence into our community at the midnight hour and beat us and leave us half dead, and we shall still love you. But be ye assured that we will wear you down by our capacity to suffer. One day we shall win freedom, not only for ourselves. We shall so appeal to your heart and conscience that we shall win *you* in the process, and our victory will be a double victory."
> —Martin Luther King, Jr.

The Nonviolent Spirit

Nonviolence, then, means actively seeking the truth and ending injustice, all the while keeping in mind the common humanity of all of our sisters and brothers and being willing to suffer in some ways for the pursuit of truth. When one does this, a spirit of nonviolence is cultivated. Among other characteristics, the spirit of nonviolence involves respect, confidence, courage, and hope.

The nonviolent person respects the dignity of all people and of creation, oppressor as well as oppressed, opponent as well as self. As King wrote, the practitioner of nonviolence does not seek to humiliate or defeat but to win friendship and understanding. (See Appendix D for King's six-point philosophy and practice of nonviolence.) The nonviolent person respects others by being open to the truth they may have.

Confidence comes from the realization that nonviolence works better than violence in the long run, certainly, but it is especially strong because of the example and teaching of Jesus. In his power and through the Spirit, we know we're on the right track when we try to act as he did, relying on Jesus' help as we struggle to do what is right. We can create a world founded in justice, starting with our own lives and relationships.

And so we're inspired to summon the courage to move forward and actively engage in the struggle to right wrongs and create helpful bonds to take the place of aggressive hostility. "I can do all things through the One who gives me strength." (Philippians 4:13) We have the courage to take risks and to enter into possible difficulty.

Through it all we have hope. People can change, structures can be improved, conflicts can be resolved, swords can be beaten into plowshares. No one is a prisoner of the past. This world and the people who inhabit it are fundamentally good. As the theologian Walter Wink writes, "History belongs to the intercessors, who believe the future into being . . .The future belongs to whoever can envision in the manifold of its potentials a new and desirable possibility, which faith then fixes upon as inevitable. This is the politics of hope. Hope envisages the future and then acts as if that future is now irresistible, thus helping to create the reality for which it longs."

Ultimately, as the Spirit spreads to more and more people, the whole world can become a better place, taking on more dimensions of the Reign of God's justice. We ourselves become ever closer to God. Father John Dear, a Jesuit author and activist, writes, "A spirituality of nonviolence means consciously living in the presence of God, growing ever more aware of God's presence in our hearts, disarming us, moving us ever deeper into God."

My optimism rests on my belief in the infinite possibilities of the individual to develop non-violence. The more you develop it in your own being, the more infectious it becomes till it overwhelms your surroundings and by and by might oversweep the world. —Gandhi

What about anger?

Some people say that anger has no place in a nonviolent person. But this is not necessarily true. Jesus got angry, such as when he cleansed the temple (Mark 11:15-17). Anger can be a part of our search for the truth. When we recognize injustice, it is appropriate to be angry. In this recognition are seeds of hope for a better way. What we must be cautious of is appropriately channeling our anger at unjust systems and actions. We must work to find new, just ways of being in the world.

Closing Prayer

Reader 1:

Loving God, You call us to act, to live out a vision of nonviolence as shown to us through Jesus and other prophets. We remember the covenant you made with your holy people and the sacrifices of your son Jesus. Your words remind us of these promises.

"Thus says God,
who created the heavens
and stretched them out,
who spread out the earth
and what comes from it,
who gives breath
to the people upon it
and spirit to those who walk in it:
I am God, I have called you in righteousness,
I have taken you by the hand and kept you;
I have given you as a covenant to the people,
a light to the nations,
to open the eyes that are blind,
to bring out prisoners from the dungeon,
from the prison those who sit in darkness. . .
See, the former things have come to pass,
and new things I now declare. . ." **(Isaiah 42:5-7; 9a)**

Reader2:

May we learn to recognize and enact this vision and reality of your creation, God.

Side 1: Teach us always to act and live in love and justice.

Side 2: Teach us to act each moment with respect for people and all of creation.

All: Give us your spirit, O God; make us a light to the nations.

Side 1: Help us to see the truth and to proclaim it to others.

Side 2: Help us be open to the truth that others may teach us.

All: Give us your spirit, O God; make us a light to the nations.

Side 1: Remind us to respect all life at all times.

Side 2: Remind us to seek not only peace, but peace with justice.

All: Give us your spirit, O God; make us a light to the nations.

Side 1: Guide us with hope through easy times and difficult ones.

Side 2: Guide us with every step on the way of your peace.

All: Give us your spirit, O God; make us a light to the nations.

Take us by the hand and transform our hearts and minds, making all things new.

Amen.

Part Four: Reflections

1. List people you know who demonstrate in some manner the qualities or attitudes discussed here:

> Active, not passive:
> Non-harming:
> Truth-seeking:
> Justice-seeking:
> Willing to accept suffering:
> Respecting of all:
> Courage:
> Hope for the future:

  A. What do you find attractive and appealing about these people?

  B. What "puts you off" or is problematic about them?

2. The spirit of nonviolence is active, not passive; tries not to harm; seeks truth and justice; is willing to accept suffering. Which of these areas is easiest for you? Which is more difficult? Are there any that you can begin to implement or further in your daily life?

3. Where do you encounter the peacemaking God in your day-to-day life?

4. How have I allowed God to disarm your heart; how are you resisting this disarming?

5. How are you being called to go deeper into the active nonviolence of God?

Suggestions for Action

- Gandhi and King, two great prophets of nonviolence, both spent much time working against racial injustice and oppression. Despite their work and the work of thousands of people, racism still flourishes in our society. Work against this violence: take a workshop on undoing racism, join a national group working on racism, work to challenge stereotypes and prejudices. Pax Christi USA recently committed to a twenty year process to dismantle racism within the organization and transform the organization into a multi-cultural, anti-racist organization. Contact Pax Christi USA for information on its Anti-Racism Team which conducts workshops for people of faith and their groups in the work of dismantling racism.

- This week, try being active in a situation of violence or injustice in which you normally might have kept quiet. For instance, take a stand when someone makes an offensive remark or refuse to give in to violence. This is often much more difficult than it may sound, but be creative. You might try, for example, refusing to go to a violent movie and telling your friends why you are doing so.

- Try to recognize the humanity in someone or a group of people with whom you disagree or might typically be considered your "enemy." For instance, think about a country with whom the U.S. disagrees and simply remember that the people of that country are human, too: they have families, work or school, fears, hungers, dreams.

- Look at the mass media with a critical eye. What assumptions are they making or whose viewpoints are they promoting? Try to find another source of news, to find another piece of the truth. For instance, FAIR (Fairness and Accuracy in Reporting) is a national media watchdog that criticizes media biases and censorship.

A Sampling of Sources and Resources:

Mohandas Gandhi:
Alexander, Horace. Gandhi Through Western Eyes. Philadelphia: New Society Publishers, 1984.

Fischer, Louis, ed. The Essential Gandhi: His Life, Work, and Ideas. An Anthology. New York: Vintage, 1983.

Gandhi, Mohandas K. An Autobiography: The Story of My Experiments With Truth. Boston: Beacon Press, 1957.

Gandhi, Mohandas K. Hind Swaraj and Other Writings. Cambridge: Cambridge University Press, 1997.

Gandhi, Mohandas K. Non-Violent Resistance (Satyagraha). New York: Schocken Books, 1961.

Jack, Homer A., ed. The Gandhi Reader: A Sourcebook of his Life and Writings. New York: Grove Press, 1956.

King, Mary. Mahatma Gandhi and Martin Luther King Jr.: The Power of Nonviolent Action. Paris, France: UNESCO (United Nations Educational, Scientific and Cultural Organization) Publishing, 1999.

Merton, Thomas, ed. Gandhi on Non-Violence: A Selection from the Writings of Mahatma Gandhi. New York: New Directions, 1965.

Martin Luther King, Jr.: (See also Part Eight for resources on the U.S. Civil Rights Movement.)
Carson, Clayborne, ed. The Autobiography of Martin Luther King, Jr. New York: Intellectual Property Management, Inc. and Warner Books, 1998.

King, Martin Luther, Jr. Stride Toward Freedom: The Montgomery Story. San Francisco: Harper & Row Publishers, 1958. (Written after the Montgomery bus boycott.)

Washington, James M., ed. A Testament of Hope: The Essential Writings and Speeches of Martin Luther King, Jr. San Francisco: Harper & Row Publishers, 1986.

Miscellaneous Resources:
Bristol, James E. "Primer on Pacifism," Reprinted from Fellowship by the American Friends Service Committee, Philadelphia.

Bristol, James E. "Nonviolence Not First for Export," Gandhi MARG, October 1972. (Available from the American Friends Service Committee, Peace Building Unit.)

FAIR (Fairness & Accuracy in Reporting): 130 W. 25th Street; New York, NY 10001; phone: 212/633-6700; e-mail: fair@fair.org; http://www.fair.org

Harper San Francisco staff, ed. Peace Prayers: Mediations, Affirmations, Invocations, Poems, and Prayers for Peace. San Francisco: Harper San Francisco, 1992.

King, Martin Luther, Jr. Strength to Love. Philadelphia: Fortress Press, 1963.

McGinnis, James et al. Educating for Peace and Justice: Religious Dimensions. St. Louis, MO: Institute for Peace and Justice, 1984.

Wink, Walter. Engaging the Powers: Discernment and Resistance in a World of Domination. Minneapolis: Fortress Press, 1992.

Wink, Walter. The Powers That Be: Theology for a New Millennium. New York: Galilee Doubleday, 1998. (Based on Wink's Powers series; less academic.)

Part Five

Nonviolence and Christianity

Mohandas Gandhi, a strong believer in the connections between faith and nonviolence, once said, "The only people on earth who do not see Christ and his teachings as nonviolent are Christians." What did Gandhi mean? How does the life of Jesus and his demonstration of the "Third Way" offer an alternative to the violence that surrounds us? What does it demand of those of us who call ourselves followers of Christ?

Opening Prayer

Reader 1:

Jesus, we ask you to show us your way of nonviolence. Teach us to truly believe in you and to share that belief with our Church. Help us to be part of the birthing of your reign of justice and peace here on earth and to recognize the ways we realize it each day, as well as the ways in which we fail. We ask that you send your Spirit upon us, upon the leaders of our Church, and upon all God's children so that we may live out your message of nonviolence.

All: Amen.

Reader 1:

A reflection from "This Land is Home to Me," the 1975 Pastoral Letter of the Appalachian bishops that expresses their sense of the needs and hopes of the people of Appalachia, who are often poor, oppressed, and struggling.

Side 1: "Dear sisters and brothers,
　　　　we urge all of you
　　　　not to stop living,
　　　　to be a part of the rebirth of utopias,
　　　　to recover and defend the struggling dream. . . .

Side 2: For it is the weak things of this world,
　　　　which seem like folly,
　　　　that the Spirit takes up
　　　　and makes its own.

Side 1: The dream of the mountains' struggle,
　　　　the dream of simplicity
　　　　and of justice,
　　　　like so many other repressed visions,
　　　　is, we believe,
　　　　the voice of [God] among us.

Side 2: In taking them up, hopefully the Church
might once again be known as

All: - a center of the Spirit,
    - a place where poetry dares to speak,
    - where the song reigns unchallenged,
    - where art flourishes,
    - where nature is welcome,
    - where little people and little needs come first,
    - where justice speaks loudly,
    - where in a wilderness of idolatrous destruction
     the great voice of God still cries out for life."

Please add, in silence or aloud, your hopes and visions for the world and for God's kindom.

Reader 1:
We humbly ask that you work in us, great God, so that your kindom,
beyond our wildest imaginings, may come about in our world.

All: Amen.

Nonviolence and Faith

The violence of our world might seem so widespread as to be overwhelming or unavoidable. But the world's great religious prophets have all held out hope for a better way. The ancient Taoist teaching of "creative quietude," the Hindu and Buddhist ideal of "non-injury," the Jewish vision of the full peace of "shalom," the Muslim dream of a "world of peace," Jesus' example of unconditional love: all these express a nonviolent approach to conflicts.

It's also possible to be nonviolent without being explicitly religious. Many sincere, dedicated people of good will embrace a nonviolent way of life without embracing a spiritual base for their lives. Humanitarian concerns have led them to the realization that a nonviolent approach is in accord with the deepest laws of human nature.

It is our conviction that a deep spirituality based especially on the spirit of the Gospels is a powerful aid for those who call themselves Christians. The Scriptures provide a basis for examining the violence and injustice of the world and for naming and opposing these occurrences. Both the Hebrew and the Christian Scriptures condemn not only personal sin but also evil social structures. For example, Isaiah 5 condemns economic injustice, Amos 5

injustices in the legal system, and Amos 4 materialism. One of Jesus' most dramatic actions, the cleansing of the temple, recorded in all four canonical Gospels (see John 2:12-17), was a response to a religious system that put profits above both people and worship of God. The Gospels record Jesus' way of responding to injustice not with violence, but always with love, healing, and inclusion.

Nonviolence has been practiced by courageous Christians over the centuries but until recently has not been stressed as an important consequence of following the Gospel. (However, in the first several centuries after Jesus' death, nonviolence was part of being Christian. Those people who called themselves his followers refused to fight in wars.) For Christians, the basis of nonviolence is faith in Jesus and a desire to follow his command to love, a commandment that points to nonviolence. Recently, the U.S. bishops' peace pastoral, *The Challenge of Peace: God's Promise and Our Response,* declared, "Peacemaking is not an optional commitment. It is a requirement of our faith. We are called to be peacemakers, not by some movement of the moment, but by our Lord Jesus Christ." For us as Christians, nonviolence must be rooted in a spiritual basis.

"FAITH DOES NOT insulate us from the challenges of life; rather, it intensifies our desire to help solve them precisely in light of the good news which has come to us in the person of Jesus, the Lord of history."   *–The Challenge of Peace*

The Way of Jesus

When we read the Gospels with "peace eyes," with a mindset nurtured by love and a desire for peace, we find a clear message. Angie O'Gorman writes, "The dynamic of nonviolence is woven like the warp of a loom throughout the entire Christian Scripture. Hidden, it holds the other threads together. It forms the fabric. To miss it is to misunderstand the primary design in the Christian pattern: the power to apply love to hate." This message is of nonviolent love.

It is also a message of suffering servanthood (articulated in Isaiah 42 and 49-55). Jesus first proclaimed his mission while in Nazareth, where he read from the prophet Isaiah: "[T]o preach good news to the poor. . .to proclaim freedom for the prisoners and recovery of sight for the blind, to release the oppressed, to proclaim the year of the Lord's favor." (Luke 4:14-21) By no means is this an easy path. In fact, it eventually led to Jesus' crucifixion as a state criminal. Jesus had so much love for the world that he was willing both to serve others and to go through painful suffering. The suffering Jesus went through was for the transformation of relationships–the relationship between God and human beings, and the relationship of human beings with each other. Saint Paul expressed it: "God demonstrates his own love for us in this: While we were still sinners, Christ died for us . . ." (Romans 5:8). Jesus' way was the way of God, the way of suffering love.

Jesus was the compassionate one, the reconciler, the peacemaker. He lovingly accepted suffering–even to the point of death. He was the one "who loves us and has freed us from our sins by his blood." (Revelation 1:5) Jesus responded with love, especially to those on the margins of society: women, children, the sick, prostitutes, tax collectors. Not satisfied with the status quo, he sought to reconcile people and to create community.

Jesus' Third Way (see part 4) demonstrates an alternative, one that has many characteristics. As we reflect on his life, on the words and actions that revealed his suffering love, it is helpful to concentrate on four principles that are especially relevant to the nonviolent dimensions of peacemaking.

1. Love of Enemies

If there is any message Jesus consistently preached, it was the message of love: love God above all and love your neighbor as yourself. In the parable of the Good Samaritan, Jesus defined neighbor in the widest possible terms: as anyone in need. We can tell whether we really love our neighbor by how we act toward our "enemies." Jesus spelled out the hard answer: "Love your enemies, do good to those who hate you, bless those who curse you, pray for those who mistreat you." (Luke 6:27-28)

We may at first be inclined to take this teaching as a personal and individualistic one, to say that it applies only to our relationships with those around us. It certainly does apply to those relationships, and it is hard enough to live up to in these cases.

But when we look at the historical context in which Jesus preached this message, we see the broader dimensions of loving our neighbor, of loving our enemies. His country was occupied and ruled by foreigners–the Romans. The people of Jesus' time reacted to those enemies in three different ways. Some, the Zealots, felt that the only appropriate response was violence–revolt, overthrow the occupiers, and get rid of them. Others, the Sadducees especially, believed it was best to make some sort of accommodation with the Roman establishment. Then there were those, the most numerous, whose response was patient, passive endurance.

Jesus proclaimed and acted in a way that differed from all these. Jesus was not passive. He did not shrink from conflict. He never compromised his principles. Nor did he ever promote the sword. His way was different. "If someone forces you to go one mile," (as Roman soldiers forced people to carry their military baggage) "go with him two miles." (Matthew 5:41)

This advice was more than just a role of suffering and submission: it turned relationships upside down. By law, Roman soldiers could force someone to carry their packs for one mile and one mile only. By voluntarily carrying the pack another mile, the person broke this law, forcing the Roman soldier to see the person in a new light. It demonstrated love, rather than hostility.

In Jesus' day, "love your enemies" meant especially to love the Romans. In our day it means love the Chinese, love the Iraqis, love the Cubans, love those labeled as "terrorists," love all those who are hostile to us or whom are enemies of our government. Jesus' unconditional love is not an easy principle. It's certainly not a popular one. To believe in nonviolence, we must believe in the power of love.

Questions:

What does "unconditional love" mean to you? How might this principle have applied to a Jewish Palestinian asked to carry the pack of a Roman soldier (an occupying military)?

How are we harmed when we hate another person?

Close your eyes for a minute and think of a person, a situation, or an event in which you can apply the principle of unconditional love. "Walk" through it, examining your feelings. What additional demands might be asked of you? What changes in YOU might you anticipate?

2. God as Giver of Life

The second principle is that God is our Mother/Father, our Creator in whose image and likeness we are made and the One who gives us life and nurtures us. If God is our Mother/Father, then all people are sisters and brothers. This image has great consequences when we talk about issues of war and peace. It helps us move beyond the tendency that citizens of every nation have—to believe that God is on *our* side and will give us victory over the other side.

People who believe that God is on their side can hate, kill, threaten, and watch each other starve, and feel no obligation to do anything about it as long as it's happening to those others, on whose side God is not. But the barriers that divide us—nation-states, ethnic groups, races, religions, classes, political parties—are all brought down by the truth that we, every one of us in this world, are sisters and brothers.

This idea also has profound effects on the ways we live our everyday lives. If we see God all around us and believe that God gives all life, we will be much less likely to engage in any behaviors—from small put-downs to participating in unjust structures to war—that hurt others. Why would we want to kill, oppress, hurt, or ignore members of our own family? In addition, this principle should extend to all of creation, for God gives life not only to humans, but to plants and animals and the whole of the world. All of creation reflects God's beauty, and thus we must respect and nurture it.

Questions:

Find and cut out pictures of people who might be classified as "enemies" and include them in your prayer space and time. Let their presence help lead to our stretching our idea of family to include all people.

3. Human Dignity

A third principle important for our understanding of nonviolence is the infinite value of the human person. God loves each of us. The stories of the prodigal son (Luke 15:11-32), of Zaccheus (Luke 19:1-10), of the woman caught in adultery (John 8:1-11)—these and others make it clear that love for every individual person is central to Jesus' teaching and the way he acted toward people. We do not have to prove ourselves worthy of this love; our human dignity does not depend on what we do or don't do. This principle is the foundation for our own sense of self-worth and for our respect for the immeasurable dignity of every other woman and man we will ever encounter.

Catholic social teaching echoes this theme. (See Appendix E for a listing of the building blocks of Catholic social teaching.)

The Challenge of Peace declares, "No society can live at peace with itself, or with the world, without a full awareness of the worth and dignity of every human person, and of the sacredness of all human life." Each person has a right to the fulfillment of basic needs, such as health care, education, shelter, and work. Anything that denies this dignity or blocks the realization of the fulfillment of these needs is violent. In *Economic Justice for All*, the National Council of Catholic Bishops stated that this human dignity can be realized and practiced only in community.

Questions:

What is one thing you find unlovable about yourself? How can you remember that God always loves you...and every other human being?

4. Forgiveness

Closely tied to the infinite value of every human being is the fourth principle: forgiveness. "Peter came up and asked Jesus, 'When a sister or brother wrongs me, how many times must I forgive? Seven times?' 'No,' Jesus replied. 'Not seven times; I tell you seventy times seven.'" (Matthew 18:21-22) When he said seven, Peter thought he was being generous. Jesus again showed another way. Seven was the number of perfection; the value of seventy times seven was a symbol for infinity. We are to forgive, to forgive, and then to forgive again.

Jesus taught us to pray, "Forgive us our sins (debts), as we also forgive everyone who sins against us (our debtors)." (Luke 11:4; Matthew 6:12) He urged us to be compassionate as God is compassionate. (Luke 6:36) In his own life, Jesus was compassionate, merciful, reconciling. He forgave Peter, who had denied him three times. At the very end he even forgave his executioners "for they don't know what they are doing." (Luke 23:34)

Forgiving is not easy. When someone wrongs us, we are likely to feel hurt, bitter, and angry. Forgiving does not mean that we deny those feelings or that what the other person did is okay. Instead, forgiving involves acknowledging both our own feelings and the wrongdoing—and the fact that we all sin and need forgiveness. It does mean that we work to let go of our hurt and anger, a process that often takes time. Again, it helps to remember that the other person is also a child of God. With God's help and love, forgiving—not necessarily the same as forgetting—moves us toward reconciliation.

Being able to rise above the hurts we receive from others is a key element in nonviolent peacemaking. Jesus praised those who followed this way: "If you forgive the faults of others, Abba God will forgive you yours." (Matthew 6:14)

Catholic social teaching tells us the same: "As disciples and as children of God, it is our task to seek for ways in which to make the forgiveness, justice and mercy and love of God visible in a world where violence and enmity are too often the norm." (*The Challenge of Peace*) We must go even further than forgiving and work for reconciliation, bringing people back together, repairing not only the damage, but building new relationships. Reconciliation is key in working to bring about the peace of God's reign.

Questions:

Name a personal conflict that you are currently experiencing with someone. Plan in your heart/mind how you can "make the first move" to resolve and reconcile the conflict, misunderstanding, or bad feelings involved.

BECAUSE YOU are God's chosen ones, holy and beloved clothe yourselves with heartfelt compassion, with kindness, humility, gentleness and patience. Bear with one another; forgive whatever grievances you have against one another–forgive in the same way God has forgiven you. Above all else, put on love, which binds the rest together and makes them perfect. Let Christ's peace reign in your hearts since, as members of one body, you have been called to that peace. **—Colossians 3:12-15a**

Followers of Jesus' Way

Those who are serious about these principles taught and lived by Jesus recognize that the world is far different. We see exploitation and cruelty: child abuse, family quarrels, poverty, greed, sweatshops in Asia, war in sub-Saharan Africa, fanatical violence for a cause. We may be upset because so many things in the world around us are not right. The Dutch theologian Edward Schillebeeckx has written that the peace of Christ, in our time, consists "in an inward discontent, in a prophetic protest against the situation as it is, and which is precisely not right the way it is." As followers of Jesus' nonviolent way, we have ample reason to be "inwardly discontent."

Our inward discontent is a small price to pay for looking at the world through "peace eyes." James 4:4 says that to be friends with the world is to be enemies with God. We can expect that our desire to live according to Jesus' way of nonviolence and love will put us at odds with our culture. Attempting to follow Jesus' Third Way is not popular; it is "thinking outside the box," not following the rules our society gives us. And it is sometimes difficult to find examples of people who try to solve all types of problems and difficulties this way. We must work to be the examples.

This way is difficult at times. *Economic Justice for All* tells us, "We should not be surprised if we find Catholic social teaching to be demanding. The Gospel is demanding. We are always in need of conversion, of a change in heart. . .We know that, at times, in order to remain truly a community of Jesus' disciples, we will have to say 'no' to certain aspects in our culture, to certain trends and ways of acting that are opposed to a life of faith, love and justice. . .No one may claim the name Christian and be comfortable in the face of the hunger, homelessness, insecurity found in this country and the world." Looking at the world with "peace eyes" means recognizing the injustices that our culture tells us are not polite to discuss and acting in nonviolence to change ourselves and the injustices of our society.

The Reign of God

Through his words and deeds, Jesus proclaimed the Good News that the kindom of God was near at hand. As his followers, our ultimate goal is to be involved in establishing the reign of God. Indeed, the original vision of the church was to carry out the difficult work of living out and announcing the Gospel of God's love, justice, and peace.

The reign of God is here among and within us: how do we as Christians reveal it? We can only do so nonviolently. Thomas Merton wrote that: "Christian non-violence is nothing if not first of all a formal profession of faith in the Gospel message that the [Reign] has been established and that the [God] of truth is indeed risen and reigning over [God's Kindom], defending the deepest values of those who dwell in it." Part of this kindom is peace, Jesus' first gift to his disciples after resurrection. (John 20:19)

This vision is rooted in love for each other, respect for human dignity, and knowledge of God. The bishops' peace pastoral highlighted the meaning of the kindom as Jesus expressed it in the Sermon on the Mount: "In God's reign the poor are given the [kindom], the mourners are comforted, the meek inherit the earth, those hungry for righteousness are satisfied, the merciful know mercy, the pure see God, the persecuted know the [kindom], and peacemakers are called the children of God." (*The Challenge of Peace*)

Our vision goes beyond any immediate conflict however pressing it might be. We help to realize the kindom when we live according to its ideals right now. Jesus' teaching urges us to live according to the future we most desire to see. The future fullness of the kindom can begin to be a reality for us when we act in peace and love and freedom, that is, nonviolently, now. We get a taste of the glory that is to come "on earth as it is in heaven." (Matthew 6:10)

> ALL CREATIVE people are moved by some great idea. . .Jesus, too, was motivated by a central vision that kept everything in focus and gave life its richest meaning. Jesus called his vision the "[kindom] of God," that is, the fullness of God's work of love in creation. Jesus' vocation was to labor for the coming of this [kindom].
>
> —Mary Evelyn Jegen, SND

God shall wipe every tear from their eyes,
and there shall be no more death or mourning,
crying out or pain,
for the former world has passed away.
The One who sat on the throne said to me,
"See, I make all things new!"
Then this one said,
"Write these matters down,
for the words are trustworthy and true!"

—Revelation 21:4-5

Questions:

How can God use you to make things new? What talents, gifts, and resources do you have to use to work for a new earth?

List five actions you've performed this year that fit into your vision of "building the kindom." Were these conscious or unconscious happenings?

Christian People of Nonviolence

Nonviolence has been practiced throughout the history of Christianity. The early Christians understood God to be peace and nonviolence. One early Christian who proclaimed this was St. Martin of Tours. A convert to Christianity, he was one of the first Christian conscientious objectors to war and a man who encountered Christ in the poor. He later became a bishop. Another was St. Justin, a martyr, who said, "We who once killed each other not only do not make war on each other, but in order not to lie or deceive our inquisitors we gladly die for the confession of Christ."

Dom Helder Camara (1909-1999), Roman Catholic archbishop of Recife, Brazil, was a great witness and prophet of nonviolence, despite being silenced by the Brazilian government as well as targeted for persecution. He worked for social justice, empowering poor people to be agents of change. He lived a simple life based on the Church's "preferential option for the poor," rooted in prayer.

If it depended on me, doors and windows . . . would remain open, generously letting in the air and light and life!

Dom Helder Camara

St. Francis of Assisi (1182-1226), born to an Italian family of privilege, heard a call to live out the Gospel in a radically simple lifestyle. He rejected all violence as contrary to the Gospel vision of love. He is known for his joy in life and for his wonder for all of God's creation. He founded the Franciscan order, based on the Gospel command of poverty.

Peter Maurin (1877-1949) and Dorothy Day (1897-1980) founded the Catholic Worker movement to live out the Gospel vision of love. Maurin was a traveling worker who developed a social philosophy based on his Catholic faith. He felt that modern life had been separated from the Gospel and called for a "personalist revolution" in which people recognized the worth of every human being and lived their lives accordingly. A convert to Catholicism, Day had been involved in women's and worker's rights movements. Together, they combined their religious faith and social vision into a movement to practice the works of mercy and nonviolence. They started shelters and soup kitchens, a newspaper, and farming communities. This highly localized movement of intentional communities continues today.

Thomas Merton (1915-1968) was a Trappist monk who felt a solidarity with the human race. This feeling brought him to try to make connections between the monastic life and the world, especially issues such as war and racism, and made him into a prophet of peace and nonviolence.

Oscar Romero (1917-1980) was a pious and relatively conservative bishop who, after his appointment as Roman Catholic archbishop of San Salvador, El Salvador, underwent a conversion and became an outspoken witness for peace, justice, and nonviolence during the Salvadoran civil war. His commitment to human rights and dignity and his advocacy on behalf of the poor of El Salvador led to his assassination while saying Mass in 1980.

Thomas Merton

Ben Salmon (1889-1932) was imprisoned in the U.S. during World War I for his refusal to fight. His conscientious objection to all war–pacifism–was based on his firm Catholic faith. Salmon was the only man in World War I to base this belief on his Catholicism. Originally sentenced to death, he endured solitary confinement for much of his two-year imprisonment. Finally, he went on a hunger strike, was transferred to a psychiatric hospital, and eventually released. He wrote an extensive critique of the Catholic Church's Just War Theory.

Hans and Sophie Scholl (d. 1943), under the name "The White Rose," were among the authors of a series of leaflets condemning the Nazi regime and calling for resistance. These university students were inspired by their Christian faith, believing resistance to evil to be part of their Christian duty. At the ages of 24 and 21, they, along with 23-year-old Christoph Probst, were beheaded for treason in Germany.

A civilization of love that did not demand justice of people would not be a true civilization . . . it is a caricature of love to try to cover over with alms what is lacking in justice.

Oscar Romero

These short biographies are excerpted primarily from Robert Ellsberg's book, All Saints. It is an excellent collection of "daily reflections on saints, prophets, and witnesses for our times."

Another good source is Cloud of Witnesses, edited by Jim Wallis and Joyce Hollyday. Included in this book are interviews and brief biographical profiles of modern witnesses and prophets who have lived the Gospel, such as Clarence Jordan (theologian, farmer, and racial healer in the U.S. South), Penny Lernoux (journalist and advocate for the poor of Latin America), William Stringfellow (U.S. theologian, social critic, and writer), and Desmond Tutu (Anglican bishop from South Africa and 1984 winner of the Nobel Peace Prize).

Closing Prayer

If possible, have many candles in the prayer space. Enter the time of prayer in semi-darkness.

Reader 1:
Loving Creator and Giver of All Life,
We thank you for the many people who have gone before us:

Reader 2:
For those who have lived out Jesus' example of love

Reader 1:
For those who have worked tirelessly to make sure that all people are treated with dignity

Reader 2:
For those who have taught us how to pray

Reader 1:
For those who have shown us how to forgive

Reader 2:
For those who have helped us to cross boundaries

Reader 1:
For those who have tried to live your way of nonviolence

Reader 2:
For those who have lived out your kindom of justice, love, and peace

Reader 1:
Even for those we've struggled with.
We name them now before you.

Please name people you know or have read about who have been an example to you.
As each witness to God's love and nonviolence is lifted up, someone should light a candle.

Reader 1:
We know that we do not go alone, for the path is brightened by those who have gone before us. May our lives also be shining examples to others.

All:
Jesus, following your way is not easy. Give us courage, strength, and wisdom. Convert our hearts to your way of nonviolence. When we are afraid, help us to remember your words, "Peace I leave with you, my peace I give to you; but the kind of peace I give you is not like the world's peace." (John 14:27) As we attempt to travel outside of the ways of the world, we know that you walk with us. Thank you for giving us this example and forgive us for the many times we fail. Amen.

Part Five: Reflections

1. What in the life and teaching of Jesus do you find most significant in your examination of nonviolence as a way of life?

2. What in your life is the greatest obstacle to following the teaching of Jesus on nonviolence?

3. What effect do you think that nonviolence will have on your life in the near future? Five years from now? How will it or can it affect your choices about jobs, schools, relationships?

4. The values of our culture and world are often at odds with the Gospel values that call us to nonviolence. Make a list of U.S. values versus Gospel values (including such areas as the worth of humans, money, personal strengths). With which areas do you particularly need to struggle to live out the Gospel values?

5. With whom do you need to be reconciled, in your family, friendships, community, city, nation, or world? When you pray, ask for healing in these broken relationships and try to take small steps toward this healing.

Suggestions for Action

• Find out more about the nonviolence tradition of another faith.

• Reach out to someone in your community whom you might consider an enemy or someone very different from you. Start a conversation.

• Get involved with a group, such as Amnesty International (which has many local chapters), that works for human rights and dignity.

• Think about who might currently be considered our "enemies" (such as the people of Iraq) and support a group working with these people.

• Work on forgiving someone who has hurt you and then tell him or her that you have forgiven, even if the hurt was small or long ago.

• Bring peace and justice issues to your faith community, perhaps using some of the social teachings listed below.

A Sampling of Sources and Resources

On Catholic Social Teaching and Thought:
(See Appendix E for a listing of building blocks of Catholic Social Teaching.)

Center of Concern: 1225 Otis Street NE; Washington, DC 20017; phone: 202/635-2757; http://www.coc.org (Catholic Social Teaching and social justice projects)

Coleman, John and Gregory Baum, eds. Rerum Novarum: A Hundred Years of Catholic social teaching. London: SCM Press, 1991.

Curran, Charles. Many books on Catholic social thought.

Gremillion, Joseph, ed. The Gospel of Peace and Justice: Catholic social teaching Since Pope John XXIII. Maryknoll, NY: Orbis Books, 1976.

O'Brien, David J. and Thomas A. Shannon. Catholic Social Thought: The Documentary Heritage. Maryknoll, NY: Orbis Books, 1992.

Phan, Peter C. Social Thought. Wilmington, DE: Michael Glazier, Inc., 1984.

Walsh, Michael and Brian Davies. *Proclaiming Justice and Peace: Documents from John XXIII–John Paul II.* Mystic, CT: Twenty-Third Publications, 1984.

Some documents from the Catholic Church:
National Conference of Catholic Bishops, The Challenge of Peace: God's Promise and Our Response. Boston: St. Paul Editions, 1983.

National Conference of Catholic Bishops. Economic Justice For All: Pastoral Letter on Catholic Social Teaching and the U.S. Economy. Washington, DC: United States Catholic Conference, 1986.

National Conference of Catholic Bishops. The Harvest of Justice is Sown in Peace: A Reflection of the National Catholic Council of Bishops on the Tenth Anniversary of The Challenge of Peace. Washington, DC: United States Catholic Conference, 1993.

Pope John XXIII. Pacem in Terris (On Establishing Universal Peace in Truth, Justice, Charity and Liberty), April 11, 1963.

Second Vatican Council. Gaudium et Spes (Pastoral Constitution on the Church in the Modern World), December 7, 1965.

Other Resources on Christians, Christianity, and/or Nonviolence:
Dear, John, S. J. The God of Peace: Toward a Theology of Nonviolence. Maryknoll, NY: Orbis Books, 1994.

Ellsberg, Robert. All Saints. New York: Crossroad Publishing Company, 1997.

Ellsberg, Robert, ed. Gandhi on Christianity. Maryknoll, NY: Orbis Books, 1991.

Love Your Enemies brochure/bulletin insert–fifty-two ways to love your enemies. Simple, far-reaching ways of prayer, study and action to be practiced each week during the year. Pax Christi USA, 532 W.8th St., Erie, PA 16502; phone: 814-453-4955 x231; e-mail: sales@paxchristiusa.org; http://www.paxchristiusa.org

O'Gorman, Angie, ed. The Universe Bends Toward Justice: A Reader on Christian Nonviolence in the U.S.. Philadelphia: New Society Publishers, 1990.

Wallis, Jim and Joyce Hollyday, eds. Cloud of Witnesses. Maryknoll, NY and Washington, DC: Orbis Books and Sojourners, 1991.

Part Six

Cultivating Peace in Our Daily Lives

A group of political activists were attempting to show the Master how their beliefs would change the world. The Master listened carefully. The following day he said, "An ideology is as good or bad as the people who make use of it. If a million wolves were to organize for justice, would they cease to be a million wolves?"

In the final analysis, any discussion of nonviolence must address an ancient saying: to have peace in our world, we must first have peace within ourselves. Again, we will be challenged: Can we simplify our lives? Can we identify and root out our negative assumptions, prejudices, and judgments of others? Can we see those who are different from ourselves as fully human? Can we learn to respect all of creation? How can our spiritual life help us to work toward a more nonviolent attitude and character?

"A journey of a thousand miles begins with one step," observed the Chinese philosopher Confucius. If many people are to take up the nonviolent journey, a few have to take it up first. Then it can spread. Let us begin.

> **Cultivating Peace in Our Daily Lives**
>
> - *Opening Prayer*
> - *Cultivating Nonviolence Within*
> - *Spirituality*
>   - *—Prayer*
> - *A Nonviolent Attitude and Character*
> - *Simpler Living*
> - *Risking the Journey*
> - *Closing Prayer*
> - *Reflections*
> - *Suggestions for Action*
> - *A Sampling of Sources and Resources*

Opening Prayer

Reader 1:
God, we give you thanks for the wonders of your creation and for the gift of this day, ordinary as it may seem. We praise you for all parts of our lives, the challenges, the surprises, the wonders–for they all reveal you to us. Teach us to live in gratitude. Remind us that we do not walk on this journey alone. Teach us to listen to those around us and to your word within us. Forgive us for the times when we fail to acknowledge the humanity of others and when we do not listen with open minds and hearts. Make us mindful of the presence of your son Jesus in all of our sisters and brothers. Amen.

(Time for silent reflection)

All:
God, make me an instrument of your peace.

Side 1:
Where there is hatred, let me sow love;
Where there is injury, pardon;
Where there is doubt, faith;

Side 2:
Where there is despair, hope;
Where there is darkness, light;
Where there is sadness, joy.

All:
O Divine One,
grant that I may not so much seek

Side 1:
To be consoled as to console,
To be understood as to understand,
To be loved as to love;

Side 2:
For it is in giving that we receive,
It is in pardoning that we are pardoned,
It is in dying that we are born to eternal life.

All:
Amen.

Cultivating Nonviolence Within

We live in a culture that encourages–at times even demands–us to be very self-centered, yet at the same time discourages us from treating ourselves well in any but shallow ways. We are bombarded with images encouraging us to think of our own wants and desires first. We are told that the way to "take care of ourselves" is to buy more, to do more, to concentrate on the external. Yet we are not encouraged to tend to our spiritual side or to be kind to our bodies. Often, we are violent toward our very selves, we push ourselves too far and skip sleep, eat poorly, fail to value our bodies (and their limitations), and neglect our spiritual selves.

To attempt to live nonviolently means that we must develop nonviolence within ourselves. We cannot hope for nonviolence for the world if we do not try to live it in our daily lives. We must become centered in peace. Only then can we hope that nonviolence will spill over into our relationships and our world. Becoming firmly grounded in nonviolence is a process–a never-ending one. Yet each step brings us closer, as well as helps us to model new ways of being in the world.

This nonviolent approach needs to be developed. The starting point is a conscious decision to allow nonviolence to fill all aspects of our lives as well as a desire to disarm our hearts, minds, and spirits. This decision must be taken in the face of opposing social pressures for violence–expressed in movies, television, newspaper reporting, the way history is presented, the national spirit. Decidedly counter-cultural, it requires a conversion of the heart.

Encouraging nonviolence means a daily attempt to be nonviolent toward ourselves, toward the earth, in our relationships with family and friends, in school and work exchanges, in our career and professional lives. This takes effort and study; it takes community and spirituality.

Questions:

What are examples of the ways our society encourages us to be violent toward ourselves?

In what ways are you violent toward yourself?
What steps can you take to be more nonviolent?

> "I REALLY SEE no other solution than to turn inwards and to root out all the rottenness there. I no longer believe that we can change anything in the world until we have first changed ourselves."
>
> **—Etty Hillesum (World War II concentration camp victim)**

Spirituality

Many followers of nonviolence have stated that they did not feel that one could practice nonviolence apart from God or some higher force, whatever they chose to call that Being. (Gandhi, for instance, named the force "Truth.") As Christians (followers of Christ), our faith motivates us to try to live nonviolently, as Jesus did. A healthy spirituality provides a firm foundation for nonviolence.

In the Catholic tradition, the U.S. bishops' peace pastoral (*The Challenge of Peace*) suggests ways that we can begin to develop a spirituality that will allow us to "disarm our hearts" and become a peaceful people. The bishops remind us that we cannot have peace in the world unless we have peace within ourselves. We are to work on a heart empty of hate, a spirit of calm and inward quiet that touches everything we do.

One way to develop staying power for the long, difficult road to peace is to develop a sense of solidarity. . .with mature and exemplary Christians. This means becoming acquainted with peacemakers, living and dead, who are prophets of nonviolence. Reading and reflection can nurture our spirit and provide new insights. It is important to drink deeply of sources that inspire and communicate strength: Mohandas Gandhi, Martin Luther King, Eileen Egan, Leo Tolstoy, Daniel Berrigan, Dorothy Day.

Our faith also requires us to work for peace and justice. The Catholic bishops ask us to become physically involved in the work of recognizing the kindom of God. Because we are all capable of violence, the bishops call us to personal discipline—to penance and fasting —in order that "we become more conformed to Christ." They remind us that those who want to live a spirituality of peace must become involved with the poor, the oppressed, and those who suffer violence anywhere in the world.

Our spirituality should be deeply inter-twined with nonviolence and vice versa. Nonviolence allows us to grow more deeply in our individual and interpersonal spirituality, but it also invites us into a corporate spirituality. We become involved with the world and work to change it according to the richness of the kindom. We work nonviolently to overcome those systems that prevent people from living as God intends us to live and which limit God's love in the world. In this way, our spirituality grows to include the good of the whole earth.

Ultimately, our inspiration to try to be nonviolent comes from a deeper source. In the peace pastoral, the bishops expressed it well: "Let us have the courage to believe in the bright future and in a God who wills it for us–not a perfect world, but a better one. The perfect world, we Christians believe, is beyond the horizon, in an endless eternity where God will be all in all. But a better world is here for human hands and human hearts and minds to make." The prayer and discipline of a spiritually-rooted life will help to bring about this world.

THE SPIRITUALITY of the peacemaker is permeated by a deep reverence for all life and a commitment to hope, a hope whose offspring are anger and courage. St. Augustine said it well:

Hope has two lovely daughters:

anger and courage.

Anger so that what must not be may not be;

courage so that what should be can be.

Reflect on the quote from St. Augustine.

"LIKEWISE, discovering God's peace, which exceeds all understanding, in prayer is essential to peacemaking" (Phil 4:7). The peace given in prayer draws us into God, quieting our anxieties, challenging our old values and deepening wells of new energy. It arouses in us a compassionate love for all humanity and gives us heart to persevere beyond frustration, suffering and defeat. We should never forget that peace is not merely something that we ourselves as creatures do and can accomplish, but it is, in the ultimate analysis, a gift and a grace from God.

—The Harvest of Justice is Sown in Peace

OTHER FAITH traditions also emphasize nonviolence and spirituality. One person who studied such connections is Sri Eknath Easwaran. A writer, lecturer, professor, and the founder of the Blue Mountain Center of Meditation in California, he wove together spiritual growth, ecological healing, and nonviolent social change, all of which come, he wrote, from a change of heart. He was convinced that "there is no instrument of change more powerful than the well-lived life."

Prayer

Prayer is the search for God, the encounter with God, and the relationship we have with God. It plays an important part in our spiritual and peace journey, not only in asking for peace for our lives and world, but in allowing us to move more deeply into the nonviolence of God. Prayer helps us to search for clarity or vision and to decide how God would want us to live or act. Through prayer, we become more aware of God in our lives and in our world and come to wonder at the many ways God is revealed to us. Prayer, both individual and communal, invites us into unity with the whole body of Christ.

Yes, prayer shakes the universe.
—**William Johnston**

How one prays is very personal. For many people, prayer does not always seem natural; sometimes it may be difficult to pray or we may not feel like doing so. But prayer is extremely important, even essential, for a person of nonviolence.

Many of us have been taught that praying is words, and words or writings clearly can be one form of prayer. But we should recognize that there are many other forms of prayer, such as silence or the beauty of nature. Prayer is that which makes us aware of God's constant presence in our lives.

What is important is that each of us finds one or more ways of praying that work for us. Then we must take time each day in prayer, time reserved for God alone, even if it is only several minutes. As Henri Nouwen wrote, "We do not take the spiritual life seriously if we do not set aside some time to be with, and listen to, God. We may have to write it in black and white in our daily calendar so that nobody else can take away this period of time." It may be helpful to set aside not only a specific time, but also a special space for prayer, such as a corner of your room. Here you can put sacred objects or images. When entering the prayer space and time, some people find it helpful to start with some sign that designates sacred time, such as lighting a candle.

Here are some examples of prayer disciplines:

- *Start your day by recalling God's presence and asking that God be with you throughout your day and all that you do in it.*
- *End your day by reflecting on what or who brought God's love to you or what has drawn you closer to God. Where do you find or recognize God in your daily life?*
- *Read and reflect on sacred scriptures from various faith traditions.*
- *Meditate in silence, especially using a "mantra," the repetition of sacred words (for instance, some Christians simply repeat "Jesus"), or by concentrating on breath moving in and out of your body.*
- *Attend community prayer, such as liturgies.*
- *Read a scene from the Gospels and place yourself in it. What do you see, smell, feel, and hear? What character in the story are you? How does God speak to you?*
- *Have a conversation with Jesus. Tell him about your day, your fears, your hopes, your dreams.*
- *Write out a favorite scripture passage, carry it with you, and reflect on it throughout the day.*
- *Lectio Divina (divine reading): Read a scripture passage through slowly, perhaps several times. Choose a word or phrase that speaks to you; repeat that word or phrase. How does it connect to your life? What is God trying to show you?*
- *Walk, especially in nature, in a slow and observant manner. How is God revealed to you in your surroundings?*
- *After you pray, think or write about how you felt during prayer. What things came up for you? How was the experience? What had you hoped for?*

"IN A SOCIETY that seems to be filled with urgencies and emergencies, prayer appears to be an unnatural form of behavior. Without fully realizing it, we have accepted the idea that 'doing things' is more important than prayer and have come to think of prayer as something for times when there is nothing urgent to do. . .This predicament shows how necessary it is to view prayer as a discipline. Concentrated human effort is necessary because prayer is not our most natural response to the world. . .Prayer requires that we stand in God's presence with open hands, naked and vulnerable, proclaiming to ourselves and to others that without God we can do nothing."
—**Henri Nouwen**

Questions:

What do you see as the relationship between nonviolence and spirituality?

What are the sources of your spiritual nourishment?

What role does prayer play in your life?

A Nonviolent Attitude and Character

Cultivating nonviolence within oneself and developing a spirituality to support this are never-ending tasks, but regardless of where we are in the process, this spirit will affect all our interactions and relationships. Often, it is extremely difficult to be loving and peaceful with those around us. Working on being nonviolent in our closest relationships is extremely important.

The person who tries to let the spirit of nonviolence enter all areas of life finds many opportunities to practice. The ideal approach of a nonviolent person toward others is to be straightforward but not intimidating. People normally don't like being pressured, forced, or put into positions where they are expected to bow to someone else's wishes. The nonviolent person tries to avoid giving the impression of forcing others along.

At the same time, the nonviolent person does not behave like a victim or appear to be frightened. Fear is perceived and can encourage a hostile party to continue an undesired activity. We often feel fear in the face of hostility, but must try to maintain self-control. Acting like a victim usually encourages people to take advantage of us.

Here are several areas in which it is important to attempt nonviolence. They are also often the most difficult, as they require constant attention. However, it is through living nonviolently in these situations that we will bring about a nonviolent world.

1. Speech

Words can be weapons to hurt another or to defend ourselves when attacked. The nonviolent person tries to refrain from getting the better of people in conversation, from striking back verbally when someone has spoken unfairly, and from putting people down behind their backs.

Respect for others' dignity also means using inclusive language–addressing both men and women, all of humanity–in casual conversation, at worship services, in public forums. Ignoring one half of the human race by refusing to "call women by name" is violence. We must also be aware of other ways in which we put people down or dismiss them, on the basis of race, class, sexual orientation, etc.

A nonviolent consciousness will also make us alert to phrases that have become part of our common vocabulary. Sayings such as "killing two birds with one stone" can become more nonviolent by transformation to "feeding two birds with one crust." While this may seem overly dramatic, our language definitely influences how we think and react. By attempting to modify our violent language, we also change our own assumptions, attitudes, and ways of reacting.

Words can be weapons...

Questions:

How do you respond to sarcastic or insulting remarks?

Rework other violent idioms that are part of our language.

2. Routine Activities

Many acts we take for granted can be done in a consciously nonviolent way. There is such a thing as nonviolent driving, for example. The nonviolent driver is no weakling, allowing others to take improper advantage. The trick is to drive firmly but respectfully. One driver, when a large truck cut in on her, reacted instinctively at first by waving her fist in frustration. The truck driver saw her in his rear view mirror, stuck his arm out the window, and shook his fist back at her. A few minutes later, after she had calmed down and remembered some nonviolent principles, she passed the truck and deliberately smiled at the driver. He smiled back.

Many acts. . . can be done in a consciously nonviolent way.

Questions:

What are some other "everyday" actions that spark violent feelings? (For instance, someone cutting in line at a store.) How do you react? How could you react more nonviolently?

3. Active Listening

We have all heard or taken part in conversations that essentially consist in alternate monologues–one person saying what is on her or his mind, then waiting while the other person does the same. Active listening, by contrast, shows respect for the speaker by giving a response directly related to what the speaker has said, perhaps by repeating a phrase, asking a clarifying question, or simply indicating, "I understand." Sometimes, active listening is difficult because we may feel that we don't have an opportunity to say what is on our minds. Nonviolence, however, means putting other people first and really respecting them–in this case, by truly listening to what they have to say.

Active listening shows respect for the speaker. . .

Questions:

Name one situation when you tried to force your opinion on others. What was the response? How did you feel afterwards?

How could you have made the point you were trying to make in a different way?

4. Non-Cooperation

The nonviolent person needs to look hard at cooperation with violent systems. Just as a morally sensitive person would not take a job with a mob group that is engaged in bribery and murder, even if the job is on the fringe such as bookkeeping or typing and does not involve direct brutality, so the nonviolent person will look at his or her employment and avoid taking a job with an institution that is spreading violence. If one's government is felt to be an unjust and violent institution, the nonviolent person will consider the possibility of refusing to support that government in various ways.

The nonviolent person needs to look hard at cooperation with violent systems.

Questions:

List the ways your workplace or school promote justice.

List the areas of injustice present in your school or work situation. In what ways can you confront this injustice?

In what areas of your life are you most in need of a nonviolent attitude?

Simpler Living

We Who Prayed and Wept

Wendell Berry (1980)

We who prayed and wept
for liberty from kings
and the yoke of liberty
accept the tyranny of things
we do not need.
In plentitude too free,
we have become adept
beneath the yoke of greed.

Those who will not learn
in plenty to keep their place
must learn it by their need
when they have had their way
and the fields spurn their seed.
We have failed Thy grace.
Lord, I flinch and pray,
send Thy necessity.

In addition to examining our attitudes and everyday actions, we who are trying to be nonviolent need to reflect on our lifestyles. In a consumer society it's easy to be caught up in the swirl of feeling the need for more–or better –clothes, cars, music, food, homes, furniture, gadgets. Just as it's important to resist cultural pressures that advocate violence, it's also important to stand firm and not be seduced by the cultural pressures for excess comfort, which is actually another form of violence. We need to slow down and truly enjoy what and who is around us, not always trying to do and to have more.

For many of us in industrialized nations, consumption is not determined by our needs (since our physical needs are all met) but by desires and wants, especially those created by advertising. It's clear that a nonviolent person should oppose the excessive consumption that occurs in the western world while elsewhere billions suffer from the lack of basic necessities. Consumption of ever-increasing amounts is only possible at the expense of the environment–the earth that shelters us–and humans who live and toil in poverty to meet the demands of others.

Fundamental to considering a simpler lifestyle is examining our attitudes and desires about money and financial security. Our society tells us that we can never have enough money. But the ways we have of getting money are quite often destructive to our lives, to our relationships, to our fellow human beings, and to the earth, contradicting an attempt to live nonviolently. Even if our job doesn't exploit others or the earth, it may prevent us from doing what we would really like to do, from practicing nonviolence, from living in community. More money leads us to consume more, further damaging the earth. Likewise, a perceived need for financial security can turn us away from a path of nonviolence.

To grow in our personal nonviolence, we must also examine the place of consumer goods in human life. They cannot make up for personal insecurity, although many people pursue that illusion. They sometimes substitute for human beings as objects of our attention and affection. It seems easier to fix a machine than mend a mind or a relationship.

But the value of material things actually lies in how they enhance human dignity. They help us achieve a level of decency when they are used to relieve some unnecessary burdens and free people for creative occupations. In so many parts of the world, and in our own country, people are burdened by poverty, by hunger, by homelessness. Everyone in the world should have the opportunity for a decent life. So everyone in the world should have access to a sufficient amount of material goods to assure that decency.

Decency is not the same as luxury. To live decently is to have enough food, clothing, shelter, and medical care to sustain physical life and to have access to works of art and literature to nourish spiritual life. It is to be free from worry about survival, free to contribute to the well-being of others. Anything more than that is not necessary for a nonviolent person. Gandhi put it this way: "If each retained possession only of what (was) needed, no one would be in want, and all would live in contentment. . .The rich should take the initiative in dispossession with a view to a universal diffusion of the spirit of contentment. If only they keep their property within moderate limits, the starving will be easily fed, and will learn the lesson of contentment along with the rich."

It is clear that our overconsumption and desire for more, bigger, faster is killing the earth God made. Not only has our disposable and product-oriented culture taken us further and further from the land, it has destroyed that very land. Living more simply, doing with less, and using local resources and services show respect for creation, cut down on waste, and encourage more human community.

Knowing this, what are our choices?

Some nonviolent people choose voluntary poverty as their personal path. They see this as a way of identifying more closely with the poor and oppressed who are forced to live that way. People who choose voluntary poverty believe in conserving the world's natural resources in the interest of a more just distribution of them. They try to live simply so that others may simply live.

Others do not see voluntary poverty as a necessary condition for personal nonviolence. To cut back on one's own standard of living by itself will not end others' poverty, unless it is accompanied by actions to change the system that keeps people poor. But simpler living frees one's energies from a preoccupation with things, so energy and time can be channeled in the direction of constructive, cooperative action to improve the social system. Reducing consumption, finding more sustainable ways of living, and nurturing community and relationships are all part of this process.

Questions:

React to Gandhi's words. What might they mean in your life?

What are your feelings and goals toward and about money?
How do or don't they fit with living nonviolently?

What do you see as the relationship between nonviolence and lifestyle?

How can you begin to invest in relationships rather than things?

Care of the Earth

In industrialized societies, we, for the most part, have become very disconnected from the land, from the earth, from the source of our food, from the source of our being. Living simply–and living nonviolently–means making connections between what we do in our daily lives and the health of the planet. The earth is not just a tool for our use and exploitation; what we do has consequences for our survival as a species and for the survival of all other life species.

What are some of the choices that we have made, individually and collectively, that have been so devastating to the earth?

- *Not being satisfied with the bounty of the earth and thus genetically engineering plants*
- *Not buying locally and thus wasting resources, especially oil, on transport and forcing the growth of crops which do not feed local people and may not be suitable for the land*
- *Using tons of pesticides and fertilizers rather than working with organic products or having dandelions in our yards*

- *Surrounding store-bought products in layers and layers of non-recyclable packaging which gets added to our dumps*
- *Using chemicals and crops that lead to soil erosion*
- *Poisoning our water supply with hazardous waste, fertilizers, and other chemicals*
- *Endangering thousands of species through pollution, hunting, and clearing their natural habitats*
- *Clearing rainforests, especially to provide grazing land for the cattle which end up in our fast-food restaurants*
- *Creating tons of greenhouse gases through vehicle emissions and the burning of fossil fuels*

In the natural world, waste is unheard of. Everything is recycled in some way. Our use of the earth and its resources, on the other hand, creates tons of waste every day. Too often, our very lifestyles are acts of violence toward the earth. As Pope John Paul II said, "Today the dramatic threat of ecological breakdown is teaching us the extent to which greed and selfishness, both individual and collective, are contrary to the order of creation."

In addition, a huge connection exists between violence toward the earth and the oppression of weak and vulnerable people by the greedy and dominating. Not only have we in essence attempted to revise creation to bring wealth to the few, but we have done so by controlling the poor. Nearly always, after exploiting the bodies and the land of the poor and disenfranchised, we dispose of our garbage and hazardous waste in "their backyards." While this harms the poor the most, it hurts all of us.

We must recognize that we are intimately connected to all life on the planet: our brothers and sisters in our neighborhood and in our country, but also those 3000 miles away; the trees outside our homes, schools, and workplaces, but also those in a rainforest in Cameroon. Petra Kelly, an activist and Green politician, wrote, "Using power to dominate humans and nature has brought us to an impasse and can never take us beyond it. We must learn to think and act from our hearts, to recognize the interconnectedness of all living creatures, and to respect the value of each thread in the vast web of life." We cannot live apart from the natural world.

In attempting to live nonviolently, we must treat the earth with reverence and awe. After all, our faith teaches us that God created not just humans but the whole of creation; God's covenant includes nature (in the story of the ark, the animals are essential and God's sign

We did not weave the web of life; we are merely a strand in it. Whatever we do to the web we do to ourselves.

–Chief Seattle

of the covenant–the rainbow–is given through nature). All creation is a sign of the divine presence and reveals the divine to us. This is a reason to celebrate and to give praise to God for the wonder and beauty of creation.

This realization also calls us into right relationship–to realize the connections and interdependence between all living things. There are no boundaries in nature; we are all part of creation. The Bible calls us to choose life. We must extend this call to all life. William James Riley, in a poem entitled "Dwelling," writes, "Each of us/is responsible/to those who dwelled here before us/and those who will inherit our decisions./What we do now/will be recorded/not only in the mind of God/but in the bowels of the Earth/where trees invent their roots."

Prophets such as John the Baptist and Moses recognized the sacredness of creation; when they wanted to be close to God, they journeyed to the wilderness. Benedict of Nursia, Francis of Assisi, and Hildegard of Bingen are among others who demonstrated care for and love of the earth. Like these prophets, we must reconnect with creation. Some people have termed this eco-spirituality: seeking and finding God in creation. We must ask our churches to do so as well, by forming committees on environmental justice, praying for the earth, and attempting to treat the earth with more care.

The first step is changing our personal habits of excessive consumption and wastefulness. But while these personal changes are important, structural changes are desperately needed. Governments and corporations are usually behind great ecological devastation. For instance, in Los Angeles (and many other cities), an auto manufacturer bought and dismantled a rail transit system, forcing people to be more dependent upon cars, which are extremely harmful to the environment.

IN ACTUALITY, humans are but a very small part of creation. There are slightly more than 1.4 million named species on this planet–99% of which have only scientific, not common, names. Scientists estimate that there are 10-100 million species on the planet.

Questions:

How does your lifestyle impact the earth?

Buying locally, "reducing, reusing, and recycling," and limiting consumption are some ways to start. What are some other ways you can begin to change?

In what ways can we call on governments and corporations to be more responsible to the earth and its future?

Prayer

Recognizing the interconnectedness of all life–not just human–we pray,

We join with the earth and with each other,
　　To bring new life to the land.
　　To restore the waters.
　　To refresh the air.

We join with the earth and with each other,
　　To renew the forests.
　　To care for the plants.
　　To protect the creatures.

We join with the earth and with each other,
　　To celebrate the seas.
　　To rejoice in the sunlight.
　　To sing the song of the stars.

We join with the earth and with each other,
　　To recreate the human community.
　　To promote justice and peace.
　　To remember our children.

We join with the earth and with each other.
　　We join together as many and diverse expressions
　　of one loving mystery, for the healing of the earth
　　and the renewal of all life. Amen.

("We Join with the Earth," from the UN Environmental Sabbath Program)

Questions:

What connections do you see between respecting all of creation and what we eat? How might this principle ask us to change our diets? Have you considered becoming vegetarian (no meat) or vegan (no animal products)?

Risking the Journey

If any or all of this sounds terribly difficult, we need not become discouraged. The human spirit has great powers. When we take the basic step of wanting to pursue the path of nonviolence, we have made the conversion that leads us in the direction of true peace. We are attempting to live the Gospel message in a way that's particularly appropriate to our time.

The direction is certain, but the details along the way are not. We don't have all the answers yet. The ultimate textbook on nonviolence hasn't been written. In all probability it never will be. Gandhi called nonviolence an "experiment" in truth, not knowing where the experiment would lead. He abandoned some steps he had taken when they backfired or when he found others that were more effective.

Our attempts to live nonviolently are certain not to work all of the time. But we are not called to success but to faithfulness, to live our lives in imitation of the nonviolence of Jesus. We will not be perfect in this journey, and the conversion of our hearts will be slow and difficult at times. No person–including the great prophets of nonviolence–has been completely successful at nonviolence. This should not discourage us from attempting the journey. Indeed, as Walter Wink writes in *Engaging the Powers*, "in a certain sense, nonviolence never fails, because every nonviolent act is a revelation of God's new order breaking in upon the world."

Our lives, lived nonviolently, are experiments in truth. Nonviolence takes us beyond comfort and certainty into risk. It's the kind of risk a follower of Jesus will find familiar. "Therefore I tell you, do not worry about your life, what you will eat, or about your body, what you will wear. Life is more than food, and the body more than clothes. Consider the ravens: They do not sow or reap, they have no storeroom or barn; yet God feeds them. . .Do not set your heart on what you will eat or drink; do not worry about it. All the nations of the world seek these things, yet your Abba God knows well what you need. Set your sights on the kindom of God, and all these other things will be given to you as well." (Luke 12:22-24, 29-31)

We seek the reign of God through active nonviolence. Our lives become part of a pattern of peacemaking that can spread throughout the world. Every individual act of nonviolence helps to create and spread that pattern. When we consciously adopt a nonviolent approach, we adopt the mode of thinking and acting necessary in our time, not only to avoid catastrophe, but to renew the face of the earth, starting with our own little piece of it.

Closing Prayer

Reader 1:

God has moved within us; God walks with us on the journey. This is indeed cause for celebration. And all of creation rejoices with us! Let us give thanks to God for the stirrings in our hearts, for the transformation of our lives!

Side 1:
Sing to Yahweh a new song!
Sing to Yahweh, you lands!

Side 2:
Sing to Yahweh; bless God's name.
Proclaim God's salvation day after day.

Side 1:
Tell God's glory among the nations;
tell God's wondrous deeds to all people.

Side 2:
Let the heavens be glad, and the earth rejoice;
let the sea and all that it holds resound.

Side 1:
Let the fields and all that is in them exult;
let all the forests cry out for joy
at the presence of Yahweh. . .
(from Psalm 96)

Reader 1:

We cry out for joy at your presence among us, God. We ask your blessing upon us; may we feel your guidance on the way of peace.
And so we pray,

All:

O Holy Mystery, Creator God, pour into me your Sanctifying Spirit, that I may water the world with the love and example of Jesus.

Help me to strive for peace within, and to make peace in my life this day.

Strengthen me to accept suffering rather than inflict it. In the face of provocation and violence, be my calm.

Preserve me in nonviolence of tongue and heart. Quench my inner violence with your life-giving Word.

Help me drink deeply of the small joys of life. Sustain me in a simple life, so others may simply live.

Energize me to work against injustice and to actively resist evil. Empower me to overcome the sins of racism, sexism, and materialism.

Stream through me to abolish war from my own heart and from the face of the earth. Equip me to build the reign of justice and peace.

O Holy Mystery, Creator God, I trust in your sustaining love and power. I believe that just as you gave me the desire to offer this prayer, so you will also bestow abundant grace to fulfill it. Amen.

("**Prayer for a Nonviolent Heart**," adapted by Kathy Schmitt from *The Vow of Nonviolence* by Pax Christi USA)

Part Six: Reflections

1. What do you think about taking a "vow of nonviolence?"

2. What stands in the way of my making a conscious decision to allow nonviolence to enter all parts of your life?

3. What small actions can you take to gain more inward peace and peace in your daily life?

4. Gandhi called nonviolence an experiment in truth. From your experience, do you find this an appropriate description?

5. List the "steps" that you've taken in the past year in your own "thousand mile" journey toward nonviolence.

6. In what ways can you praise God for the beauty and joy of creation? How can you be more conscious of how your decisions affect the earth? Read Psalm 104 as a reminder of the vast wonder and wisdom of God's creation.

Suggestions for Action

- Slow down. Be conscious of what is around you. Notice something that you've never noticed before. Where is the wonder around you?

- Begin a spiritual discipline, perhaps using one of the examples of prayer listed above.

- Try to eliminate words of violence from your speech.

- Each day, try at least once to listen really and completely to what someone is saying to you. Concentrate only on that person, not on what his or her words might mean to you or affect you.

- Reduce your consumption. Before you buy a product, ask yourself if you really need it, how long it will last, if you could use something that you already have, if you could borrow it from someone else. Pay attention to whether it comes in lots of extra packaging, where it was made, who will benefit from your purchase and who will be harmed.

- Recycle whatever you can, even if it means going a little out of your way (such as taking something home to be recycled rather than throwing it away when you are out).

- Think of two ways that you can take better care of the earth and begin to practice them. Some examples: carpooling or walking instead of driving separately, buying local produce at the farmers market rather than from the chain supermarket, conserving water by taking shorter showers, using natural products rather than artificial chemicals to clean your house or fertilize your plants or garden.

A Sampling of Sources and Resources

Prayer, Spirituality, Nonviolence:
Durback, Robert, ed. *Seeds of Hope: A Henri Nouwen Reader.* Toronto: Bantam Books, 1989.

Easwaran, Sri Eknath. *Meditation: A Simple Eight Step Program for Translating Spiritual Ideals into Daily Life, and Your Life is Your Message.* Tomales, CA: The Blue Mountain Center of Meditation/ Nilgiri Press.

Johnston, William. *Being In Love: The Practice of Christian Prayer.* San Francisco: Harper & Row Publishers, 1989.

Kownacki, Mary Lou, ed. *The Fire of Peace: A Prayer Book.* Erie, PA: Pax Christi USA, 1992.

National Catholic Conference of Bishops. *The Harvest of Justice is Sown in Peace: A Reflection of the National Conference of Catholic Bishops on the Tenth Anniversary of The Challenge of Peace.* Washington, DC: United States Catholic Conference, 1994.

Nouwen, Henri. *With Open Hands.* Notre Dame, IN: Ave Maria, 1972.

Schreck, OSF, Nancy and Maureen Leach, OSF. *Psalms Anew: In Inclusive Language.* Winona, MN: Saint Mary's Press, 1986.

Vanderhaar, Gerard A. *Beyond Violence: In the Spirit of the Non-Violent Christ.* Mystic, CT: Twenty-Third Publications, 1998.

Simpler Living and Care of the Earth:
GROUPS: (See also groups in Part Two.)
"Defending Those Who Give the Earth a Voice," a joint project of the Sierra Club and Amnesty International USA; phone: 800/213-2650; http://www.defendtheearth.org; (Produced a 20 minute video, "Environmentalists Under Fire: Defending Those Who Give the Earth a Voice," that ties together environmental and human rights issues from around the globe.)

Friends of the Earth: 1025 Vermont Avenue NW; Washington, DC 20005; phone: 202/783-7400; e-mail: foe@foe.org; http://www.foe.org

Student Environmental Action Coalition (SEAC): PO Box 31909; Philadelphia, PA 19104-0609; phone: 215/222-4711; e-mail: seac@seac.org; http://www.seac.org (See Part Eight.)

United States Catholic Conference Environmental Justice Program: Office of Social Development & World Peace; National Conference of Catholic Bishops/United States Catholic Conference; 3211 4th Street NE; Washington, DC 20017-1194; phone: 202/541-3000; http://www.nccbuscc.org/sdwp/eip/index.htm

AUTHORS:
Thomas Berry, Wendell Berry, Annie Dillard, Pierre Teilhard de Chardin.

BOOKS:

Bhagat, Shantilal P. *Creation in Crisis: Responding to God's Covenant.* Elgin, IL: Brethren Press, 1990. (Includes Biblical perspectives on creation, examples of human destruction of the earth, looks at the interaction of faith and environmentalism, and includes study questions and resources.)

Cummings, Charles. *Eco-Spirituality: Toward a Reverent Life.* Mahwah, NJ: Paulist Press, 1991. (Integrates Judeo-Christian scriptures and Catholic and monastic spiritual traditions with scientific exploration; examines reconciliation and healing.)

Elgin, Duane. *Voluntary Simplicity: Toward a Way of Life that is Outwardly Simple, Inwardly Rich.* New York: Quill, 1993.

Gould, Lisa Lofland. *Caring for Creation: Reflections on the Biblical Basis of Earthcare.* Burlington, VT: Friends Committee on Unity With Nature, 1999. (A series of reflections done for Quakers on the Bible and environmental stewardship and relations with the Earth.)

Kelly, Petra K. *Thinking Green! Essays on Environmentalism, Feminism, and Nonviolence.* Berkeley, CA: Parallax Press, 1994. (Written by a German activist and Green politician, weaving together many issues.)

Longacre, Doris. *Living More With Less.* Scottdale, PA: Herald Press, 1980.

McDonagh, Sean. *To Care for the Earth: A Call to a New Theology.* Santa Fe, NM: Bear & Company, 1986. (Written by a missionary, incorporates Christian theology, history, and biological and earth science.)

Roberts, Elizabeth J. and Elias L. Amidon, eds. *Earth Prayers: From Around the World, 365 Prayers, Poems, and Invocations for Honoring the Earth.* San Francisco: Harper San Francisco, 1991.

Part Seven

Nonviolent Witnesses

"To change the world for the better you must begin by changing your own life. There is no other way. You begin by accepting your own worth as a part of the universe and by granting every other being that same recognition. You begin by honoring life in all of its forms. You begin by changing your thoughts toward your contemporaries, your country, your family, your working companions. If the ideal of loving your neighbor like yourself seems remote, you will at least absolutely refrain from killing your neighbor. And your neighbor is any other person on the face of the planet. You cannot love your neighbor, in fact, until you love yourself, and if you believe that it is wrong to love yourself, then you are indeed unable to love anyone else." –Jane Roberts (Seth) (in *The Individual and the Nature of Mass Events*)

The previous section emphasized that nonviolence is a journey that begins with a gradual conversion of one's own heart and life. It involves recognizing the common humanity in all persons, regardless of their actions, and treating others with the respect each child of God deserves. It means overcoming the fears that bind us and keep us from loving. It means seeking healing and creative measures of resolving conflict.

Along the way, we grow personally and jointly and move nearer to the vision of the peaceable kindom that God has created for us.

We have many examples and stories of and about the great prophets of nonviolence. (More examples and campaigns are shared in Parts 8 and 9.) Too often, however, these people have been glorified to the point where we may feel unable to follow their examples of nonviolence.

In this chapter, we read stories–all but one of which are true–of how ordinary people called on the power of love and nonviolence to change their world and themselves. These individuals, from around the world, broke cycles of violence both in their everyday lives and during times of organized violence and struggle. May their examples be more food for our journey.

Nonviolent Witnesses

- *Opening Prayer*
- *The Rabbi's Gift*
  - *–Recognizing Christ in Each Person*
- *Responses to Violence:*
  Overcoming Fear and Living Creatively
  - *–Resisting Assault*
  - *–The Power of Love*
  - *–A Visit to South Africa*
  - *–Reconciliation in Northern Ireland*
  - *–Profile: Pia Deas*
- *Conclusion*
- *Closing Prayer*
- *Reflections*
- *Suggestions for Action*
- *A Sampling of Sources and Resources*
- *Credits*

Opening Prayer

Reader 1:
We pause from our thoughts and actions, from all the things that occupy our minds. We recall God's presence in our lives, in this moment and all moments. To what is God calling us today? How are we to live with others? How can we bring God's love more fully into the world? How can we walk the way of peace more completely?

Reader 2: The words of St. Paul (Romans 12:9-18):
Your love must be sincere. Hate what is evil and cling to what is good.
Love one another with the affection of sisters and brothers.
        Try to outdo one another in showing respect.
Don't grow slack, but be fervent in spirit; the One you serve is Christ.
Rejoice in hope; be patient under trial; persevere in prayer.
Look on the needs of God's holy people as your own; be generous in offering hospitality.
Bless your persecutors–bless and don't curse them.

Rejoice with those who rejoice, weep with those who weep.
    Have the same attitude toward everyone.
Don't be condescending to those who aren't as well off as you; don't be conceited.
Don't repay evil with evil.
Be concerned with the highest ideal in the eyes of all people.
Do all you can to be at peace with everyone.

(After a pause)

Reader 1:

All around the world, individuals are following your way of peace, God. Give us the courage to hear their stories and to learn from their examples. Teach us to see you in every person we meet, even in those who might try to hurt us. Inspire us with your divine love and creativity to end violence and to start healing. With the women of Brazil, we pray,

Blessed God, you who know each of our fears,
release us from them all by your love and give us courage to act

Side 1: against rejection,
    and for your love,
Side 2: against oppression,
    and for justice,
Side 1: against poverty,
    and for life abundant,
Side 2: against loneliness,
    and for companionship,
All: against violence,
    and for peace,
    against death,
    and for life.

(adapted from "Give Us Courage," by the women of Brazil, from *Women of Prayer*)

The Rabbi's Gift

by Francis Dorff

There was a famous monastery which had fallen on very hard times. Formerly its many buildings were filled with young monks and its big church resounded with the singing of the chant, but now it was deserted. People no longer came there to be nourished by prayer. A handful of old monks shuffled through the cloisters and praised God with heavy hearts.

On the edge of the monastery woods, an old rabbi had built a little hut. He would come there from time to time to fast and pray. No one ever spoke with him, but whenever he appeared, the word would be passed from monk to monk: "The rabbi walks in the woods." And, for as long as he was there, the monks would feel sustained by his prayerful presence.

One day the abbot decided to visit the rabbi and to open his heart to him. So, after the morning Eucharist, he set out through the woods. As he approached the hut, the abbot saw the rabbi standing in the doorway, his arms outstretched in welcome. It was as though he had been waiting there for some time. The two

embraced like long-lost brothers. Then they stepped back and just stood there, smiling at one another with smiles their faces could hardly contain.

After a while the rabbi motioned the abbot to enter. In the middle of the room was a wooden table with the Scriptures open on it. They sat there for a moment, in the presence of the Book. Then the rabbi began to cry. The abbot could not contain himself. He covered his face with his hands and began to cry too. For the first time in his life, he cried his heart out. The two men sat there like lost children, filling the hut with their sobs and wetting the wood of the table with their tears.

After the tears had ceased to flow and all was quiet again, the rabbi lifted his head. "You and your brothers are serving God with heavy hearts," he said. "You have come to ask a teaching of me. I will give you a teaching, but you can only repeat it once. After that, no one must ever say it aloud again."

The rabbi looked straight at the abbot and

said, "The Messiah is among you."

For a while, all was silent. Then the rabbi said, "Now you must go."

The abbot left without a word and without ever looking back.

The next morning, the abbot called his monks together in the chapter room. He told them he had received a teaching from "the rabbi who walks in the woods" and that this teaching was never again to be spoken aloud. Then he looked at each of his brothers and said, "The rabbi said that one of us is the Messiah."

The monks were startled by this saying. "What could it mean?" they asked themselves. "Is Brother John the Messiah? Or Father Matthew? Or Brother Thomas? Am I the Messiah? What could this mean?"

They were all deeply puzzled by the rabbi's teaching. But no one ever mentioned it again.

As time went by, the monks began to treat one another with a very special reverence. There was a gentle, wholehearted, human quality about them now which was hard to describe but easy to notice. They lived with one another as men who had finally found something. But they prayed the Scriptures together as men who were always looking for something. Occasional visitors found themselves deeply moved by the life of these monks. Before long, people were coming from far and wide to be nourished by the prayer life of the monks, and young men were asking once again to become part of the community.

In those days, the rabbi no longer walked in the woods. His hut had fallen into ruins. But, somehow or other, the old monks who had taken his teaching to heart still felt sustained by his prayerful presence. **(from New Catholic World)**

Recognizing Christ in Each Person

Nothing in this story openly speaks of nonviolence, yet the values it portrays are critical to our understanding of nonviolence. Just as the monks never mentioned the saying again, they did not say that their lives became more nonviolent. But their changed lives witnessed to the power of love, the power of nonviolence and the principles upon which it is based.

A Brazilian archbishop said that what we call nonviolence is simply living out the Gospel. And the Gospel calls us to realize that God/Jesus and the kindom are here in our midst. The monks in this story, by living as if Christ were among them—indeed, in them (as Christ truly is)—transformed themselves and their world. This is what nonviolence calls us to do.

Thomas Merton writes, "Then it was as if I suddenly saw the secret beauty of their hearts, the depths of their hearts where neither sin nor desire nor self-knowledge can reach, the core of their reality, the person that each one is in God's eyes. If only they could see themselves as they really are. If only we could see each other that way all the time, there would be no more war, no more hatred, no more cruelty, no more greed. . .I suppose the big problem would be that we would fall down and worship each other."

How can we encourage this sense of reverence and awe for the part of God which lives in all of us? How will it help us in all that we do to be nonviolent witnesses to each other and to the world?

ANNE FRANK was a Jewish teenager in the Netherlands during World War II. Hidden in an attic along with her family, she was eventually discovered by the Nazis. She later died in a concentration camp. Despite living day in and day out with the horror of how humans can abuse their brothers and sisters, she remained optimistic. She wrote, "I keep my ideals because in spite of everything I still believe that people are really good at heart. I simply can't build up my hopes on a foundation consisting of confusion, misery and death. I can feel the sufferings of millions, and yet, if I look up into the heavens, I think that it will come right, that this cruelty too will end, and that peace and tranquility will return again." How can you, despite the violence of our world, "keep the faith" and continue to reverence each person?

I . . . believe that people are really good at heart.

–Anne Frank

Responses to Violence:
Overcoming Fear and Living Creatively

Each day, each of us faces some form of violence, usually on a small scale, but sometimes on a larger one. Responding nonviolently takes preparation. We must work to build peace within ourselves. We must learn to recognize the sacred in all people, including ourselves. Respecting the dignity of all people means that we cannot (intentionally) hurt others, but also that we do not allow them to take advantage of us or to disrespect or destroy our humanity.

Nonviolence helps us both to overcome violence in specific situations and to live our whole lives creatively, to give something positive to the world. A commitment to nonviolence can prepare us for the unexpected and for daily challenges.

The following stories show how ordinary individuals, through a commitment to nonviolence and love, used creative responses to violence in their lives and world. When the world expected them to give in to violence, to seek revenge, or simply to give up, they demonstrated another way. They listened to others, quietly demonstrated their love and faith, and used writing and theater to work through violence. For some of these people, training in nonviolence or in the power of the Gospel was critical.

These individuals also worked to overcome their fears, whether of an armed individual, of going to jail or being tortured, or of losing acceptance in the community. By doing so, they broke the cycle of violence and instead began the process of healing and reconciliation.

We too have fears. Since most of us do not live in armed conflict zones, our fears may be different and less concrete: the fear of losing respect, the fear of giving up our material possessions, the fear of not finding a good job. Living nonviolently requires that we face these fears and place our trust in the God of nonviolence, the God who will sustain us.

In the first three stories below, people faced personal physical attack or threat. Their responses demonstrate that there is another way. They provide answers to the type of question often asked of people of nonviolence, "What would you do if an armed robber attacked your grandmother, your child, etc.?" The fourth story demonstrates how humans can respond with love and a desire for healing when faced with tremendous personal pain. The final story is an example of how to apply nonviolence to one's life, to live in a way that is creative and sustainable.

Resisting Assault

Angie O'Gorman gives workshops in nonviolent resistance to personal assault. The following is part of a letter that a woman who attended one of these workshops wrote to Angie.

Dear Angie,

Training in nonviolence and my reflection and reading on it have been extremely freeing. . . . I've got some wonderful stories to tell. . . One time I was home alone for the weekend and on Friday evening went for my daily run. It got dark sooner than I expected and I ended up on a path by the railroad tracks in the dark facing this tall, wild-eyed man. He took me rather forcefully by the arm, and I can remember feeling profoundly ungraced, very uncreative, out of control and profoundly aware of the fact that I was home alone and no one would begin to miss me until Sunday night.

To my rescue came a dog followed by its owner—a man of puny stature. The assailant looked at me—I knew he knew I was going to call for help—and released my shoulders from the tree where he had pinned them. Rather than feel frightened for myself, however, I began to feel sorry for the puny guy with the dog who was about to be dragged into a violent scene. So I took my assailant by the arm and used his line, "Come on, we're going this way." Once we were out of earshot of the little guy but by no means out of danger, he pulled back and said, "What are you doing?" I told him I could see by his eyes that he had experienced a lot of pain and that he didn't need to get hurt any further and that hurting me certainly wouldn't do anything but add to his pain. I suggested we sit down and talk.

I sat him down on a piece of concrete under a bridge, not sure if this was going to work. I thought it best to start with small talk and asked if he had a family, taking the opportunity to tell him about my family as soon as possible. To make a long story short, he was an executioner in Vietnam—the one who shot everyone in the village after they were lined up by other Marines and ended up in a POW camp for 19 months. Along with a rather rough childhood and being unemployed he was a very, very broken person. We talked for about an hour and a half. Not knowing how to get out of there or how free I was to go, but sensing the danger was over, I asked him to walk me home. He did and the upshot of the whole deal was—are you ready for this—the next day I got a small bouquet of flowers from him with a card saying, "Thank you for being my friend." Sounds unbelievable, but true. . .

Love,

Maggie (Pharris)

Question:

If you were confronted by someone who was going to attack you, how would you respond? Why?

The Power of Love

Ordinary people took great risks for nonviolence in the brutal wars in Central America in the late 20th century. These people remind us that we too can work for justice and that nonviolence can overcome violence. Sarah Corson, a U.S. missionary in Latin America, had been told that soldiers would try to eliminate foreigners in the area. When soldiers surrounded her house, she prayed to die unafraid and trusting God. At once, she felt God's presence.

I found myself speaking to the nearest soldier, "Welcome—come in. You don't need guns. You're all welcome."

The commander pushed into the house with his gun; thirty soldiers rushed into the house and began pulling everything off the shelves and out of the drawers looking for guns. They herded us into the kitchen where we sat quietly in the candlelight.

The commander turned his gun on me and demanded to know why Americans were there, trying to stop his revolution. I told him we were there for two reasons only—to teach the Bible and to teach self-help projects to the hungry. But he had never read the Bible. "That tells me nothing—maybe it is a communist book."

I picked up a Spanish Bible and turned to the Sermon on the Mount. "We teach about Jesus, the Son of God, who came into the world to save us, to show us a better way than violence, the way of love. Because of him I can tell you that even though you kill me, I will die loving you. God loves you. To follow God, I have to

love you, too."

The soldier burst out. "That's not humanly possible!"

I answered, "Humanly impossible, but, with God's help, possible."

"I don't believe it."

"You can prove it—kill me slowly and I will die praying for you because God loves you."

"You almost convince me, but I have orders to take everyone in the house."

They marched us down the trail to a truck waiting on the road from the village. Others had been taken from the village and were waiting to be loaded onto the truck with us. But the commander changed his mind. He took the men and let the women go free saying that he had never before disobeyed an order but that he could not take us women to a jungle camp to be abused by a thousand soldiers. He began to walk away, hesitated, and came back. "If my superior finds out that you were here when I raided your house, he will kill me. I could have fought guns, but there is something here I don't understand—I can't fight it. I have fought many battles and killed many people—it was just my job. But I never knew them—this is the first time I ever knew my enemy. I believe if we knew each other our guns would be unnecessary." He went away, leaving us alone.

(Full accounts of this episode appeared in *Sojourners* and *The Other Side*)

Questions:

How do you think that you might have responded in this situation?

What steps can you take so that you might be able to react like Corson?

Thousands of ordinary people brought about the transformation of South Africa, a great many of them through nonviolent means. When Joyce Hollyday, the author of the next story, first went to South Africa in 1988, nearly everyone with whom she talked thought that apartheid (racial separation and discrimination) would not end in his or her lifetime. However, it didn't take nearly that long. Hundreds of thousands of South Africans struggled for racial justice, and apartheid has been declared illegal.

Because often the stories of nonviolence we are told are of older people, we may not know that young people are committed to nonviolence and to Gospel witness. Their lives also provide us with powerful inspiration. The following is the story of one young man's courage and commitment to the truth.

A Visit to South Africa
by Joyce Hollyday

"I made my first visit to [South Africa] in the spring of 1988, back when that country was still very much in the stranglehold of the system of racial hatred known as apartheid. . .

Since a state of emergency had been imposed in June 1986, 30,000 people had been detained by the police, 10,000 of them children. Torture and assassination were routine state policy. The townships were under military occupation.

Military eyes peered constantly from the tower that rose above the township of Duncan Village, outside East London. The eyes were aided at night by powerful floodlights that could search out activity in any corner. I arrived in the early afternoon and was greeted by Jam-Jam, a young man active in the freedom struggle.

We walked unhindered for almost an hour. Then a *casspir*–a huge armored personnel carrier–appeared on the horizon and lumbered toward us. Eight members of the South African Defense Forces, pointing rifles, surrounded us and ordered us to the military strong point.

We were escorted in the direction of the tower, taken past rows of razor wire that surrounded the military headquarters, and ushered into an interrogation room. A member of the security police arrived and interrogated me, warning me that it was illegal for a white person to be in a black area, and against the law under the state of emergency to take pictures. Then he turned to Jam-Jam. Shaking his finger and uttering stern and threatening warnings, he said, 'Didn't you just get out?' He was referring to Jam-Jam's recent release from ten months in detention, where he was kept in a cold cell, fed cornmeal infested with worms, and tortured. He finished with the threat that Jam-Jam would be back in soon if he didn't give up his subversive activities.

I will never forget what happened then. Jam-Jam's only response to the threats was to reach calmly into his back pocket and take out his small New Testament. Displaying it in front of the officer's face, he said simply, 'Sir, I am a Christian.' A brief moment of silence descended as the arrogance of evil met the quiet power of the gospel."

(From Hollyday, Joyce. "Discovering Hope in the Nevada Desert," in *Fellowship*, March-April 2000.)

Reconciliation in Northern Ireland

On another continent, the faith of several women also overcame centuries of hate and brought them to do the hard work of healing and reconciliation.

The island known as Ireland is divided into two parts: the South, called the Republic of Ireland and an independent nation, and the North, called Northern Ireland and part of Great Britain. This island and its people have centuries of background, history, and conflict. While the conflict presently occurring in Northern Ireland (called "the Troubles") is often called religious, it is much more than that. It is about political power, social justice, civil participation, economic opportunity, and civil rights.

Essentially, it is a state of civil war which pits two groups against each other: the Orange/Protestants/Unionists and the Green/Catholics. The first group makes up the majority of Northern Ireland. They desire union with Great Britain. They have a history of discriminating against Catholics who live in Northern Ireland, denying them civil rights, such as housing and jobs, leading in some cases to Catholics leaving the area. In other cases, Catholics/Greens in Northern Ireland have taken up arms and fought. This conflict has led to several thousand deaths in the past few decades and the existence of several armies (the British army occupying Northern Ireland) and paramilitaries (the most famous being the Irish Republican Army–the IRA). Catholics generally desire that the whole island be part of the Republic of Ireland (which is a majority Catholic).

"Mission of hope binds mothers of violence"

by Mark Patinkin

Belfast, Northern Ireland–She had never involved herself with the Troubles. Most people are that way here. Let the rest kill each other if they choose. Let braver souls try to stop it. Maura Kiely would find her corner of peace. Even in Northern Ireland, you can do that. You can close a door.

And she did. As a devout Catholic, she found her center in church and family. She made a life in her house, and made babies there. She would not let any of it touch her.

She named her firstborn son Gerard. He came into the world with a fervor, screaming and full of life. He was the loudest of babies. He became the gentlest of young men.

He was not quite 19 when it happened. He was in college at the time, in Belfast. She later learned that he left his room at exactly 6:55 p.m. The church was the shortest of walks. Sunday night Mass went quickly. At 7:35, Gerard began to leave with the rest of the congregation.

"Two gunmen began to fire indiscriminately," said Maura. "They were in a car."

The police would later say that the incident was just what it appeared to be: Someone had decided to kill Catholics. They chose a church to make sure.

There were 700 people inside. At the moment of the shooting, her son happened to be in the doorway. The bullets struck three people. Gerard was one of two who died.

"Just one bullet," said his mother. She pointed to her own heart. "Right there."

I asked Maura what she had done with her bitterness.

She said she is reaching out to Protestants in reconciliation.

There was another woman with us in this room. Her name was Pearl McKeown. She, too, had closed a door on the Troubles and found her corner of peace.

She was a Protestant, a committed Christian, and that was her center, her church, and her family, too.

She named her daughter Karen. The child came into the world with a contentment. She was the happiest of babies. The family would joke about her being born with no tear ducts.

As a young woman, she taught Sunday school and drove fast cars. Her mother would later say it was not a contradiction. Karen loved life. She loved speed and she loved life.

She was so young when it happened. She had just passed 19. She was in college at the time, in Belfast.

She, too, died at her church. The two had gone there together, mother and daughter, for the installation of a new minister. She was a member of the ladies' club, and scheduled to help with the dishes afterward. But it had been a difficult day for her. Pearl is a nurse, and the hours this day had been long.

"So Karen looked at me," she recalled, "and said, 'Mom, I'll drop you off at home and do the dishes for you.'"

Soon, Karen was back at the church. Pearl later would hear that it happened just as she locked her car in the lot. The day before, a Catholic girl had been shot in the next neighborhood. The injury was slight, but someone decided there would be vengeance.

"This fella just came up to her," said Pearl. "He put a gun to her neck and said, 'I'm going to shoot you.' And he shot her. Straight through the neck. It severed her spine completely."

She did not die as quickly as Gerard. She lingered for three weeks.

I asked Pearl how she felt about Catholics now. She said her mission is to reach out in reconciliation.

I asked Maura about her work of reconciliation. What brought her to it?

Something unexpected happened after the

murder. Mail began coming in. Soon, there were 400 letters. Most were from strangers. They seemed to help even more than friends.

What she did next was more by instinct than design. She went to the office of one of Belfast's newspapers. She spent a day researching the names of others who, like herself, had lost a child. She made a point of listing just as many Protestants.

And one night, she began. She knocked on a door in the dark. "My name is Maura Kiely," she said, "and my son was murdered."

Two strangers sat together, and it was four hours before she left. The next night she did the same thing, this time with a Protestant.

Soon, she saw it was bigger than knocking on doors in the night. Invitations went out for a gathering. She made it clear it would be a mix of religions. She expected a dozen people. More than 60 showed up.

And a group was formed. And for the first time, survivors stopped speaking of husbands having been killed by Catholic or Protestant. They just spoke of husbands having been killed.

It remains the only such group in Northern Ireland with a mix of faiths.

I turned to Pearl. I asked how she came to her own work.

Karen had not yet died, and already the letters began for her as well. One was unexpected. It was from an imprisoned Catholic terrorist. He'd heard about Karen; he'd heard that people of his faith had shot her only because she was Protestant. He wrote that he and some other Catholics inside had come to understand this wasn't the way.

I asked Pearl why she did not condemn these men who once were a part of the violence.

Because her death was such a waste, said Pearl. It would be less so if something could come out of it.

And this was something. She saw a special power in organizing exterrorists into speaking out against it. There are few calls for peace as credible as those from men of violence.

The name of the group she now works with is the Prison Fellowship. They go to schools and neighborhoods, and they preach that the gun is not an answer. Pearl goes with them.

She said there has been a price.

"I have Protestant friends who don't want to know me anymore because I'm associating with Catholics. They told me Karen's death had flipped my lid."

If there was one subject they spoke of the most, it was the solace of faith.

"Yes," said Pearl, "if you hadn't had that, you'd have been in some bar."

She stressed that she was a committed Christian.

I'd heard many people in Northern Ireland use the cloak of Christianity as an excuse for intolerance. It is the cry of the Free Presbyterians, the followers of the Rev. Ian Paisley. They proclaim it from both the pulpit and the political podium. They have given their lives to the one true Lord, they say, and those who have not aren't true Christians.

I asked Pearl if it was the same for her. Are those who have not accepted God as she has somehow unChristian?

She said she is only angered by those who preach such gospel. It was the first time she showed the trace of bitterness. "If you say you love the Lord, but hate your brother," she said, "you're a liar!"

I had one more question for them. Their work is good, but it's so small, and the problem so big. Can they really touch it? "It is the only way with such problems," said Maura. "You don't solve them, you just touch lives one at a time. You go person by person."

"You hope the ripples spread," said Pearl.

We walked toward the door. On the way, the two women discovered an unexpected commonality.

"Karen's in Roselawn [cemetery], too?" said Maura. "I didn't know that. What's her number?"

"It's 2295," said Pearl. "What's Gerard's?"

"It's 1236."

(Mark Patinkin, a columnist for the *Providence Journal*, took a two month tour of Northern Ireland, India, and Lebanon.)

You don't solve [such problems,]

you just touch lives one at a time.

You go person by person.

Has violent death ever affected you or anyone you know personally?
How did you/they handle it?

Reflect on the grace of reconciliation—and how to feed that desire—
as the lives of Maura Kiely and Pearl McKeown demonstrate it.

Profile: Pia Deas

The story of Pia Deas, a woman in her late twenties, would probably not be one that comes immediately to mind when we think about people who are living nonviolently. We are more likely to picture someone who takes to the streets or sends off letter after letter to elected officials. Yet Pia is an example of someone who has allowed the principles of nonviolence to fill her life. Her active attempts to live out her creativity, to communicate with others (through writing, theater, and teaching), and to connect with other people—especially those marginalized in our society—are the kind of relationships and actions that are the basis of living a life of nonviolence. She is using her voice to make a unique contribution to the type of world in which a nonviolent person would like to live.

During her late teens and early twenties, Pia worked for social change on many levels, from working against racism to leading nonviolence trainings for young people. This work was not always easy. In fact, at times, she found these experiences quite tiring.

Pia realized that there had to be other ways of living nonviolently. Her experience as a woman of color at her mostly white college led her to another expression of nonviolence. She belonged to a group of women of color who worked on issues of multiculturism on campus. These women discovered that it is not enough to be active all of the time; we must also explore our inner selves. As activists, a busy schedule and a recognition of the great violence and injustice of the world can actually bring us to commit violence against ourselves, such as through trying to do too much. The group decided to spend a whole semester nurturing and being nonviolent toward themselves, through art and other creative forms.

Pia later expanded upon this creative side by working with Philadelphia's Freedom Theater, a theater company expressing the African-American experience. While she enjoyed being part of a community and working on a local level, she also heard a calling to write. She is currently exploring issues of violence in writing. She draws upon her own experiences of violence: as a person of color and as someone who lived in Germany during the Cold War and the 1986 nuclear accident (explosion) at the Chernobyl (USSR) nuclear power plant. Through her writing, she both expresses identity and explores the impact of violence in her life and the lives of those around her.

As a teacher, she uses writing to help people, especially those not accepted in our society because of racism, violence, poverty, and lack of access to education, express themselves. Working with other people gives her hope and inspiration.

For Pia, creativity is a spiritual journey: writing gives her a way to connect to the spirit. Expressing and nurturing her creative side are an important way to take care of herself. They allow her to travel with others on this journey.

(Pia was also profiled by Neera Singh in *Fellowship*, January/February 2000, Vol. 66, No. 1-2.)

In what ways do you nurture yourself?

Are there ways in which you are already living nonviolently
that you haven't before recognized or named?

Conclusion

The people in this chapter are by no means "exceptional." While they may have dedicated some or all of their lives to nonviolence and to healing, there is no reason that we can't do the same. Their stories illustrate the importance of cultivating peace within and developing a spirituality and faith that can change both ourselves and our world. They demonstrate the importance of prayer, of a nonviolent attitude, of listening, and of developing creative ways of working outside of a system of violence and creating a new way of being in the world. With many ordinary people living out such examples and witnessing daily to the power of nonviolence, we will bring about the nonviolent reign of God.

Closing Prayer

("More than we can dream of," by Jan S. Pickard, in *Women of Prayer*)

Reader 1:
We thank you, God
because you give us
more than we would ever dream of asking:
daily bread and shared meals that become feasts,
the breath of life and voices to celebrate,
the understanding of our history
and the hope of our future.
Work we can do, and time to be recreated,
people to love and trust,
people who love and trust us,
gifts and responsibilities.

Reader 2:
We thank you, God
because you ask of us
more than we dream of giving:
skills we have never developed,
care for a world whose problems we cannot solve,
listening which hurts us,
giving which leaves us empty-handed,
love which makes us vulnerable,
faith which seems impossible.

Readers 1 and 2:
But you do not ask us to be supermen and women.
You challenge us to be human.
Give us the courage to be human

Reader 1:
because you yourself became human
and lived our lives,
knowing our imperfections,

Reader 2:
sharing our joy and pain,
making us your people
so that we can say together,

All: "Our Father and Mother..."

Part Seven: Reflections

1. Many of these stories tell about overcoming fear. Of whom or what are you afraid? Why? How can youbegin to lessen this fear? How might overcoming these fears help you to live more nonviolently?

2. Have you experienced the feeling of "burn-out" or been overwhelmed at any point in your nonviolent journey? What ways do you have or can you start to prevent this?

3. How does a nonviolent society or community allow for creativity? Is this is an important or good reason to choose nonviolence?

4. How might your personal journey of nonviolence be a way of living out the Gospel?

5. How might nonviolence transform you? Your relationships? Your communities?

6. How can you make prayer a part of your attempts to live nonviolently?

Suggestions for Action

- Spend an entire day believing that the Messiah is in your midst.
  In the evening write down your reactions and feelings. Try to live out any changes that you felt.
- Role play an alternative response to a situation in which you might feel frightened or attacked.
- Write about your commitment to nonviolence and what motivates that stand.
  Share it if you feel comfortable.
- Work against gun violence. Find out about gun violence where you live and see
  if there are any groups working against it. See Part Two for groups that research gun violence.
- Do something creative; work with your hands, body, or voice.
  Paint, draw, write, sculpt, sing, garden, dance.
- Listen to music or spoken word, such as hip hop or folk music, that expresses alternatives
  to violent and unjust systems.

A Sampling of Sources and Resources

Miscellaneous:
Donnelly, Doris. Seventy Times Seven. Erie, PA: Pax Christi USA. (Resource about the subject of forgiveness and how it touches everyone's life. Offers concrete steps in the process of complete forgiveness. Explores how forgiveness makes the difference between hatred and love, hope and despair, war and peace.)

Frank, Anne. Anne Frank: The Diary of a Young Girl. New York: Bantam Books, 1993.

Linn, Dennis, Sheila Fabricant Linn, and Matthew Linn. Don't Forgive Too Soon: Extending the Two Hands That Heal. Mahwah, NJ: Paulist Press, 1997. (Contains stories of people reacting in creative, nonviolent ways when threatened as well as how to undertake the process of forgiveness and reconciliation without retaliation. Uses the concept of Jesus' Third Way.)

Murder Victims Families for Reconciliation. 2161 Massachusetts Avenue; Cambridge, MA 02140; phone: 617/868-0007; website: http://www.mvfr.org (An organization for people who have lost family members to violence and others who work for healing, for an end to the death penalty, for the rights of victims, and for a more just criminal justice system.)

Stewart, Dorothy. Women of Prayer: An Anthology of Everyday Prayers From Women Around the World. Chicago: Loyola Press, 1999.

On Thomas Merton:
Cunningham, Lawrence S., ed. Thomas Merton: Spiritual Master. The Essential Writings. Mahwah, NJ: Paulist Press, 1992.

Merton, Thomas. Faith and Violence: Christian Teaching and Christian Practice. Notre Dame, IN: University of Notre Dame Press, 1968.

Merton, Thomas. The Nonviolent Alternative. New York: Farrar, Straus, Giroux, 1980.

Credits

"The Rabbi's Gift" reprinted with permission from New Catholic World, 997 Macarthur Blvd., Mahwah, NJ 07430.

"Mission of hope . . ." written by Mark Patinkin, a columnist for the Providence Journal, Providence, RI. Reprinted with permission.

Part Eight

Nonviolence in Action: Campaigns in the United States

In the United States, thousands of people have taken journeys of nonviolence and used the nonviolent spirit to respond to indignity, hatred, oppression, dehumanization, destruction, and injustice. Martin Luther King, Jr., said, "Our lives begin to end the day we become silent about things that matter." These men and women, in a variety of times and places and for a wide range of causes, have refused to be silent. They have acted, marched, written, and spoken about the things that matter. They have started to live the society that they wanted to see and by so doing helped to bring it about, if only for a moment or a small space.

This chapter provides examples of nonviolent campaigns or movements in the United States over the past century. Some of the more famous examples you may have heard of; others are not so well-known. Some may not at first even necessarily seem as if they are specifically examples of nonviolence in action. But all are ways people have addressed injustices and worked to shape a new society in exciting, creative ways, without using violence or damaging the lives of others.

Opening Prayer

Reader 1:

"What we would like to do is change the world–make it a little simpler for people to feed, clothe, and shelter themselves as God intended them to do. And to a certain extent, by fighting for better conditions, by crying out unceasingly for the rights of the workers, of the poor, of the destitute–the rights of the worthy and the unworthy poor, in other words–we can to a certain extent change the world; we can work for the oasis, the little cell of joy and peace in a harried world. We can throw our pebble in the pond and be confident that its ever-widening circle will reach around the world.

We repeat, there is nothing that we can do but love, and dear God–please enlarge our hearts to love each other, to love our neighbor, to love our enemy as well as our friend." **–Dorothy Day**

Silence.

All: O God of timelessness and time
Thank you for those things that are possible and precious
Thank you

Side 1:   for justice which repairs the devastations of poverty;
for liberty which extends to the captives of violence;
for healing which binds up the broken bodied and broken hearted;

Side 2: for bread broken for all the hungry of the earth;
for good news of love which is stronger than death;
and for peace so that no one is afraid.

All: Thank you
for the undeniable awareness
that we need you
and that your presence is always with us,
setting us free, for others, for joy, and for you;
Thank you for your grace, our lives, forever.
Amen.

(adapted from "I Thank You for Those Things that Are Yet Possible," by Ted Loder, in Guerrillas of Grace*)*

The Civil Rights Movement

"NONVIOLENT RESISTANCE . . . avoids not only external physical violence but also internal violence of spirit. The nonviolent resister not only refuses to shoot an opponent but also refuses to hate him or her. At the center of nonviolence stands the principle of love. Along the way of life someone must have sense enough and morality enough to cut off the chain of hate. This can only be done by projecting the ethic of love to the center of our lives." **—Martin Luther King, Jr.**

The lasting legacy of the Civil Rights Movement is the model it sets for seemingly powerless people who want to change society. Farm workers, denied the right to organize; women, struggling for equal rights; ordinary citizens convinced that U.S. intervention around the globe is immoral; lesbian, gay, bisexual, and transgendered persons working for civil rights–all use the nonviolent direct actions demonstrated effectively by the Civil Rights Movement in this country.

In a country often divided by race, resistance to racial domination had been around for centuries. In the 1940s, Blacks around the country and their white allies began mass actions against segregation and injustice. They sponsored "Freedom Rides" to desegregate mass transportation and took part in sit-ins. They established groups such as the Congress for Racial Equality (CORE), the first bi-racial organization to focus on gaining civil rights through nonviolent action.

But although people had been organizing and training for a long time, 1955 in Montgomery, Alabama, is often viewed as the birth of the Civil Rights Movement. In that year, the Black people of Montgomery, after a mass meeting, decided to boycott the city busses. They stated that they would not ride until they could sit anywhere in the bus and did not have to give up their seats to white folks. For over a year, they organized carpools and walked–often in the face of violence from whites–until the city desegregated the busses.

A wave of actions and awareness-raising swept the South. In 1960, several students sat at a Woolworth's lunch counter in Greensboro, NC, calling attention to the fact that segregation did not allow them to have even a cup of coffee at the counter. Such sit-ins quickly spread to 15 cities in 5 Southern states. In a year, 50,000 people, mostly Black, participated in demonstrations. In 1963, 200,000 people gathered in Washington, D.C. to protest segregation. This was the largest demonstration in U.S. history up to this time and was a key factor in the passing of the Civil Rights Act of 1964. Once the movement started, it would not be stopped–sit-ins, civil disobedience demonstrations, marches, and boycotts became the tools for change and the signature of the movement. Numerous groups, such as the Student Nonviolent Coordinating Committee (SNCC) and the Southern Christian Leadership Conference (SCLC), did great organizing work.

The 1960s saw the passage of several civil rights laws, due to the pressure of this nonviolent people's movement. Decades later, though, racism still exists in this country, and people continue to struggle nonviolently to end its brutal grip.

Question:

How can we "project the ethic of love to the center of our lives?"

The Catholic Worker

The Catholic Worker was founded in New York City during the Great Depression when Peter Maurin, a wandering French laborer and thinker, met Dorothy Day, a U.S. journalist who had recently become a Catholic. Both saw the need to work for social justice and peace by taking literally the Christian teachings to feed the hungry, shelter the homeless, clothe the naked, and love the enemy. Maurin stated that Christ's commandments are before us; we just need to put them into action.

Under their leadership and inspiration, the Catholic Worker movement began printing a newspaper, running "houses of hospitality" where people could stay, opening soup kitchens, and expressing a courageous and consistent resistance to war and all forms of violence. Maurin's vision included establishing "agronomic universities" that would provide meaningful work and be more organic than commercial farms; this was the beginning of Catholic Worker farms.

The Catholic Worker emphasizes both doing the works of mercy and resisting structures that deny human dignity. Ending war and

Peter and Dorothy outside Catholic Worker House 1933

the methods of war have been particularly important. During the Spanish Civil War (1936), people urged the Worker to give up its stand against war because it took away from the great work the Worker was doing with the poor. However, in the vision of Maurin, Day, and the other Catholic Workers, the two were (and today are) inseparable,

Day's impact on the Church's social teaching, identification with the poor, and witness for peace was such that, when she died in 1980, a church historian called her "the most significant, interesting and influential person in the history of American Catholicism." Today more than 100 Catholic Worker communities, coordinated by people who choose to live in voluntary poverty and thus resist materialism and consumerism, continue this legacy of love. Using the teachings of the Gospels, they critique the economic, social, and political system. At the same time, they take personal responsibility for the defense of life and human dignity by meeting human needs.

Questions:

What can you do *today* to put Christ's commandments into action?

Do you see a connection between the works of mercy and resistance? Why or why not?

United Farm Workers

Migrant farm workers were considered unorganizable, and that is how many growers and politicians wanted them to stay. Farm workers were exploited. They lacked health care, education, and grievance procedures (to challenge discrimination, hiring, or firing practices). They were paid very little and forced to work in fields where dangerous pesticides were used. They had no protection under national labor laws and regulations.

That was before Cesar Chavez. Chavez, a former migrant farm worker, organized farm labor into a powerful union and led one of the most successful boycotts in U.S. history. When Chavez joined the farm workers' struggle in the early 1960s, he brought a belief in nonviolence both as a personal commitment and as a strategy for social change. He encouraged farm workers to discipline themselves in nonviolence in order to be successful, not just on the picket line, but in the hard work of organizing.

In 1962, Chavez helped to form the National Farm Workers Association (NFWA; later the United Farm Workers or UFW) to address the workers' conditions. Chavez, Delores Huerta, and many other farm workers set up a store, a gas station, a service center, and began a modest life insurance policy.

In 1965, when another union called for a strike of grape workers, they voted to join. They also voted to maintain nonviolent tactics in their struggle. The farm workers went on to use hunger fasts and consumer boycotts, the latter of which were very effective in reaching the conscience of the middle class. They marched, sang, picketed, went to jail, and traveled around the country. They organized against many companies and in many fields. Besides pressuring California grape growers to sign the first wide-scale union contracts in the state, the union was influential in obtaining the right for farm workers to vote for the union of their choice.

Nonviolence remained vital to their struggles. Chavez in an appeal to the president of the California Grape and Tree Fruit League, wrote, "our strikers here in Delano and those who represent us throughout the world are well trained for this struggle. They have been under the gun, they have been kicked and beaten and herded by dogs, they have been cursed and ridiculed, they have been stripped and chained and jailed, they have been sprayed with the poisons used in the vineyards; but they have been taught not to lie down and die nor to flee in shame, but to resist with every ounce of human endurance and spirit. To resist not with retaliation in kind but to overcome with love and compassion, with ingenuity and creativity, with hard work and longer hours, with stamina and patient tenacity, with truth and public appeal, with friends and al-

> "WHEN WE are really honest with ourselves, we must admit that our lives are all that really belong to us. So, it is how we use our lives that determines what kind of persons we are. It is my deepest belief that only by giving our lives do we find life. I am convinced that the truest act of courage, the strongest act of humanity is to sacrifice ourselves for others in a totally nonviolent struggle for justice. To be human is to suffer for others. God help us to be human."
>
> —Cesar Chavez

lies, with mobility and discipline, with politics and law, and with prayer and fasting."

Chavez himself never stopped working for the rights of farm workers. One of his last campaigns was against the use of pesticides in commercial agriculture. He always encouraged people to be involved. When asked what he would advise young people to do with their lives, Chavez responded. "I would ask them to choose one important area of human need and focus their energies in that direction so much so that their lives are touched and changed by the people they work with."

The White Train Campaign

Since the mid-1970s, the Ground Zero Center for Nonviolent Action in Washington state has worked for nonviolence and against one of the world's deadliest weapons: the Trident nuclear submarine. The Ground Zero Center house borders a large Navy base that became "home" to Trident submarines in 1982. In the 1980s, Ground Zero began a campaign to monitor and protest trains carrying nuclear bombs from a plant in Texas to these submarines.

A network of people in over a dozen states –an extended nonviolent community called the Agape Community–became involved in the White Train Campaign. These people recognized that they, as people in the U.S., had a responsibility for those weapons and the violence they could create, as well as how dangerous it was to transport them across the country. They trusted in love and nonviolence to overcome violence: "We believe the spiritual force capable of both changing us and stopping the arms race is that of *agape*: the love of God operating in the human heart."

For three years, the community monitored the armored white (painted to deflect heat) train's location as it went to both Washington and South Carolina. Hundreds were arrested for sitting on the tracks to stop the train; hundreds more vigiled alongside the tracks against nuclear weapons, often 24 hours a day. Demonstrators successfully stopped the trains for a few minutes with their actions. They also maintained good relations with local authorities and reached out to those operating the trains by offering fresh bread and messages.

The movement began to receive wide support and led to many conversions. In 1984, in Orchard, Idaho, the 6 o'clock news announced the train. Eight women who had been playing bridge left their cards to go to the vigil. Two of these women had never before been to a public protest. In 1984, 12 Catholic bishops urged direct action to block the deployment of nuclear weapons and urged their parishioners to join the prayer vigils. A lawyer who had prosecuted White Train protestors became the defense attorney for the next White Train trial. A jury ruled not guilty in the trial of a group of protestors who said that international law gave them the responsibility to block nuclear weapons.

Because of the protests, the Department of Energy (DoE) rerouted the train. But this only resulted in an ever-widening campaign. According to a secret 1984 memorandum, the DoE also changed strategy by painting the sides of the train red, green, gray, and blue (the top stayed white to reduce heat for safety reasons). But these strategies were not enough. Public opposition was too great. The last White Train to Washington was in February 1985 and the last to South Carolina in February 1986.

The DoE melted the train down and began putting the weapons on trucks. Nukewatch in Madison, Wisconsin, followed such nuclear warhead shipments from Texas and contacted people along the route. Other groups monitored various other shipments of parts for the nuclear weapons.

The group's goal, to raise awareness of the destructive power of nuclear weapons and eventually to stop the arms race, is far from accomplished. The Washington Trident base still houses Trident submarines with more nuclear weapons than Great Britain, France, China, Israel, India, and Pakistan combined – all the nuclear powers but Russia. But many more people are aware of the horrors of nuclear weapons and the U.S. government's participation in this crime. Glen Milner, one of the activists, wrote, "We were reminded with each trip of what the arms race had ultimately brought to us–to witness our own spiritual deaths in the nuclear age. With each White Train, hearts and minds were transformed and the tracks became a sign of an extended nonviolent community."

> "WE CANNOT cooperate massively with Trident and other nuclear weapons and then expect God's intervention to prevent our being burned by the evil we have chosen. To continue doing evil and then expect God to save us from its consequences is to mold the Creator in our own image."
>
> **–Jim Douglass (from his book, *The Nonviolent Coming of God*)**

Questions:

What difference do you think reaching out to the military personnel made? What about Ground Zero folks living in the community (next to the base)? What challenges and opportunities do you think it presents?

Solidarity with South Africa

It may seem odd to have a story about South Africa in the section on nonviolence in the United States. But the increasing interconnectedness of our globe has allowed the struggles of one people to be taken up by another half a world away.

Until the 1980s, a brutal system of racial apartheid dominated South Africa. The smaller numbers of white people viciously oppressed the vast majority of people, who were Black. While South African activists had faith that this domination system would fall, many thought that it would take several lifetimes.

One reason that it fell much more quickly was that the movement to end apartheid had strong support from outside of South Africa. For instance, many people in the United States took up this struggle. They used several methods: demonstrations and civil disobedience and divestment strategies (taking financial investments out of South Africa and companies based there).

In November of 1984, people began daily civil disobedience in front of the South African Embassy in Washington, DC. Students, community leaders, members of Congress, national labor and religious leaders, and teachers were among those who, in solidarity with their sisters and brothers in South Africa who were denied basic human rights, risked arrest every weekday for over a year. Thirty-one hundred were arrested. Twenty-six other cities had campaigns that resulted in five thousand arrests.

The second method of calling attention to the oppression of apartheid was through the movement to divest. South Africa had many foreign investors. In order to protest the government that denied humanity to the majority of the country's people, divestment began. Students were leaders in this movement. They built shantytowns and held sit-ins in attempts to force their colleges and universities to divest from South Africa. Hundreds were arrested. Eventually, 130 campuses divested over $4 billion from South Africa.

Along with detailed documentation of the violence occurring in South Africa, the solidarity displayed by thousands of people abroad who were willing to risk arrest, sleep outside, and educate their peers helped to bring down apartheid. In the end, the government of South Africa could not resist the pressures of such a movement.

Question:

How can we support other people's struggles while still allowing them to make their own decisions and resisting the domination and exploitation that has often been part of U.S. involvement in the world? For instance, in the work to end apartheid, South African activists made the decisions about what kind of support they needed—for example corporate divestment—then requested that their U.S. counterparts pressure corporations to divest.

Mothers of East LA

In the mid-1980s, Juana Gutiérrez, mother of nine, decided she had enough of neighborhood decay and corporations' abuse of her community in East Los Angeles. She gathered a group of mothers who formed "*Madres del Este de Los Angeles, Santa Isabel*" (Mothers of East LA), Their rallying cry is, "*Las Madres Unidas Contra Todas Las Injusticias!*" (Mothers

United Against All Injustices). Their broad definition of both community and injustice allows them to work for many kinds of change.

In a community with very few financial resources, this group of women, concerned about their children's futures, is transforming their neighborhood and protecting the environment. They use a broad range of nonviolent techniques to promote the environmental, political, and educational awareness, advancement, and well-being of the Latino population of this community. They work both to stop harmful practices (especially relating to the environment and health impacts) and to create and use positive alternatives. They have set up neighborhood watch systems to keep the neighborhood safe, defeated an oil company pipeline and two hazardous waste treatment centers that threatened to pollute their neighborhood greatly, organized a recycling program that has traded in nearly 70,000 high-water-use toilets for ultra-low flush toilets, and provided scholarships. They have organized, educated, and mobilized to make their community a better, more ecologically sound, and safer place for all children to live.

Questions:

Do you think that "all injustices" are related? Why or why not?

What connections do you see between some of the different types of work that *Las Madres del Este de Los Angeles* have done?

SEAC: Student Environmental Action Coalition

SEAC–pronounced "seek," as in "seeking"– is a student and youth-run network that addresses environmental injustices of all types. While its members now come from over 1500 college and high school campuses, it started very modestly.

In 1986, two University of North Carolina students restarted a campus environmental group with a focus on recycling. In 1988, they approached several national environmental organizations about launching a student movement. These organizations were nervous about starting a group over which they would ultimately have no say. Eventually, Greenpeace magazine agreed to run an ad asking to hear from student environmentalists interested in forming a network. The group's budget was $200. At its conference the next fall, the organizers hoped to get a few hundred students from several different campuses. Instead, 1700 students from 44 states arrived. A movement had begun.

The students began writing grants and hiring staff. SEAC, the Student Environmental Action Coalition, went on to boycott Coors beer and to pressure DuPont and BP over environmental ruin.

SEAC has had its problems, such as internal disagreements over politics. But it has continued to unite young people around the country. It runs an office that provides resources, such as publications, campaigns, and skills training, for a diverse variety of young activists working on education and action at the grassroots level. It works to create change on both the local and global levels, sharing resources, building coalitions, and challenging the limited definition of "environmental issues."

Starting with a small focus on recycling, SEAC now aims to uproot all environmental injustices, including physical, economic, political, and cultural. It is unique in that it does not limit its environmental concerns to what many people usually think of, such as pollution and recycling. The environment, says SEAC, is everything around us. Thus, SEAC works not only to end environmental abuses and to recognize the impact of humans on the environment, but to support human and animal rights, to demand corporate responsibility, and to end classism, racism, sexism, heterosexism, imperialism, and militarism.

Nonviolence in Action

Questions:

What do you think about SEAC's definition of the environment?

Does it make sense to you? Why or why not?

How would you define the environment?

Devising a New System: Ithaca's HOURS

Violence can be economic. Wealth is becoming increasingly concentrated in the hands of a few; our economic system pits people against each other. Awareness of this violence has led to many forms of protest. One of these is the creation of local currencies, a (legal) way of helping local business, services, and friendships while maintaining awareness of social concerns. These currencies involve systems of trade and exchange that do not use U.S. dollars. Alternative economic systems and arrangements allow people to remove themselves from an economic system that values profits over people. They encourage community building.

Ithaca, New York's HOURS system is an example of how over 1300 participants and tens of thousands of dollars have helped area residents "gain control of the social and environmental effects of commerce. . ." Started in 1991, HOURS helps support local people and community trading, allows people to exchange goods and services–such as plumbing, nursing, child care, food, gifts, rent, hospital services, no-interest loans, grants for community organizations, and entertainment–and raises the minimum wage. As the creator, Paul Glover, wrote, "We're making a community while making a living. As we do, we relieve the social desperation which has led to compulsive shopping and wasted resources." HOURS are printed in 5 denominations and are backed by "real people, real time, real skills and tools."

Hate Crimes: Billings, Montana

In the 1990s, especially after the brutal murders of a Black man in Jasper, Texas, and a gay man in Laramie, Wyoming, people began increasingly to be aware of certain acts of violence that can be called "hate crimes." These are violent acts against a person or group of people who are or are thought to belong to a different race, ethnicity, religion, or sexual orientation. While lawmakers consider increasingly punishing and revengeful laws to deal with people who commit hate crimes, other people are choosing to respond to these acts with creativity and community. Their nonviolence demonstrates that there is a better way to respond, a way that draws people together, educates, and leads to a more peaceful society.

In Montana, for instance, various white supremacy groups have increasingly violently targeted people of color, Jews, and gays and lesbians. For instance, in the city of Billings, a Jewish cemetery was vandalized and swastikas were painted on the home of an interracial couple.

In some ways, such actions in Billings came to a head in December of 1993, when a brick was thrown through the window of five-year-old Isaac Schnitzer's bedroom. Isaac's window displayed a menorah and other symbols of Judaism in celebration of the Jewish holiday Hanukkah. The investigating officer advised Isaac's mother, Tammie, to remove the symbols. But Schnitzer wondered how she would explain this to her son and decided to leave the menorahs up.

Another mother, Margaret MacDonald, reading the story in the paper, thought about this dilemma. She remembered hearing that during World War II, Danish people chose to wear yellow stars in solidarity with the Jews. MacDonald called her pastor, who called other clergy in town. The following week, hundreds of children put cut-out menorahs in their windows. The Billings paper printed a full-page drawing of a menorah, inviting people to put it up. Shopkeepers distributed them. By the end of the week, between 6000 and 10,000 homes had menorahs in their widows.

The solidarity went beyond the display of menorahs. A sporting goods store posted a sign saying, "Not in Our Town! No hate. No violence. Peace on Earth." People organized a vigil outside the synagogue on the Sabbath. The Catholic school put up a sign saying "Happy Hanukkah to our Jewish Friends" and placed menorahs in the windows. These displays of solidarity and love were met with some violence–several homes, cars, and churches had windows broken, for example.

But the people of Billings, for the most part, grew closer. Inter-religious relationships have developed. The next year, menorahs once again appeared in thousands of windows. The people of Billings, rather than reacting with fear and violence to the fear and violence of certain individuals, tried the way of nonviolence, love, and respect–and grew in the process.

(Also reported in *Fellowship*, January-February 1995; *Woman's Day*, November 22, 1994.)

The people of Billings . . .
tried the way of nonviolence, love and respect
—and grew in the process.

Voices in the Wilderness

In 1991, the United States and its allies went to war against Iraq, supposedly to stop Iraq's oppression of the people of Kuwait. Many in the U.S. and elsewhere saw it as a war over oil, and officials later admitted that this was a major factor.

In the 45 days of the First Gulf War, the small country of Iraq had more bombs dropped on it than were dropped in the Second World War. But actually the war did not end in 45 days, even though many of the troops went home and the issue faded from consciousness. The United States and Britain continued to bomb. This bombing (which in 1991 included depleted uranium, whose dust is toxic and radioactive) has had devastating effects. Much of the country's infrastructure (e.g., hospitals, sewage systems, water purification plants, and transportation routes) was destroyed.

Physical destruction is not the only punishment the people of Iraq have faced. Even up to and through the Second Gulf War, again led by the U.S. despite lack of UN approval, Iraqis lived under the most comprehensive set of economic sanctions ever enforced against a country. These sanctions prevented even basic supplies, such as spare parts, from entering the country. Sometimes when materials did enter the country, there were not ways to transport or distribute them effectively. The sanctions devastated the country in nearly every way: financially, socially, educationally.

Reports from human rights organizations, including UNICEF and other UN bodies, estimated that 5000-6000 children died unnecessarily every month as a result of the sanctions, even after UN measures to trade Iraqi oil for food.

Well over one million people died during the twelve years of the sanctions, the majority of whom were children. Many died from easily preventable causes such as diarrhea and malnutrition. Sanctions targeted the weakest and most vulnerable members of society: children, the elderly, and the poor.

In response to this grave crisis, people from the United States, calling themselves Voices in the Wilderness (VitW), put themselves at risk to deliver needed supplies such as aspirin and vitamins to Iraq, to build connections with Iraqi civilians, and to document and draw attention to the devastation. Because of the sanctions, U.S. citizens were not allowed to travel to Iraq. But since 1996, more than 50 delegations composed of teachers, social workers, authors, health care professionals, tradespeople, and church leaders have gone to Iraq. They and others broke the sanctions, knowing that their simple gestures of humanity could land them in prison for 12 years and $1 million in fines. And as the U.S.-led attack against Iraq began anew in the spring of 2003, members of VitW remained in Iraq, in solidarity and suffering with the many Iraqi friends they had made over the years.

Profile: Ben Grosscup

Just three days after his 18th birthday, in December 1999, Ben Grosscup of Minnesota traveled to Iraq with VitW. Ben later wrote in a song,

"I went to Iraq on a truck from Amman [Jordan] / Because to get there by air you have to carry bombs / I had come to see the human tragedy / That our country has been inflicting against the Iraqis. . ." Ben did witness the devastation of Iraq. He also made new friends. His personal connections with Iraqis have made him even more committed to ending the war against the people of Iraq.

Ben's work against the sanctions is just one part of his work against injustice, one way of creating a different or new world. For instance, he also lives at a Catholic Worker house. Activism for Ben isn't just issues of the world. He also recognizes that he can't stand against the political and economic violence of our system without changing his own lifestyle and interactions. He is committed to changing not only the world, but himself.

Because of his participation in various struggles, Ben has questioned certain aspects or principles of nonviolence and also labels (like "pacifist") that we use to describe ourselves. Too often, he believes, labels become too rigid, not allowing for change and dialogue, and thus untruthful. He emphasizes that nonviolence must always be inclusive and open to critique and question. Despite his questions and concerns, Ben remains "deeply convinced that nonviolence is the best way to create meaningful social change."

Prayer to End the War Against Iraq

by Art Laffin

Loving God,
We beg your forgiveness for the war the U.S. is waging against the Iraqi people, for destroying Iraq's infrastructure by massive bombings, for using highly toxic weapons that contaminate Iraqi land and water, and are causing major increases in cancers among children. Forgive us for imposing economic sanctions that have killed over one million Iraqis, mostly children. Forgive us for placing oil interests above human welfare. Heal us of our moral blindness and fill our hearts with love. Help us to renounce all killing, to stop demonizing our adversaries, to value all life as sacred, and to see the Iraqi people as our brothers and sisters. Empower us to engage in nonviolent action to end this slaughter of the innocents.

O God, make us channels of your peace and reconciliation. Amen.

(available as a prayer card from Pax Christi USA)

Questions:

Voices in the Wilderness says that we must all accept responsibility for Iraq's devastation: for our failure to educate ourselves and others, for our materialism which drives us to acquire more at the expense of others, for accepting violence as a legitimate way to solve problems, for allowing half of the U.S. discretionary federal budget to be spent on the military. Their website says, "Every person has the right and obligation to understand the world they live in. This includes being aware of oppression and fighting to end it. When we remain complacent, we become part of the system that oppresses people." Do you agree? What is your responsibility?

SOA: New Name, Same Shame

Established in Panama in 1946 and moved to Fort Benning, Georgia, in 1984, the U.S. Army School of the Americas (SOA) states that it trains Central and South American soldiers and officers to promote stability and democracy in their home countries. Instead, the record of the school's nearly 60,000 graduates shows a trail of suffering, murder, torture, and terror, leading many to call it the "School of Assassins."

Countries with the worst human rights violations or the most violent internal conflicts (Mexico and Colombia in the late 1990s) consistently send the most soldiers to the SOA. Graduates of the SOA were the majority of those named in El Salvador for the murders of Oscar Romero and the four U.S. church missionaries and the El Junquillo, El Mozote, Las Hojas, San Sebastian, and Jesuit massacres. Religious leaders, labor and union organizers, students, human rights workers, and educators have been particularly targeted in such repression.

In September of 1996, under pressure, the school released some of its training manuals. They included information on interrogation "techniques" such as torture, execution, blackmail, and arresting relatives of suspects. Soldiers have been trained in low-intensity conflict: using the soldiers of a country to repress the people and to keep power, land, and wealth in the hands of the elite through terror and intimidation.

In the spring of 2000, the U.S. House of Representatives voted, 214-204, to close the SOA. However, they also voted to open another school, the Western Hemisphere Institute for Security Cooperation, in its place. Despite the U.S. Army's insistence that the school has reformed and now teaches human rights, it continues to be a combat training school.

But the school and its supporters have definitely encountered resistance. In 1983, two priests (one a Vietnam veteran) and a woman in the Army Reserves went onto Fort Benning where Salvadoran soldiers were. They played the sermon Oscar Romero gave the day before his assassination, asking soldiers to stop murdering their brothers and sisters. In 1990, one of these priests founded SOA Watch to call attention to the horrors of this school. SOA Watch has sponsored vigils, fasts, demonstrations, public education, and media work. It informs U.S. citizens that tens of millions of their tax dollars fund the school.

Mass action is also part of this campaign. Every year, starting in 1990, on the anniversary of the 1989 murders of six Jesuits, their housekeeper, and her daughter in San Salvador (capital of El Salvador), people have gathered at Fort Benning to call for the school's closure. The first year 25 people demonstrated. In 1996, 500 people gathered to protest the school and 60 crossed onto the base and were arrested. By 1999, an estimated 12,000 people vigiled at the gates of Fort Benning. After attending nonviolence training, 4408 risked arrest by walking onto the base in a solemn funeral procession to honor those killed by SOA graduates. Dozens of activists have served many months–and several have served years–in jail for their nonviolent actions to close the SOA.

Among the groups that have passed resolutions to close the SOA are dozens of labor unions and religious bodies (churches, dioceses, etc.), city councils such as Philadelphia, the state assemblies of New York and New Jersey, the VFW (Veterans of Foreign Wars) of Santa Cruz, CA, and peace, justice, nonprofit, and humanitarian groups such as the NAACP, the Center for Defense Information, Women's Action for New Directions, and Pax Christi USA.

Nonviolently, thousands of people around the U.S. educate their fellow citizens about the horrors of this school and work to close it. Despite the name change, this movement will not stop until the school is closed.

"THE DEMONSTRATIONS, the marches, the public speaking and the imprisonment that has followed are all of a piece and together constitute an act of hope. Coming from a generation dubbed 'X' means having grown up malnourished of hope. It means having grown up watching visions of social change being sold out for nice homes in the suburbs and fast cars with which to escape them. It means having grown up with the world running from the devil of nuclear holocaust towards the deep blue sea of global environmental catastrophe. It also meant seeing that the affluence and prosperity of our America [sic] came bolstered by an economic and military violence executed upon the world's poorest in Latin America, Africa and Asia. What I and many of my peers learned from our coming of age in the 80s and 90s was a dark cynicism about the state of the world and a sense of the futility of trying to do anything to change it. . .

I hope and believe that it will always be worth it to act towards your better impulses rather than to cede your soul and conscience to a state of belief in their own futility even if the consequences mean persecution, imprisonment or even death."

—Christopher Jones in August 1998, completing a 6-month jail term for walking onto Fort Benning in November 1997 (age 23).

Civilian-Based Defense

Suppose the United States adopted nonviolent strategies to prevent invasion. To develop such a civilian defense system, large amounts of time and money would need to be spent on preparation, as is done with military defense. Psychological, social, economic, and political tactics would be included.

The entire population would be trained in ways of resisting an invader's demands: U.S. police and government officials would refuse to cooperate. Records would be hidden so that invaders could not find and arrest leaders. Workers would refuse to manufacture goods the invaders needed. Essential machinery in factories would temporarily disappear. Groups would be trained for specific jobs: one team would be in charge of shutting down all essential services—water, electricity, gas, food services, transportation, and communications systems. Any invaders would arrive to total shutdown and blackout. Others would be in charge of setting up an underground resistance: secret presses and an organized communications system. To demonstrate to potential invaders the disadvantages of invasion, public training exercises would be held in which the citizens of entire cities or states would put this into action, disrupting mock efforts by an "invading army" to "occupy" their territory.

All citizens would be trained to confront the invaders politely, but firmly, telling them to return home. Massive noncooperation and defiance would be used to prevent attackers from establishing control. The success of this type of defense would depend on people taking the initiative by denying authority to attackers and by gaining sympathy for the resistance. It would also be greatly strengthened by support from established institutions such as unions, religions, political parties, and social organizations.

Peace researcher, international lecturer, and educator on nonviolence Gene Sharp has labeled the process of switching to such a civilian-based defense "transarmament." It would involve research into nonviolent resistance, in-depth analysis of the political system of potential attackers, and problem-solving research, such as how to maintain communications systems during an attack. But, it would still cost less than current defense systems.

This system would not be "the easy way out." It would require much courage and training. Dave Dellinger, a life-long activist, wrote in a 1965 essay that a nonviolent defense system requires not only a willingness to risk one's life but also "renunciation of all claims to special privileges and power at the expense of other people." It means recognizing the contributions of all people.

Such a system can use the skills of all people—young, old, differently abled, women, men. Civilian-based defense applies the power of society itself to deter and defend both against internal power struggles and foreign invaders. Through such a system, people gain a greater awareness of their own power as well as confidence in their ability to influence their surroundings. Most importantly, it would respect the fundamental rights and dignity of all persons, including the invaders.

It has been successful in several places.

• *Germany, 1920*: Strikes and noncooperation by the government and the general population overcame an internal attempt to overthrow the government.

• *Germany, 1923*: Germans refused to obey orders, dismantled equipment, and published defiance in newspapers and other publications to resist French and Belgian occupation.

• *Algeria and France, 1961*: French President Charles DeGaulle said that he was abandoning attempts to keep Algiers (Algeria) French. This led to conflicts between the French in Algeria and the French in Paris. Rebel military commanders seized Algiers. However, the people closed airports, pilots pretended to have mechanical failures, and others blocked airfields or disappeared files. Communications were deliberately delayed. Algeria became independent from France in 1962.

• *Czechoslovakia, 1968-69*: The armies of the five Warsaw Pact nations invaded in an attempt to crush the Czechoslovak government. The people began a campaign of resistance, even though they had not been trained. They organized strikes, established underground communications, blocked transportation routes, distributed leaflets to the invaders, changed street signs and markers, gave wrong directions to Army units, and opened discussion with the soldiers. These direct appeals made some of the invading soldiers feel so badly that they left. Because of the resistance, three Soviet armies with half a million troops were unable to gain control for eight months, when they had anticipated a quick victory. Eventually, they were successful not because the people gave in, but because the government did. In 1989, a nonviolent revolution (known as the "Velvet Revolution") ended Soviet rule in Czechoslovakia.

Peace Teams

OTHER MODELS include the creation of peace teams, Global Peace Services, for instance, aims to develop a professional peace service through education and skills training based in a philosophy of active nonviolence. Teams would manage, resolve, and transform conflicts, prevent violence from occurring, rebuild communities torn apart by violence, and protect and preserve the environment. Other groups, such as Peace Brigades International, Christian Peacemaker Teams, Witness for Peace, and Michigan Peace Teams, currently work around the world, serving human needs, building community, accompanying peacebuilders, changing policies of violence, using peacemaking skills and nonviolent direct action, and bringing God's love to situations of violence.

Questions:

Would you feel safer with
   a. a nonviolent civilian defense system
   b. an ordinary military defense system
   c. a nuclear defense system
   d. some combination of the above

Do you think there is any value in promoting, researching, and experimenting with nonviolent civilian defense? Why or why not?

Closing Prayer

After each short phrase, all should respond "The people are rising!"

Reader 1:
   Everywhere, the people are rising.
   Everywhere, the people are rising,
      rising from the dead.

   From our silence. . .

All:
   The people are rising!

Reader 2:
   From our bondage. . .
   From exclusion. . .
   From exploitation. . .
   From violence. . .
   From our guilt. . .
   From all affliction. . .
   From all addiction. . .
   Against all odds. . .

All:
   Everywhere, the people are rising.
   Everywhere, the people are rising,
      rising from the dead.

Reader 2:
   Like the sun. . .

All:
   The people are rising!

Reader 1:
   Like the moon. . .
   Like a kite. . .
   Like an eagle. . .
   Like the tide. . .
   Like a prayer. . .
   Just like incense. . .
   Just like bread. . .
   Just like Jesus. . .

All:
   Everywhere, the people are rising.
   Everywhere, the people are rising,
      rising from the dead.

Reader 2:
   Into hope. . .

All:
   The people are rising!

Reader 1:
   Into freedom. . .
   Into speech. . .

Into power. . .
Into love. . .
Into significance. . .
Into the future. . .

All:

Everywhere, the people are rising.
Everywhere, the people are rising,
   rising from the dead.

Reader 2:

Across the nation. . .

All:

The people are rising!

Reader 1:

Around the world. . .
Across false boundaries. . .

All:

Everywhere, the people are rising.
Everywhere, the people are rising,
   rising from the dead.

(Adapted by Robin Small-McCarthy from Miriam Therese Winter's "A Psalm of Women Rising." Found in Our Prayers Rise Like Incense: Liturgies for Peace, *published by Pax Christi USA, edited by Cindy Pile.)*

Part Eight: Reflections

1.What questions, if any, did these stories of nonviolence raise for you?

2. Have you heard any of these stories of nonviolence in the media? If not, why do you think that this is so?

3. What kind of training and discipline does a person involved in a nonviolent campaign need? What can we do to become more skilled in nonviolence?

4. King said that we must end both external physical violence and internal violence of the spirit. Do you agree? Why or why not? If you do agree, what can you do to end both kinds?

5. Chavez advised young people to "choose one important area of human need" and focus energy and attention on it. Do you agree with this advice? Is there one such area that stands out for you in your life today?

Suggestions for Action

- Get involved in a campaign of nonviolence. If you are interested in one of the examples above, please see the resources section for contacts or more information.

- Try to find out more information about the farm workers who grow your food. Ask in the produce department or in your school cafeteria where food is grown, by whom, under what growing conditions, with what pesticides, etc. Try to buy food that is grown locally, organically, and by businesses or corporations that pay decent wages.

- Support an initiative to decrease military spending and abolish nuclear weapons. Pax Christi USA's Bread Not Stones campaign, for instance, has many resources and information on how to get involved.

- Speak out against hate crimes that occur in your community. Be conscious of little ways and attitudes that lead to such actions (such as ethnic jokes).

- Take action to close the School of the Americas, such as writing to your Congresspeople.

A Sampling of Sources and Resources

(For general resources, please see the listing in Part One.)

Civil Rights Movement:

Branch, Taylor. Parting the Waters: America in the King Years, 1954-63. New York: Simon and Schuster, 1988.

Branch, Taylor. Pillar of Fire: America in the King Years, 1963-68. New York: Simon & Schuster, 1988.

Carson, Clayborne et al., eds. Eyes on the Prize: Civil Rights Reader, Documents, Speeches, and Firsthand Accounts from the Black Freedom Struggle. 1954-1990, New York: Viking Penguin, 1991.

Garrow, David J. Bearing the Cross: Martin Luther King, Jr., and the Southern Leadership Conference. New York: Marrow, 1986.

Hampton, Henry and Steve Fayer with Sarah Flynn. Voices of Freedom: An Oral History of the Civil Rights Movement from the 1950s through the 1980s. New York: Bantam Books, 1991.

Catholic Worker:

Cornell, Thomas C., Robert Ellsberg, and Jim Forest. A Penny a Copy: Readings from the Catholic Worker. Maryknoll, NY: Orbis Books, 1995.

Ellsberg, Robert, ed. By Little and By Little: The Selected Writings of Dorothy Day. New York: Alfred A. Knopf, 1983.

Forest, Jim. Love is the Measure. New York: Paulist Press, 1986.

Maurin, Peter. Easy Essays. Chicago: Franciscan Herald Press, 1977.

Troester, Rosalie Riegle. Voices from the Catholic Worker. Philadelphia: Temple University Press, 1993.

Farm Workers' Movement

Levy, Jacques E. Cesar Chavez: Autobiography of La Causa. New York: W. W. Norton & Company, Inc., 1975.

Smith, Sydney D. Grapes of Conflict. Pasadena, CA: Hope Publishing House, 1987.

White Train:

Douglass, James W. The Nonviolent Coming of God. Maryknoll, NY: Orbis Books, 1991. (White Train Campaign participant and founder–with Shelley Douglass–of the Ground Zero Center for Nonviolent Action.)

Ground Zero Center for Nonviolent Action: 6159 Clear Creek Road NW; Poulsbo, WA 98370; phone: 360/377-2586; e-mail: info@gzcenter.org; http://www.gzcenter.org

South Africa:

Wink, Walter. Violence and Nonviolence in South Africa: Jesus' Third Way. Philadelphia: New Society Publishers, 1987.

Madres del Este de Los Angeles:

924 S. Mott Street; Los Angeles, CA 90023-1412; phone: 213/269-9898; http://clnet.ucr.edu/community/intercambios/melasi/

SEAC:

PO Box 31909; Philadelphia, PA 19104-0609 ; phone: 215/222-4711; e-mail: seac@seac.org; http://www.seac.org

Ithaca HOURS:

PO BOX 6731; Ithaca, NY 14851; phone: 607/272-3738; e-mail: ithacahours@lightlink.com; http://www.lightlink.com/hours/ithacahours or http://www.ithacahours.org

Voices in the Wilderness and Iraq:

Arnove, Anthony, ed. *Iraq Under Siege: The Deadly Impact of Sanctions and War.* Cambridge, MA: South End Press, 2000.

Bennis, Phyllis and Michel Moushabeck, eds. *Beyond the Storm: A Gulf Crisis Reader.* Brooklyn, NY: Interlink, 1991.

Briemberg, Mordecai. *It Was, It Was Not: Essays & Art on the War Against Iraq.* Vancouver, BC: New Star Books, 1992.

EPIC (Education for Peace in Iraq Center) 1101 Pennsylvania Avenue SE; Washington, DC 20003; phone: 202-543-6176; e-mail: info@epic-usa.org: info@epic-usa.org; http://www.epic-usa.org

Iraq Action Coalition: e-mail: IAC@leb.net; http://leb.net/IAC

Khadduri, Majid and Edmund Ghareeb, eds. *War in the Gulf: The Iraq-Kuwait Conflict and Its Implications.* Oxford: Oxford University Press, 1997.

Laffin, Art. "Prayer to End the War Against Iraq" with action suggestions. Erie, PA: Pax Christi USA.

Pilger, John. *Paying the Price: Killing the Children of Iraq.* (Video.) 2000.

VitW: 1460 West Carmen Avenue; Chicago, IL 60640; phone: 773/784-8065; http://www.nonviolence.org/vitw

School of the Americas:

Nelson-Pallmeyer, Jack. *School of Assassins: The Case for Closing the School of the Americas and for Fundamentally Changing U.S. Foreign Policy.* Maryknoll, NY: Orbis Books, 1997.

SOA Watch: PO Box 4566; Washington, DC 20017; phone: 202/234-3440; e-mail: info@soaw.org; http://www.soaw.org

Civilian-Based Defense and Peace Teams:

BOOKS:

Dellinger, Dave. *Revolutionary Nonviolence.* Garden City, New York: Anchor Books, 1971.

Griffin-Nolan, Ed. *Witness For Peace: A Story of Resistance.* Louisville, KY: Westminster/John Knox Press, 1991.

Sharp, Gene. *Civilian-Based Defense: A Post-Military Weapons System.* Princeton, NJ: Princeton University Press, 1990.

GROUPS:

The Albert Einstein Institute: 427 Newbury Street; Boston, MA 02115; phone: 617/247-4882; e-mail: einstein@igc.org; http://www.aeinstein.org (Nonprofit organization advancing the study and use of strategic nonviolent actions in conflicts throughout the world.)

Christian Peacemaker Teams: PO Box 6508; Chicago, IL 60680; phone: 312/455-1199; e-mail: cpt@igc.org; http://www.cpt.org

Global Nonviolent Peace Force: 801 Front Avenue; St. Paul, MN 55103; phone: 651/487-0800; e-mail: info@nonviolentpeaceforce.org ; http://www.nonviolentpeaceforce.org

Global Peace Services: PO Box 27922; Washington, DC 20038-7922; phone: 202-216-9886; http://www.globalpeaceservices.org

Michigan Peace Teams: 1516 Jerome Street; Lansing MI 48912; phone: 517/484-3178; e-mail: michpeacteam@peacenet.org; http://www.michiganpeaceteam.org

Pastors for Peace: PO Box 408130; Chicago, IL 66040; phone: 773/271-4817; e-mail: p4p@igc.apc.org; http://www.ifconews.org/p4p.html

Peace Brigades International: 1904 Franklin Street, Suite 505; Oakland, CA 94612; phone: 510/663-2362; e-mail: pbiusa@igc.apc.org; http://www.peacebrigades.org

Witness for Peace:1229 15th Street, NW; Washington, DC 20005; phone: 202/588-1471; e-mail: witness@witnessforpeace.org; http://www.witnessforpeace.org

Peace teams . . .

currently work around the world,

serving human needs,

building community,

accompanying peacebuilders,

changing policies of violence,

using peacemaking skills

and nonviolent direct action,

and bringing God's love

to situations of violence.

Part Nine

Nonviolence in Action: Campaigns Around the World

The 20th century has birthed hundreds of campaigns for human dignity and liberation around the world. People have used nonviolence to resist invasion of their country, to win freedom from outside rule, to bring down an unjust government, to ask for reforms, to bring about social change, to protect the environment, to end injustice, and to recapture human dignity.

These campaigns have not always been "successful" in the ways we typically measure success. In fact, sometimes, nonviolent actors have been killed, tortured, or imprisoned for attempting to bring about a new society. Other times, decades have passed before goals are reached. Yet, their effects are not insignificant. Walter Wink, in *Engaging the Powers*, estimates that between 1986 and 1989, the majority–64%–of humanity lived in a country touched by a nonviolent social movement, whether for independence, social justice, or another cause.

The various situations and methods used in these efforts have much to teach us. In our violent world, the following movements and individuals are beacons of hope.

Opening Prayer

Have a large bowl in the center of the room. Have several containers of water near it. While the passages from Ezekiel and Isaiah are read, have several volunteers pour the water from the containers into the large bowl.

Reader 1:
The word of God that came to the prophet Ezekiel (36:25-27a; 28b):
"I will sprinkle clean water upon you, and you shall be clean from all your uncleannesses, and from all your idols I will cleanse you. A new heart I will give you, and a new spirit I will put within you; and I will remove from your body the heart of stone and give you a heart of flesh. I will put my spirit within you. . .you shall be my people, and I will be your God."

Reader 2:
The word of God that came to the prophet Isaiah (44:1-3):
"But now hear, O Jacob my servant, Israel whom I have chosen! Thus says the Lord who made you, who formed you in the womb and will help you: Do not fear, O Jacob my servant, Jeshurun whom I have chosen. For I will pour water on the thirsty land, and streams on the dry ground; I will pour my spirit upon your descendants, and my blessing on your offspring."

As the following prayer is read, all are invited to go to the bowl of water and bless themselves in whatever way they feel comfortable, whether by washing their hands, making the sign of the cross, or another way.

Reader 1:

God of love, God of sustenance,
you are the living water of life.
You cleanse us with clean water;
with your spirit of love you change our hearts of stone into new hearts (Ezek 36:25-26),
hearts ready to follow you.
We remember your promises to us,
the assurance that you dwell with us,
that you are creating us anew moment by moment,
that you will pour water on the thirsty land–and on our thirsty souls–
and give streams on the dry ground–and in our dry hearts (Is 44:3).
We remember that you have promised your spirit
not only to us, but to those who have gone before us and those who will come after us,
to all those who listen to your word and struggle to build your kindom.
God, living water of life and love, who makes all things new (Rev 21:5),
we ask that you guide us continually,
satisfy our needs in parched places,
make us like a watered garden, like a spring of water, whose waters never fail (Is 58:11).
God of love, God of sustenance, God who creates us anew,
we are thirsting for your presence.
We are thirsty; give us the waters of your life, your spirit within us,
and with joy, we will drink of the water;
we will gulp freely the waters of life, bathe in them, delight in them.
With all of creation, watered by your unfathomable and boundless love for us,
let us give praise, work to build and recognize your kindom among us, and love each other.

All: Amen.

Independence for India

One of the largest nonviolent revolutions in history–the thirty-year struggle to free India from British colonial rule–is associated with Mohandas (also called Mahatma, meaning "great soul") K. Gandhi.

Gandhi based a nonviolent movement on the concept of *satyagraha* (roughly translated as soul-force), or the power of one mind to influence another without the use of physical force. This philosophy guided the development of a self-disciplined people who refused to cooperate with injustice and exploitation, choosing instead nonviolent noncooperation in the form of boycotts, strikes, and civil disobedience. The Indian people also actively labored to construct the society they wanted: working on village improvement, cottage industries, and education.

One of the campaigns of the movement was about salt. The British government had a complete monopoly over the salt industry in India; British authorities even made it illegal for people who were poor to gather salt that formed naturally along the sea. Gandhi started a massive civil disobedience campaign against these salt laws.

While salt may seem an insignificant item to organize around, it was not. Its extremely high price affected everyone. Additionally, it was relatively easy to manufacture outside of the rules of the British empire, making it good for a campaign.

On March 12, 1930, Gandhi and crowds of supporters began a 241-mile march to the sea. As they marched from village to village, from town to town, millions traveled far to catch a glimpse of Gandhi, to hear him speak, or to join the march. At every step, he preached the message: join the campaign of civil disobedience, break the salt laws, resist nonviolently.

After twenty-six days of walking, the party made its way into Dandi, a barren village on a isolated stretch of beach. At dawn the following day, Gandhi emerged from his cottage, prayed, and took a brief swim in the sea. Then he scooped up some seawater and took it back to shore. The water was boiled until only a small deposit of salt remained in the vessel. The salt law had been broken.

"When civil disobedience is started, my arrest is a certainty," Gandhi had written two weeks before this campaign began. "This time, on my arrest, there is to be no mute, passive nonviolence, but nonviolence of the active type should be set in motion." Indeed, Gandhi's act of defiance at Dandi sent a revolutionary spark throughout India. Indian leaders reported that in one year, over 100,000 Indians were jailed. Gandhi himself was arrested a month after breaking the salt law.

While the government held Gandhi prisoner, Sarojini Naidu, a poet, prepared 2,500 volunteers for a nonviolent raid on the Dharasana salt depot. She warned the group that they would be beaten. "India's prestige is in your hands. You must not even raise a hand to ward off a blow."

At the saltworks the group found great salt heaps surrounded by ditches filled with water and barbed wire and guarded by four hundred Indian police, under the command of six British officers.

This demonstration of willingness to suffer without inflicting suffering on others can be considered the turning point in Gandhi's nonviolent campaign.

A witness described what followed: "In complete silence the Gandhi followers drew up and halted a hundred yards from the stockade. A picked column advanced from the crowd, waded the ditches and approached the barbed wire stockade. The police officers ordered them to retreat and disperse. The Gandhi followers continued to advance. Suddenly, at a word of command, scores of native policemen rushed upon the advancing marchers and rained blows on their heads with their steel-shod clubs. Not one of the marchers even raised an arm to fend off the blows. They went down like tenpins. From where I stood I heard the sickening whack of the clubs on unprotected skulls. The waiting crowd of marchers groaned and sucked in their breath in sympathetic pain at every blow. Those struck down fell sprawling, unconscious or writhing with fractured skulls or broken shoulders. The survivors silently and doggedly marched on until struck down." Three hundred and twenty were hospitalized; two died.

This demonstration of willingness to suffer without inflicting suffering on others can be considered the turning point in Gandhi's nonviolent campaign. British authorities soon felt obliged to directly negotiate with Gandhi.

The years of preparation and discipline before these actions exposed the nature of the colonial regime. The movement did three things in 1930: it made the British people aware that they were cruelly suppressing India; it produced opposition within Britain itself; and it gave Indians the conviction that they could lift the yoke from their shoulders. After that, it was certain that Britain should someday refuse to rule India, and India should someday refuse to be ruled. In 1947, India achieved independence.

Question:

List social conditions that need to be changed in the United States. Brainstorm ways they can be met with nonviolent noncooperation. Select one that is realistic to follow through with among friends and supporters of the issue.

Norway Under Nazi Occupation

One of the questions that a believer in nonviolence always faces is the question of what to do in the face of horrific, genocidal evil. The solution is to act. Gandhi said, "Without a direct action expression of it, nonviolence, to my mind, is meaningless." The following story provides an example of people who took action in the face of evil, who made choices and commitments.

"But what would you do about enemies like the Nazis? Could they really be opposed effectively by nonviolent means?"

The answer to this question is that during World War II there was considerable nonviolent resistance taking place on various scales in a number of countries, but especially important in the Netherlands, Denmark, and Norway. The Norwegian teachers' resistance is one of the most important of these resistance campaigns.

During the Nazi occupation, the Norwegian fascist "Minister President," Vidkun Quisling, set out to establish a fascist Corporative State modeled after Mussolini's Italy, selecting teachers as the first "corporation." For this he created a new teachers' organization with compulsory (mandatory) membership. A compulsory fascist youth movement was also set up.

The underground called on teachers to resist. Between 8,000 and 10,000 of the country's 12,000 teachers signed their names and addresses to the text circulated by the underground, addressed to Quisling's Church and Education Department, saying they could not take part in the fascist education of youth and concluding: "I cannot regard myself as a member of the new teachers' organization."

The government threatened them with dismissal and then closed all schools for a month. Teachers held classes in homes. Despite censorship, news of the resistance spread. Tens of thousands of letters of protest from parents poured into the government office.

After the teachers defied the threats, about 1,000 male teachers were arrested and sent to concentration camps. Children gathered and sang at railroad stations as teachers were shipped through in cattle cars. In the camps, the Gestapo imposed an atmosphere of terror intended to induce capitulation. On starvation rations, the teachers were put through "torture gymnastics" in deep snow. Only a few gave in; "treatment" continued.

The schools reopened, but the remaining teachers told their pupils they repudiated membership in the new organization and spoke of a duty to conscience. Rumors were spread that if these teachers did not give in, some or all of those arrested would be killed. After difficult inner wrestling, the teachers who had not been arrested, almost without exception, stood firm.

Then on cattle car trains and overcrowded steamers, the arrested teachers were shipped to a camp near Kirkenes, in the far north of Norway. There they were kept in miserable conditions, doing dangerous work.

Their suffering, however, strengthened morale on the home front and posed problems for the Quisling regime, to the point that Quisling, visiting a school near Oslo, ranted and raved and screamed at the teachers, so loudly that it was heard in the schoolyard, "You teachers have destroyed everything for me!" Fearful of alienating Norwegians still further, Quisling finally ordered the teachers' release. Eight months after the arrests, the last teachers returned home to triumphal receptions.

Quisling's new organization for teachers never came into being, and the schools were never used for fascist propaganda. After Quisling encountered further difficulties in imposing the Corporative State, Hitler ordered him to abandon the plan entirely.

—**Reconciliation International**

...an example of people who took action in the face of evil, who made choices and commitments.

Questions:

Do you think that violence was the only way to stop Hitler?

Do you think that nonviolence, if widely used in such tactics as those in Norway, might be effective against a brutal dictator?

What questions do you have about such a process?

Hug the Trees:
India's Chipko Movement

Decades after a nonviolent movement freed India from colonial rule, Indians began another nonviolent struggle, again focused on the land. This time it centered on protecting the environment–the source of life for the people–and allowing people, rather than corporations, access to the land.

The Chipko methods have been influential in alternative development strategies.

Forests are critical to the survival of rural Indians because they directly provide food and fuel and because they stabilize water and soil resources. Several factors called attention to practices harmful to this relationship. In the mid-twentieth century, industry and commerce increasingly took more and more trees. In 1970, an unusually heavy monsoon caused massive flooding, destruction, and nearly 200 deaths. People began to recognize the links between increasing deforestation and such disastrous landslides and floods.

In 1973, some rural Indians in the Himalayas asked the Forest Department if they could cut down trees to make the agricultural tools they had made and used for centuries. The Forest Department denied their request, but granted that of a sporting goods corporation that wanted to cut down the same trees to make cricket bats and tennis rackets. In order to stop the logging of these trees, Indians spontaneously decided to hug the trees so that the axes of corporations could not cut them down. The people told the company that the trees would be cut down, literally, only over their dead bodies. The company saw that these people were insistent about the trees and abandoned the project.

Thus was born the Chipko ("embrace" or "hugging" in the Hindi language) movement, a poor people's movement in defense of traditional forest rights. The movement consisted of approximately 23,000 people from 150-200 villages in hundreds of locally-run initiatives, largely led by women concerned about their people's survival, their communities, and their environment. In addition to the physical act of protecting the trees, the people led marches, traveled from village to village educating others, fasted, picketed, led workshops and training sessions, held rallies, meetings, and demonstrations, and studied sacred scripture. In one instance, high school students went on strike when police used their school as a base for trying to control the people.

From a small beginning, saving a handful of trees, actions went on to save thousands. The movement has several times been successful in stopping logging, including a multi-year ban on logging and a halt to Forest Department tree auctions. The movement expanded its focus to include forest, mineral, soil, and water conservation, reforestation, and an end to quarrying which used up water supplies. It has led to improved wages for forest workers and ensured that communities arrange their own local forest management. It gave birth to other environmental movements in India (including the Appiko movement) and put the environment on the national agenda. The Chipko methods have been influential in alternative development strategies.

Although they have met opposition (especially from the media), the activists have maintained their emphasis on decentralization, nonviolence, self-reliance, survival, and the harmony between humanity and nature. They have used the resources that they had. Though poor, they could use their bodies and their communities. Through their words and actions, the activists of this movement have stated that environmental destruction and social injustice are inseparable and have called attention to the fact that through corporate domination of the natural world, people who are poor are made even poorer.

Profile: Oscar Romero

The history of El Salvador in the 20th century is filled with blood, violence, and oppression. Beginning in the 1930s, a military dictatorship ran the country. An elite 2% controlled 60% of the land while the vast majority of people lived in poverty, lacking education and employment.

But the history of El Salvador is also filled with courageous people who stood up to the violence–and often paid with their lives. In the 1970s, after nearly half a century of military rule, workers, peasants, and students began popular movements that challenged the status quo and demanded justice. They organized base communities: part religious, part political, these communities analyzed the conditions in the country and worked to support the people.

The government responded with even more repression and terror, eventually leading to a 12-year civil war, supported by $6 billion from the United States. Seventy-five thousand people were killed. Kidnappings, torture, disappearances, and the killing of clergy and activists were common. According to the UN truth commission report, the great majority–85%–of these crimes were planned and carried out by the Salvadoran military and death squads.

He spoke from a perspective of faith.

One of the most prominent figures in the nonviolent struggle in El Salvador was someone whom no one had expected. In 1977, the Vatican named a new archbishop of San Salvador: Oscar Romero. The conservative Romero was viewed as a "safe choice." However, the murder of his friend, Rutilio Grande, a Jesuit priest, that same year provoked a conversion. Romero began to speak out.

As archbishop, Romero set up an office to investigate human rights violations. He wrote a weekly column and met regularly with young clergy and nuns and members of base communities. He analyzed the social, political, and economic reality of his country and taught the social teaching of the Church and the Gospel. He spoke for the poor and called attention to institutional violence, injustice, and repression. He encouraged reconciliation. He called all people to conversion and action. In response, the Vatican urged him to tone down his speaking and writing.

But Romero did not. He spoke from a perspective of faith, believing that the Church called its members to action, to defend the rights of the people: "Some want to keep a gospel so disembodied that it doesn't get involved at all in the world it must save. Christ is now in history. Christ is in the womb of the people. Christ is now bringing about the new heaven and the new earth." Romero believed that we must convert our hearts to God: "As long as one does not live a conversion in one's heart, a teaching enlightened by faith to organize life according to the heart of God, all will be feeble, revolutionary, passing, violent."

Because he would not be silent, Romero received many death threats. Well aware of the danger, he said, "If they kill me, I shall arise in the Salvadoran people." He offered his life in love. On March 24, 1980, while saying Mass, Romero was shot and killed. One month before his murder, Romero had sent a letter to U.S. President Jimmy Carter asking that no more military aid be sent to El Salvador and expressing concern for human rights.

THE DAY BEFORE his murder, Romero pled in his homily with the Salvadoran police and military: "You are part of our own people. You kill our own *campesino* brothers and sisters. . . .the law of God must prevail that says: 'Thou shalt not kill.' No soldier is obliged to obey an order against the law of God. No one has to fulfill an immoral law. . .The church, defender of the rights of God, of the laws of God, of human dignity, the dignity of the person, cannot remain silent before such abomination. . .In the name of God, and in the name of this suffering people whose laments rise to heaven each day more tumultuous, I beg you, I ask you, I order you in the name of God: Stop the repression!"

Question:

Do you think the Gospel calls you to get involved in the world?

Why or why not and how?

Poland's Solidarity Movement

In Poland, tens of thousands of workers carried on the Solidarity freedom movement in the face of great opposition. Solidarity, begun as a trade union, was the name given to the umbrella group of workers, intellectuals, students, and farmers in 50 unions made up of 10 million members. They asked for reforms and more labor and human rights.

They asked for reforms and more labor and human rights.

Examples abound of the creativity of this struggle. In the town of Swidnik, just southeast of the capital Warsaw, dissatisfaction with government propaganda on newscasts prompted residents to stage "newswalks." For over a month, most of the 30,000 residents simply turned their television sets toward their windows during the 7:30 nightly news and began walking up and down the main street. The newswalks were so successful that they spread to the cities of Olsztyn, Lublin, Bialystok, and Warsaw.

Newswalks were just one in a long list of new techniques used by the Poles to protest government control. Dressing in black or displaying black ribbons became a popular means to symbolize national mourning over the loss of freedom. Many wore either a badge of the Black Madonna of Czestochowa (the religious emblem associated with imprisoned Solidarity leader and electrician Lech Walesa) or a tiny radio resistor to express their resistance literally. The people undertook strikes to demand higher wages, civil liberties, more time off, the right to strike, more day care for children, and the right to criticize managers.

Such protests did not proceed without opposition from the government. In Swidnik, local authorities imposed a 7:00 p.m. curfew in order to prevent newswalks. The residents responded by taking their walks during the 5:00 p.m. broadcast. Authorities fined those organizing newswalks 5,000 zlotys (US $60), the same penalty levied against those who wore the Black Madonna badges. Once, workers who participated in a work stoppage at a factory were simply fired.

The government suppressed and even banned Solidarity, but the Poles continued to use nonviolent tactics to protest the martial law declared in 1981 and to call for government reforms. A strong sense of solidarity remained among the people as evidenced by churches throughout the country that provided food and supplies to families of the unemployed and imprisoned.

In 1989, Solidarity entered into negotiations with the government. Solidarity won a sweeping victory in the June election. Two months later, the government signed an agreement with them. Walesa, released from prison, became president in 1990.

The Student Movement for Democracy in China

Many people around the world have seen the picture of Wang Weilin, the 19-year-old Chinese student who stood alone in front of a tank in Beijing's Tiananmen Square in June 1989. When the tank stopped, he climbed aboard the turret and pleaded with the soldiers to turn back and stop killing people. He returned to stand in front of the tank and was eventually led away into the crowd. Wang Weilin was later disappeared.

But many people do not know more of the story of the occurrences in the spring and early summer of 1989 in China. Nineteen eighty-nine saw a nonviolent, pro-democracy movement with broad-based support that questioned the elite and the government.

Beginning in April, students gathered in Tiananmen Square, requesting freedom of speech and press, increased money for education, an end to favoritism and corruption, and the right to hold peaceful public demonstrations. In the next six weeks, hundreds of thousands of students organized a union, a sit-in, marches, class boycotts, and a hunger strike. They composed posters, poetry, newsletters, and other written word.

Very quickly, people in Beijing moved to support the students, bringing blankets, food, and other supplies. Between one and three million people took to the streets in support of the students. Journalists, professors and university staff, and laborers from 20 different industries joined the struggle. Business people used their motorcycles to inform the students of governmental troop movements. Beijing factory workers established a trade union in support of the student movement. Dozens of other cities, including Shanghai, Nanjing, and Chang Sha, had actions. The students had such strong support that during this time there was no theft, no fighting, and no traffic accidents. For several days, the Chinese press enjoyed freedom to write about this Democracy movement.

However, the Chinese government responded to this outpouring with repression, intimidation attempts, and the declaration of martial law. In June, the government called in the troops. The military used armored vehicles, tear gas, rubber bullets, tanks, and the internationally forbidden dumdum bullets. On June 3rd, tear gassing and beatings began in earnest.

One of the students, Chai Ling, reported later, "We kept telling the crowds that ours was a peaceful demonstration and that the highest principle of peace is sacrifice. . .It was a war between love and hate, not between violence and battle forces. We felt that the patriotic democratic movement, which was based on the principles of peace, would fail if the students tried arming themselves with gas bottles and wooden clubs to resist the machine guns and tank drivers."

The students promised not to use violence against their attackers. In fact, students who had some submachine guns and bombs tried to give them to the army, which refused to take them. The students then dismantled them. Some students also tried to negotiate with the military, even when the attacks began on June 3rd.

Some people threw bricks and stones, but the massive movement of millions of people remained nearly nonviolent–except, of course, for the military and the government, which used electric cattle prods, clubs, and great brutality. In clashes in the Square and other places in the early morning hours of June 4th, thousands (estimated) were killed. Later, other students involved in the Democracy movement were executed (40 confirmed). Tens of thousands were imprisoned and charged with peaceful acts of protest, such as distributing handbills and giving speeches; many were tortured.

Despite a call for general strikes, the movement faltered, collapsing in the face of possible civil war. Censorship returned and the Democracy movement was forced underground. Many activists fled the country. Despite its lack of "success," the movement brought hope for a time. At the beginning of the 21st century, China is still widely criticized for its human rights violations, including the occupation of Tibet. Nonviolent movements there and abroad continue the struggle for justice.

> "THE DEMOCRACY MOVEMENT was characterized by one outstanding feature: demonstrators used only peaceful, rational, and nonviolent means to try to achieve their goals. In carrying out protests against the government with a nonviolent hunger strike, Beijing students completely exposed China's defects."
>
> –From Han Minzhu's book, *Cries for Democracy*

Questions:

Do you agree with the tactics of the students?

Why do you think the government responded with such repression?

"Give Life to That Which Does Not Live:"
El Salvador

Many years after the end of civil war in El Salvador, the country still struggles. Young people are often caught up in a web of poverty, drugs, and violence. Gangs, an import from the U.S., are becoming increasingly important to many young people.

But in San Salvador's Santa Cecilia base community, young people are living another vision. They are turning from violence to nonviolence.

These young people choose not to participate in gang rivalries or wars. They instead seek to create alternatives through faith, culture, and art, such as mural projects, dance, and community education. Julienne Gage, a North American journalist and cultural anthropologist who has spent time in Santa Cecilia, reflects that these young people who reject violence need to express the beautiful and creative sides of themselves that can benefit the community. "Creativity invokes humanization. Some of the worst poverty is the loss of human dignity so rescuing dignity in the midst of dire social and economic conflict is vital to rebuilding a healthy community and giving them reason to go on creating life."

Nonviolence offers hope by showing a new direction. It means trying to live together in community, caring for the environment, and treating others and selves with respect. This alternative way, says Julienne, is a "path toward life." Thus, the motto of Santa Cecilia is "give life to that which does not live." This path takes courage, for the young people face condemnation from all sides: both from an apolitical community that doesn't necessarily want to hear about social justice from a liberation theology perspective and from gang members.

By deliberately reaching out to gang members, this community is inviting people traditionally seen as "enemy" to participate in its growth. The young people, many of whom have been in a gang or have been tempted to join, recognize the social pressures that others face and thus can show compassion. They know that all young people need to belong and that peace provides an active way to stand up for the truth.

The following is excerpted from an article Julienne wrote about their efforts.

Romero's Children

In Santa Cecilia, neighbors live in close-set rows of small cinder-block houses, separated by tiny cement paths. The love and concern among residents has created both emotional and spiritual community. Their cooperative ideology means that they look out for each other's material needs as best they can. . .

[Santa Cecilia's young people's] unique strength is that they also look to ground their work in both El Salvador's history and the radical message of the gospel as reflected in liberation theology. They believe that youth who feel they have national roots and strong cultural traditions are less tempted to look for identity in an imported gang culture. And they believe that the message of Christ offers an alternative to the violence that surrounds them.

The work in Santa Cecilia began with the young people meeting on the street corners. Through casual dialogue with community leaders, these young people built a support system, then became organized within the base community, operating as a new generational movement within an older social movement.

Now they congregate in a one-room house in the barrio. In it, they are trying to set up a small space with a computer, as well as a place for youth to sleep at night when they can't go home or they don't have a home to go to. During the day the house serves as a place for formal and informal socializing and daily prayer. . .

Alvaro Rafael is twenty-one–a gang member who began participating in the Santa Cecilia community youth program five years ago and is now "nonactive." Like most Salvadoran gang members, Rafael is tattooed with gang art and gang affiliations on his back, his chest, and his arms. Among these tattoos is one of Oscar Romero. . .

Rafael attributes his conversion to Christianity to his understanding of liberation theology. He hopes to build on what he has learned about Oscar Romero's life to create a new theology for marginal Salvadoran youth in the postwar era–a takeoff on liberation theology that he calls "Theology of the Streets". . .

Mural painting educates the youth on nonviolent national leaders like Romero. The artwork reflects images of the poor of El Salvador struggling for community cooperation. Gang art and images reflecting precepts of liberation theology are often mixed in the same murals.

Other groups have revived different strands of El Salvador's cultural history—like folk dances. Seventeen-year-old Rosita believes that without the popular-education program Generation 21, she would have joined the gangs. Instead, she participates in the dance group and spends her free time teaching Salvadoran folk dance to Santa Cecilia children, some of whose parents are involved in prostitution. . .

"Because young people do not know how beautiful Salvadoran culture is," says Kony [a 17-year-old member of the group], "the majority prefer to imitate the culture of other countries." She and young people like her are committed to showing the beautiful side of the El Salvador they come from–and the El Salvador they are trying to create.

From "Romero's Children," by Julienne Gage, *The Other Side*, March/April 2000, volume 36, no. 2. Reprinted with permission from *The Other Side*.

"The nonviolent message of Christ works for them because it gives them a more valiant answer. . .It's a form of resistance. . .Christ-like Salvadoran role models like Romero also recapture their human dignity. Like Christ, he was martyred. But neither he nor Christ died weakly; they did so with a heart of love, a tough resistant love that refused to stoop to the level of their enemies by retaliating with violence or by running away."

–Interview with Julienne Gage

Vieques:
US Navy Out!

Vieques, Puerto Rico, is east of the big island of Puerto Rico and is home to 9,400 people. For more than 60 years, until 2003, the U.S. Navy used Vieques for combined land, air, and sea operations and for weapons storage and practice. The Navy controlled approximately two-thirds to three-fourths of the land. The U.S. also rented out the use of Vieques to NATO and foreign militaries for training.

Weapons training and practice have had devastating and dangerous effects for the people, land, and environment of Vieques. For instance, the Navy dropped five bombs (four of which detonated) a mile from the main town in Vieques in 1993, used napalm in 1992, and fired 263 depleted uranium shells in 1999. Between

1983 and the end of the century, the Navy and Marine Corps dropped nearly three million pounds of explosives on the eastern end of Vieques.

According to the Puerto Rico Department of Health, the cancer rate in Vieques is 27 % higher than the Puerto Rican average, believed to be due to chemical and nuclear weapons. Explosive and toxic materials have been found in the drinking water. Bombings and other testing have caused destruction to the ecosystems of Vieques, including the coastline, coral reefs, lagoons, and forests. Among the environmental pollutants found in Vieques are asbestos, lead, mercury, and nitrates.

Since 1983, the Navy and Marine Corps have dropped nearly three million pounds of explosives...

For decades, Puerto Ricans engaged in efforts to get the U.S. Navy to leave this island. In the late 20th century, these efforts were brought into the spotlight once again through large demonstrations and organizing work in Puerto Rico and in the United States.

The death of a civilian sparked new flames of outrage. In April 1999, two 500-pound bombs (being used for practice for the war in Kosovo) went miles off target and killed David Sanes and wounded four others. Bombing was temporarily halted. In January 2000, U.S. President Bill Clinton, in conjunction with Puerto Rican governor Pedro Rossell–(who reversed his earlier position), announced that bombing would begin again, using inert bombs. In response to calls from religious leaders, between 85,000 and 150,000 Puerto Ricans marched in silence in the capital city of San Juan to protest, perhaps the biggest march in Puerto Rican history. San Juan Archbishop Roberto Gonzalez Nieves said, "We are showing the consensus in Puerto Rico's heart in favor of peace and justice."

Another response to Sanes's death was to attempt to stop bombing by being a physical presence on the bombing ranges. On May 4, 2000, U.S. federal authorities removed hundreds of these protestors–including the archbishop–from their resistance camps on the island. The diverse group of nonviolent protestors included elected officials from Puerto Rico and the U.S., grassroots community leaders, students, religious leaders, union members, and community people. Some of these people had been camped out in Vieques for over a year.

Residents of a camp sponsored by a Catholic diocese were trained in nonviolence and briefed on relevant church teachings. Church leaders thought it important that people be disciplined and trained and in the camps to work and pray for peace. The presence and participation of Catholic and Protestant churches, including Methodist and Baptist, has been very important in gaining strong public support for this cause, making it clear that this is not just political, but about the violation of human rights and abuses of people and the environment.

After the arrests, students at the University of Puerto Rico went on strike in protest. Over and over, people re-entered the bombing zone, continuing their peaceful protests.

In 2001, the U.S. announced that the Navy would leave Vieques. In 2003, the land was transferred to the U.S. Department of Fishing and Wildlife, to conduct an environmental assessment. The struggle continues to clean up the environment, to return the land to Puerto Ricans, and to deal with the prosecution of activists by the U.S. government.

"WE IN THE DIOCESE have made an option for peace in Vieques, and we have to act out that option in concrete forms. So we've come here to work for peace, and to defend life, both the life of the environment and of the human beings who are threatened here. . .When there is an unjust law that violates the laws of the reign of God, then we Christians can disobey that law."

Fr. Juan Luis Negrón, Catholic seminary rector

Question:

Is your faith community involved in any struggles for human dignity, the environment, etc.?

If not, should it be? What might your role be?

Movimento dos Trabalhadores Rurais Sem Terra:
Landless Workers Movement

The Landless Workers Movement in Brazil (MST in Portuguese) began at the end of the 1970s in southern Brazil and was formally founded in 1985. This grassroots movement of the rural poor and landless has become the largest social movement in Latin America and one of the most successful grassroots movements in the world. Today, landless people in 23 Brazilian states are involved.

The movement began in response to extreme poverty and malnutrition caused by unequal land distribution. Nearly 5 million Brazilian families lack land, due to the large landholdings of the elite and privileged. Although small family farmers are 30% of Brazil's farmers, they hold only 1.5% of all agricultural land while the country's largest farm-owners (1.6% of the farming population) hold 53% of the land. Overall, less than 3% of the population of Brazil owns two-thirds of the farmable land. While 60% of the farmland lies idle, 25 million people struggle to survive by working temporary agricultural jobs.

A 1964 law says that the federal government can seize unproductive or overly large landholdings, pay the owners for it with government bonds, and then redistribute the lands. However, the political power of the landowners prevented Brazil's military dictatorship from doing so. Today, more than a decade after the end of the military dictatorship and despite land redistribution plans and a constitution that guarantees the right to land, the government continues to favor banks, multinational corporations, agribusiness (such as large cattle ranches), and export-oriented farming over the rural people's needs.

Since the government is not taking the lead in land reform, the people are. Following the country's laws, the MST identifies qualified land. Then, dozens or hundreds of families move in together, set up camps, and begin to farm the land. Once settled, the families decide how to divide the land, where to build homes, and whether to farm individually or cooperatively. Hundreds of occupations of idle land have occurred. The movement has acquired land for more than 250,000 families in 2600 settlements. In mid-2000, over 71,000 families in encampments throughout Brazil were awaiting government recognition.

Support for the MST has come from many places, including the Lutheran and Catholic churches of Brazil. International support from labor unions, religious organizations, and human rights groups is growing. Additionally, a March 1997 Brazilian public opinion poll found that 77% of the respondents approved of the MST and 85% approved of the nonviolent occupation of idle farmland.

The MST does not focus only on getting land for the landless and so guaranteeing them food. It also organizes the rural poor to include them in the economic, social, and political life of the nation. It advances an alternative development model, one that is healthier and safer for farmers and the environment. The MST organizes food cooperatives and small agricultural industries (which create jobs), conducts a literacy program for 17,000 students and runs public schools for over 100,000 children, publishes a journal and operates nearly 30 community radio stations, and takes steps to protect the environment, such as the production of organic seeds. Additionally, it critically examines the role of women and culture, monitors humans rights, and takes the movement's message around the world. Using time-honored traditions of nonviolence, the MST organizes marches, assemblies, walks, and occupations.

As demonstrations have increased, the government has responded with terror, including killings and evictions. In the 1990s, more than 1000 activists for the landless were killed. The government has been repressing social movements in the countryside and threatens to use the army to apply national security laws from the time of the military dictatorship, to prosecute the leadership, and to arrest activists. It is also leading a campaign against the MST in the Brazilian press.

Question:

What is the importance of the MST extending its struggle beyond simply gaining land?

Sudanese Women's Voice for Peace

Since gaining independence in 1956, Sudan, Africa's largest country geographically and one of its most ethnically diverse, has endured numerous civil wars. These wars have been worsened by outside intervention and massive arms transfers.

Its most recent war, focused mostly on the southern part of the country, began in 1983. The massive loss of life due to this war is greater than in any other place or war since World War II. The U.S. Committee for Refugees estimates that more than 2 million people have died of war-related causes (including famine in the late 1990s brought on by war); it is estimated that on average more than 300 people die per day. At least one out of every five people in southern Sudan has died as a result of this war. Approximately four million Sudanese are displaced internally (within the country), more than in any other country in the world, and close to half a million are refugees in other countries.

...attempts to create bonds among women ...go beyond tribal and racial boundaries

Despite several attempts at negotiation in the 1990s, the war continues to rage against the civilians of Sudan. It has been marked by torture, disappearances, aerial bombings of civilian centers, starvation as a means of combat, the deliberate obstruction of humanitarian relief operations, the use of children as soldiers, and human rights.

The war has created immense crisis; years of warfare, massive population displacement, and government neglect have devastated southern Sudan. It is one of the poorest places on earth. More than 80% of its estimated population of five million has been displaced at least once since the war began. Most of the people have absolutely no access to schools or reliable health care.

Despite the horror of the war and the many forms of terror used against civilians, there are many peace and human rights groups both in and focused on Sudan. The existence of such groups offers hope for a better future for the people of Sudan.

One active group is the Sudanese Women's Voice for Peace (SWVP), established in 1994 by exiled Sudanese women living in Nairobi, Kenya. An indigenous NGO (non-governmental organization), the SWVP promotes dialogue among all parts of Sudanese society, but focuses especially on Sudanese women. In a country overwhelmed by violence on many levels, it attempts to create bonds among women that go beyond tribal and racial boundaries.

Its three-step approach is to give women skills through peace-building training, to establish local abilities to build peace, and to encourage participation in conflict resolution and the promotion of a culture of peace. The SWVP creates peace-demonstration centers in southern villages, gives trauma workshops, helps to establish village peace committees in southern Sudan, and supports small-scale local development projects. It has worked in cooperation with churches, other women's groups, and NGOs such as Pax Christi International. By focusing on education, economics, and interpersonal relationships, SWVP advances peace and nonviolence and creates possibilities for today and tomorrow.

Question:

Do you think that the efforts of groups such as the SWVP can help to end such a long-standing and cruel civil war?

Why and how or why not?

Women the world over are spelling out a new "yes," for themselves, for their children, for the poor, who are the poorest of the poor. For peace.

Dorothee Soelle

Refusing to Kill:
Conscientious Objection in Chile

In Chile, as in many other countries, the military has much power and influence. It consumes great financial resources and people resources. All 18-year-old men must register for the military draft. The law says that failure to do so can result in two years in prison, although this is not really enforced. By September of each year, approximately 20,000 men register; a lottery chooses about 13,000 who are required to serve in the military. Students and men with certain medical conditions can get exemptions. So can the wealthy–men with money can buy their way out or at least get better assignments. Thus, the military is largely composed of poor people.

In recent years, many young men–and many women–have actively, vocally, and publicly opposed this system. For the most part, Chileans are very afraid of the military. A layer of secrecy and silence surrounds it. Declaring conscientious objection to the military is a way of ending this fright and talking about the problems and damage caused by the military and its support of big companies and the rich. The efforts of these young people are one way to struggle against the militarism that exists in Chile and throughout the world.

In the mid-1990s. about a dozen young Chileans–both men and women–began meeting and agreed to form a group to support conscientious objection and to oppose mandatory registration and the lottery system. They researched international and human rights laws that supported the right of conscientious objection and discovered that Chile had signed many of these treaties. They wrote about these documents to remind Chilean officials that they had signed them. Each person also wrote her or his own declaration against mandatory military service and asked to be granted conscientious objector status.

In August of 1998, these young men and women sent their conscientious objection declarations to the country's hierarchy. By law, the government had to respond by September, the date by which the men who were turning 18 were required to register. When the government responded that they didn't have the power to declare a person a conscientious objector, three of the conscientious objectors took their case to court in 1999. (Others had decided not to, especially under pressure from their parents.) The courts came back with the same response: they did not have the power to declare conscientious objection a legitimate reason for not doing obligatory military service.

Thus, the young people decided to take their case to an international level. They began a process to take it to the Interamerican Human Rights Commission.

At all of these steps, the conscientious objectors make their actions and declarations public. They hold press conferences. Twice a year, they return to the same public official, declaring their conscientious objection again. In the past several years, 200 people have made public declarations and hundreds more have done so privately.

Their most important action is educating in schools about conscientious objection.

The public declaration of conscientious objection raises objection to military service (and militarism) from a personal problem to a social one. It is a way of standing in solidarity with the poor, with people who can't buy their way out of service. It also connects their struggle to the struggles of people all over the world for fundamental human rights and dignity and for the right not to see each other as enemies.

The government has not completely ignored these issues. In 2000, a new Chilean government went through a four-month process to discuss military service and the country's defense. It invited the government, the military, and social institutions, including conscientious objectors. The conclusions of these discussions were released the first week of September. Even before the announcement, though, the conscientious objectors knew the results would not be favorable. They predicted that the government would say that although the system needed some changes, it worked fine and that the draft was needed for defense. Indeed, this was the outcome. In fact, the conference went even further, by suggesting that it would soon not be necessary for 18-year-olds to register, as they would be registered automatically at birth. It also favored increasing the number of women who enlist in the military.

In response, the conscientious objectors held a march and a concert. Such activities are just some of the outreach and education that these young men and women have done. Their most important action is educating in schools about conscientious objection. They also write about it and have a weekly radio program. Decidedly countercultural, their movement works to articulate alternatives to militarism.

Since the formation of the group in Santiago, others, composed mostly of 15- and 16-year-olds, have started in two Chilean cities.

Profile: Javier Garate

One of these men is Javier Garate (born 1979) of Santiago (the capital). Javier, like other conscientious objectors, believes that it is wrong to kill. He refuses to learn how to kill and finds it dangerous that so many people are being trained to do so. To justify this training, the military must encourage false rivalries between people and countries. Enemies are created. In Chile, Peruvians and Argentineans are portrayed as potentially dangerous people. This portrayal denies the importance of all human lives and hides the fact that there are no real reasons why the people of these countries are "enemies." As Javier says, it is "obvious that they are not our enemy. They are our friends, just like us, only divided by a line"–an artificial line that is used to support the idea of needing a "strong military" for the defense of the country.

In speaking of his public stance on this issue, Javier said in September 2000, "We need to stand up and say, 'Here we are.' We are going to say to everybody–to the military, country, government, schools, to everybody–'We are not afraid anymore. A lot of people think the same. We will not be in the military.'"

Public Declaration of the group

"Neither Helmet Nor Uniform"

in front of Santiago's justice tribunals, September 1999 (translated from the Spanish)

"We are here to say no to military service, again and again, each time more determinedly, with greater reason and conviction. This time we have decided not to register because we don't want to make up lies in order to get out of having to serve, because we don't have the least intention of serving in the military. We will not register. We are saying the same thing that many young Chileans have said in silence, waiting for time and forgetfulness [on the part of the government] to get them out of military service. But we show our faces, our names, our reasons.

We are not registering because we will not participate in any way with the evil military. We do not want for one second to be a part of this legal kidnapping, this military exploitation. We do not want for one second to be part of this brother/sisterhood based in violence, death, arms, war, sexism, discrimination, blind and unquestioning obedience.

We have been doing this work for more than two years. We will not tire until the right of conscientious objection is respected in this hypocritical country that ratifies it on the international level but impedes its practice on the national level. We are following and exercising our right to refuse to be part of that which violates our conscience."

Question:

What reasons can you think of that someone might become a conscientious objector?

Closing Prayer

Reader 1:	Therefore, I urge you to stir into flame the gift of God which is within you.
All:	For God did not give us a spirit of timidity, but of power and love and wisdom. (II Timothy 1:6, 7)
Reader 1:	Stir us again to flame, Lord.
All:	Light fires in us that purify our hearts, sustain our beliefs, and strengthen conviction.
Reader 2:	Light fires that burn against injustice, apathy, and neglect.
All:	Light fires that melt our hardness, open our hearts, and heal our divisions.
Reader 1:	Now the Lord is the Spirit,
All:	And where the spirit of the Lord is, there is freedom. (II Corinthians 3:17)
Reader 2:	Give us freedom, Lord.
All:	Freedom to live and act in the Spirit.
Reader 1:	Freedom to see beyond the letter of the Law,
All:	Beyond careful calculations and prudent responses.
Reader 1:	Freedom to see pain and respond with healing.
All:	Freedom to see want and to respond out of our abundance.
Reader 2:	Freedom to see hunger and starvation and to respond with our bread.
All:	Freedom to see injustice and oppression and to respond with our anger.
Reader 2:	Freedom to see death and respond with life.
All:	Freedom to give and not count the cost.
Reader 1:	You will receive power when the Holy Spirit comes upon you; and you will bear witness.
All:	In Jerusalem, and all over Judea and Samaria, and away to the ends of the earth. (Acts 1:8)
Reader 2:	Grant us the power of the Spirit, Lord, that we might be witnesses for you.
All:	Grant us the power that crumbles barriers and overcomes suspicion,
Reader 2:	That conquers fear and overwhelms hatred.
All:	That we may indeed be witnesses, away to the ends of the earth.
Reader 1:	Therefore, I urge you to stir into flame the gift of God which is within you.
All:	For God did not give us a spirit of timidity, but of power and love and wisdom.

–from *Banquet of Praise*, published by Bread for the World, with Henry G. Brinton as consulting editor

Part Nine: Reflections

1. What questions, if any, did these stories of nonviolence raise for you?

2. Of the stories in the last two parts of the book, which touched you the most? Why?

3. How does our faith or church call us to action?

4. We live in what is probably the most powerful nation in the world: militarily, socially, culturally, financially. Like it or not, our country is directly responsible for suffering and oppression around the world. What are ways that we can acknowledge our involvement in this and begin to remove ourselves from parts of it?

5. How can we become more aware of the struggles of other people around the world?

6. Gandhi felt that nonviolence is significant in reaching the hearts and minds of adversaries.

Do you agree or disagree?

7. Many of these movements and actions have focused on relationships (with others, with the land, etc.) What do you feel is the significance of this focus in these struggles?

8. What is the significance of relationships in your life?

9. What in your life has touched and changed you?

10. What characteristics did the people engaging in these nonviolent struggles have? What pushed them to become activists?

Suggestions for Action

- Rent the movie video Gandhi. Watch it with a few friends or by yourself. Share or practice what you learn from it.

- Find out about a corporation that is harming the land, through its industrial practices, by not conserving resources, by making profits more important than the earth and its people. (Groups listed in part 2 and 6 may give you some examples.) Write a letter to this corporation, letting them know why you don't approve of what they are doing. Share the information with your friends and family and ask if they will also take action.

- In the United States, families cannot get by on the minimum wage (workers in these jobs often also have few or no benefits, such as medical and dental insurance, adequate leave time, etc.). Thus, many organizations, community groups, and cities have started "living wage" campaigns, trying to get employers to pay decent wages that provide enough to live on. Find out what a living wage would be in your area and if there is a group working on a campaign. One group to contact is ACORN (Association of Community Organizations for Reform Now): http://www.livingwagecampaign.org (or http://www.acorn.org).

- Help support the young people of Santa Cecilia. Julienne Gage is interested in setting up a scholarship fund and has taken steps to set up a process. If you are interested in contributing, e-mail her at julienneg@hotmail.com. Additionally, the group is fundraising for the building that houses them. For more information, contact Yon Hui Bell at nopalita1@hotmail.com.

- Get involved in a community group that uses the arts or culture to promote nonviolence, to strengthen the community, or to share knowledge.

- Oppose U.S. military training, weapons, and money to other countries, especially countries that are at war or that oppress their own people. Groups like School of the Americas Watch (Part 8), the Center for Defense Information (Part 1), and Pax Christi have more information on specifics (letter-writing, actions, statistics, etc.).

A Sampling of Sources and Resources

(For general resources, please see the listing in Part One.)

Indian Independence:
(For sources on Mohandas Gandhi, please see the listing in Part Four.)

Attenborough, Richard, director. Gandhi (video). 1982.

Norway, World War II:
Petrow, Richard. The Bitter Years: The Invasion and Occupation of Denmark and Norway. New York: Morrow, 1974.

Semelin, Jacques. Unarmed Against Hitler: Civilian Resistance in Europe, 1939-1943. Westport, CT: Praeger, 1993.

Chipko Movement:

Hegde, Pandurang. "Chipko and Appiko: How the People Save the Trees." London: Quaker Peace & Service, 1988.

Rose, Deborah Lee. The People Who Hugged the Trees. Niwot, CO: Roberts Rinehart Publishers, 1990. (A children's book on the legend that started the movement.)

Routledge, Paul. Terrains of Resistance: Nonviolent Social Movements and the Contestation of Place in India. Westport, CT: Praeger Publishers, 1993.

Romero and El Salvador:

Dennis, Marie, Renny Golden, and Scott Wright. Oscar Romero: Reflections on His Life and Writings. Maryknoll, NY: Orbis Books, 2000.

Romero, Oscar. A Martyr's Message of Hope: Six Homilies by Archbishop Oscar Romero. Kansas City, MO: Celebration Books, 1981.

Romero, Oscar. The Violence of Love. Farmington, PA: The Plough Publishing House, 1998.

United Nations. From Madness to Hope: The 12-Year War in El Salvador. Report of the Commission on the Truth for El Salvador. New York: United Nations, 1993.

Wright, Scott. Promised Land: Death and Life in El Salvador. Maryknoll, NY: Orbis Books, 1994.

Poland:

Garton Ash, Timothy. The Magic Lantern: The Revolution of '89 Witnessed in Warsaw, Budapest, Berlin, and Prague. New York: Random House, 1990.

Goodwyn, Lawrence. Breaking the Barrier: The Rise of Solidarity in Poland. New York: Oxford University Press, 1991.

Walesa, Lech. The Struggle and the Triumph: An Autobiography. New York: Arcade Publishers, 1992.

China:

Binyan, Liu. ""Tell the World": What Happened in China and Why. New York: Pantheon Books, 1989.

Han Minzhu, ed. Cries for Democracy: Writings and Speeches from the 1989 Chinese Democracy Movement. Princeton, NJ: Princeton University Press, 1990.

Ming Pao News. June Four: A Chronicle of the Chinese Democracy Uprising. Fayetteville, AK: University of Arkansas Press, 1989.

Vieques:

Vieques Libre: http://www.viequeslibre.org

Jeffrey, Paul. "Protest Camps Grow on Vieques," National Catholic Reporter, Vol. 36, No. 19, March 10, 2000.

MST:

Friends of the MST: Run through Global Exchange, http://www.globalexchange.org/campaigns/brazil

MST English website: http://www.mstbrazil.org

Sudan and the SWVP:

Human Rights Watch; 350 Fifth Avenue, 34th Floor; New York, NY 10118-3299; phone: 212/290-4700 (one of four US offices); http://www.hrwatch.org

Pax Christi International: http://www.paxchristi.net (Search under Africa, Sudan.)

United States Committee for Refugees; 1717 Massachusetts Avenue NW, Suite 200; Washington, DC 20036; phone: 202/347-3507; http://www.refugees.org (Has a "Sudan Peace Pak" resource.)

Van de Veen, Hans, "Sudan: Who Has the Will for Peace?" European Platform for Conflict Prevention and Transformation, Searching for Peace in Africa. http://www.euforic.org/euconflict/sfp/part2/167_.htm Also, sources for further information at http://www.euforic.org/euconflict/sfp/part2/176_si.htm

Conscientious objection:
Schlissel, Lillian. Conscience in America: A Documentary History of Conscientious Objection in America, 1757-1967. New York: E.P. Dutton & Co., Inc., 1968.

Miscellaneous:
Fahey, Joseph, Pax Christi USA Ambassador of Peace. Peace, War and the Christian Conscience. A clear, concise survey of Christian thought regarding war and peace. This small booklet is an excellent guide for reflection and action. Pax Christi USA, 532 W.8th St., Erie, PA 16502; phone: 814-453-4955 ext. 231; e-mail: sales@paxchristiusa.org; www.paxchristiusa.org

Kelly, Petra K. Thinking Green! Essays on Environmentalism, Feminism, and Nonviolence. Berkeley, CA: Parallax Press, 1994.

McManus, Philip and Gerald Schlabach, eds. Relentless Persistence: Nonviolent Action in Latin America. Philadelphia: New Society Publishers, 1991.

Sutherland, Bill and Matt Meyer. Guns and Gandhi in Africa: Pan African Insights on Nonviolence, Armed Struggle and Liberation in Africa. Trenton, NJ: Africa World Press, Inc., 2000.

Vanderhaar, Gerard. Nonviolence in Christian Tradition. Survey of the nonviolent tradition from early Christian pacifism to modern times –suitable for schools and parish study/discussion groups. Pax Christi USA, 532 W.8th St., Erie, PA 16502; phone: 814-453-4955 ext. 231; e-mail: sales@paxchristiusa.org; www.paxchristiusa.org

Credits

Norway information reprinted with permission from Reconciliation International, Hof van Sonoy 17, 1811 LD Alkmaar, The Netherlands.

Excerpt from "Romero's Children," by Julienne Gage, reprinted with permission from The Other Side, (March/April 2000, volume 36, no. 2). For more information, call 1-800-700-9280 or visit http://www.theotherside.org.

Part Ten

To Tomorrow's Child

This book began with a call to imagine a world of peace. It ends with messages of hope. A mother who has devoted her life to peace writes a letter to her son describing a vision of peace for all the world's children; a peace activist and author tells us not to depend on the hope of results, but in our relationships and on the grace of God and the seeds that we plant in the service of God.

We are invited to join this journey. As Jonathan Schell (who has written extensively on nuclearism) wrote, "Because everything we do and everything we are is in jeopardy, and because the peril is immediate and unremitting, every person is the right person to act and every moment is the right moment to begin."

Where is your place in this journey of nonviolence? What messages of hope can you live out in your life? How can nonviolence transform you and the world?

Opening Prayer

Reader 1: We begin our prayer by voicing, aloud or in our hearts, any concerns, thanks, or other prayers that we may be carrying.

Please add any prayers.

Reader 1: You have promised us, God, that when we gather in your name, you are among us. Hear our prayers. Help us to trust that you answer them, even if it is not always in ways we expect. Help us to trust at all times in your presence, guiding us along the way of peace. Remind us that you ask that we do justice, love mercy, and walk humbly with you (Micah 6:8). Help us to begin this journey.

Side 1: God of history and of our hearts,
    so much has happened during these whirlwind days:
    we've been brave and scared;
    we've hurt, we've helped;
    we've destroyed, we've created;
    we've been together, we've been lonely;
    we've decided, we've waffled;
    we've laughed and we've cried.
    You know our hearts and our history–
    and now another day begins.

All: O God, help us to believe in beginnings
    and in our beginning again,
    no matter how often we've failed before.

Side 2: Help us to make beginnings:
    to begin going into fresh dreams,
    daring to make tracks into the land of now;
    to begin forgiving that we may experience mercy;
    to begin questioning the unquestionable that we may know truth;
    to begin disciplining that we may create beauty;
    to begin loving that we may realize joy;

to begin sacrificing that we may accomplish justice;
to begin risking that we may make peace.

Side 1: Help us to be a beginning for others,
to be a singer to the songless,
a storyteller to the aimless,
a befriender of the friendless;
to become a beginning of hope for the despairing,
of assurance for the doubting,
of reconciliation for the divided;

Side 2: to become a beginning of freedom for the oppressed,
of comfort for the sorrowing,
of friendship for the forgotten;
to become a beginning of beauty for the hopeless,
of sweetness for the soured,
of gentleness for the angry,
of wholeness for the broken,
of peace for the frightened and violent of the earth.

All: Loving God, help us to believe in beginnings,
to make a beginning and to be a beginning,
each day of this amazing life
that you call us to live with the passion of Jesus Christ.
Amen.

(Adapted from "Help Me to Believe in Beginnings," by Ted Loder in *Guerrillas of Grace*)

A Mother Pleads for Peace

In Northern Ireland in August 1976, a Belfast battle ended when the British Army shot an IRA (Irish Republican Army) member as he drove his car. He crashed into bystanders Ann Maguire and her children, three of whom died. After witnessing this scene, Betty Williams (Perkins) began a petition drive to end the madness. She went on television to plead for an end to the killing. Ann's sister, Mairead Corrigan (Maguire), heard this plea.

Together, they founded the Community of the Peace People. Along with a journalist, Ciaran McKeown, these women and the Peace People sponsored marches, pulling together Catholics and Protestants, middle and working classes. It became a decentralized movement committed to nonviolent action for peace in Northern Ireland. In 1977, Mairead Corrigan (Maguire) and Betty Williams (Perkins) won the Nobel Peace Prize for their efforts at nonviolent reconciliation in Northern Ireland. (The prize was actually the 1976 award, which had been reserved.)

Williams, in the Nobel lecture, said, "To those who say that we are naïve, utopian idealists, we say that we are the only realists, and that those who continue to support militarism in our time are supporting the progress towards the total self-destruction of the human race, when the only right and left, will be dead to the right and dead to the left, and death and destruction right, left, and center, east and west, north and south."

Maguire expresses similar sentiments in this letter that she wrote to her son about her hopes for the future.

In your life, Luke, pray to be a just man. Your life is precious and sacred, and your first right as a human being is your right to your life. So, as you would ask natural justice from your fellow travelers in respecting your right to life, then you too must give justice and respect every person's right to life.

This means, my little son, that you must never kill another human being. It will not be easy for you to refuse to kill. Sadly, we live in a world where those who refuse to kill and choose to live nonviolent lives are looked upon as naïve or cowards. Yes, it will take all of your courage to walk unarmed and refuse to hate and kill in a world which insists you must have enemies and be prepared to kill them before they kill you. Stand tall and strong, armed only with love, Luke, and refuse to hate, refuse to have enemies, refuse to let fear master your life. Only love can bring down the barriers of hate and enmity between people and nations. Hate and weapons only fuel the fear and bring closer the day of war.

Let no [person] plant in your heart the false seed of pride in any country's flag–a seed that produces the flower of narrow nationalism which grows so wildly, trampling and killing all life around it. Remember always, Luke, that people are more important than countries. I would not give one hair of your head for any country; you are too precious. And if I feel this passionate love for you and your life, and for my other children–Mark, Joanne, Marie Louise and John–I also feel passionately for the lives of the little children who are mine also; children who today die of starvation in Ethiopia. And the little children in Moscow and the little children in New York, who are told they must be enemies and may end up someday killing each other–in the name of the flag. Remember, Luke, you have no country, the world is your country, and you have not only two brothers and two sisters but also millions of brothers and sisters around the world.

We thank all those who in the past have courageously gone to wars, but that is the old way. Humankind must find new ways to solve its problems.

Pray also for the gift of wisdom. It is a wise [person] who soon comes to know that the human family's real enemies are injustice, war, starvation and poverty. Wise [people] also know that it is only by men and women becoming different and thinking in new ways that these things too will become different. When human life is held so sacred by everyone that no [one] is allowed to kill another, then justice will reign in all hearts and in all lands and there will be no more war. Justice will mean that no man or woman has too much while some have nothing. Greed and selfishness will be replaced by gen-

erosity and kindness, which will mean there will be enough food for the hungry. Poverty and disease will disappear from the earth.

There is nothing new in what I am telling you, Luke. Remember the Bible says, "Thou shalt not kill" and "Feed the hungry." And yet we must ask how did we get it all so wrong to end up in a world spending billions on nuclear weapons while men and women die because they have nothing to eat? It is possible, Luke, for the human family to start getting it right and to change the world. You just have to refuse to accept the old ways of thinking and doing things and begin to think and act in a way more in tune with the magnificent goodness in men's and women's hearts. All people in the world today know that killing and starvation are wrong, but it is only when all are prepared to live and work for justice and peace for all humankind that change will come.

With ever so gentle steps, Luke, walk side-by-side with all the travelers on this thorny path of life. They will differ from you in color, creed (there are many paths to God), culture and politics. But, above all, remember that your fellow travelers have the same needs as you and that our common humanity is far more important than any religious or political ideologies. Treat every man and woman justly and gently, as you would have them treat you.

And now, my little son, let me say the most important thing of all to you. Be happy, be joyous, live every minute of this beautiful, precious gift of life. When suffering comes into your life (sadly, much as I would love to protect you from suffering, I cannot, for it is part of everyone's life) and you find yourself in the winter of your life, remember to be patient. Summer will return, the sun will shine again, and the road will be covered in the beautiful roses of love.

God bless you and keep you, my little Luke.

Love, Mum

Letter to a Young Activist

Jim Forest was born in 1941. Twenty years later, in 1961, the year he became a Catholic, the U.S. Navy discharged him as a conscientious objector. He moved into a Catholic Worker house. In 1964 he was one of the founders of the Catholic Peace Fellowship (CPF), part of the Fellowship of Reconciliation (FOR). Later, he was involved in the burning of draft records to protest the war in Vietnam. He worked for both the FOR in the United States and the International Fellowship of Rec-

onciliation (IFOR).

In the early 1960s, Forest began a correspondence with Trappist monk Thomas Merton. Merton had become a Catholic at the age of 23, in 1938, and had joined the Trappist order three years later. He wrote extensively and had dozens of books published, both before and after his death in 1968. Merton made connections between the interior life, the search for God, and the most pressing questions of our age. His writings, his thought, and his speaking have been extremely influential for people all over the world.

When Forest was feeling hopeless and overwhelmed, he wrote to Merton for advice. Here is part of what Merton wrote back, in February 1966 (while the war in Vietnam was going on).

. . .do not depend on the hope of results. When you are doing the sort of work you have taken on, essentially an apostolic work, you may have to face the fact that your work will be apparently worthless and even achieve no result at all, if not perhaps results opposite to what you expect. As you get used to this idea you start more and more to concentrate not on the results but on the value, the rightness, the truth of the work itself. And there too a great deal has to be gone through, as gradually you struggle less and less for an idea and more and more for specific people. The range tends to narrow down, but it gets much more real. In the end. . .it is the reality of personal relationships that saves everything.

You are fed up with words, and I don't blame you. I am nauseated by them sometimes. I am also, to tell the truth, nauseated with ideals and with causes. This sounds like heresy, but I think you will understand what I mean. It is so easy to get engrossed with ideas and slogans and myths that in the end one is left holding the bag, empty, with no trace of meaning left in it. And then the temptation is to yell louder than ever in order to make the meaning be there again by magic. . .

This country is SICK, man. It is one of the sickest things that has happened. People are fed on myths, they are stuffed up to the eyes with illusions. They CAN'T think straight. They have a modicum of good will, and some of them have a whole lot of it, but with the mental bombardment everybody lives under, it is just not possible to see straight, no matter where you are looking. . .

The CPF is not going to stop the war in Vietnam, and it is not even going to cause very many Catholics to think differently about war and peace. It is simply going to become *another image among images, in the minds of most Catholics, something around which are centered some vague emotional reactions, for or against. Nevertheless, you will probably, if you continue as you do,* begin *the laborious job of changing the national mind and opening up the national conscience. How far will you get? God alone knows. All that you and I can ever hope for in terms of visible results is that we will have perhaps contributed* something *to a clarification of Christian truth in this society, and as a result a* few *people may have got straight about some things and opened up to the grace of God and made some sense out of their lives, helping a few more to do the same. As for the big results, these are not in your hands or mine, but they can suddenly happen, and we can share in them: but there is no point in building our lives on this personal satisfaction, which may be denied us and which after all is not that important.*

So the next step in the process is for you to see that your own thinking about what you are doing is crucially important. You are probably striving to build yourself an identity in your work and your witness. You are using it so to speak to protect yourself against nothingness, annihilation. That is not the right use of your work. All the good that you will do will come not from you but from the fact that you have allowed yourself, in the obedience of faith, to be used by God's love. Think of this more and gradually you will be free from the need to prove yourself, and you can be more open to the power that will work through you without your knowing it.

The great thing after all is to live, not to pour out your life in the service of a myth: and we turn the best things into myths. If you can get free from the domination of causes and just serve Christ's truth, you will be able to do more and will be less crushed by the inevitable disappointments. . .

The real hope, then, is not in something we think we can do, but in God who is making something good out of it in some way we cannot see. If we can do His will, we will be helping in this process. But we will not necessarily know about it beforehand. . .

Question:

In the peace work you have done, are you hoping for the good results or positive attention that may follow? Or do you trust that it is the right thing to do, that the work itself is true, regardless of the results? What are the benefits and drawbacks of each of these ways of looking at the work?

How can we learn to trust that God "is making something good out of it [our actions and lives] in some way we cannot see"?

The Journey of Nonviolence

Nonviolence is a journey. Living a life of faithful nonviolence challenges us, pushes us, makes demands on us, makes us uncomfortable at times. It requires inner strength, discipline, preparation, commitment, and courage. It allows us to walk more gently upon the earth, to respect that of God in every being, to live with integrity, and to attempt to live out the just kindom God has brought into being. The loving example of Jesus in the Gospels shows us this difficult but necessary path.

We are not alone in this journey. We are surrounded by a community of countless people all around the world, past, present, and future, who have, are, and will attempt to live in a spirit of nonviolence, love, justice, truth, compassion, and reconciliation. Our faith requires us to add our voices and actions to theirs.

As people of nonviolence—especially those with less power, such as the young, the elderly, the differently-abled, people of color, lesbians, gays, bisexuals, and transgendered persons, and women—we will be dismissed, our input not respected. We will be seen as idealistic or naïve. Others will tell us that the status quo is the way things have always and will always be, that there is no alternative to the very real violence of the world.

But this is not true. From the Philippines to South Africa to Washington state, USA to Chile, people have refused to kill, refused to commit violence against each other, the environment, or themselves, and refused to call each other enemy. In creative and varied ways, they have demanded that the dignity of each person be respected, countered oppression and the glorification of violence, and protected the earth. They have actively worked to end violence in all its forms: personal/interpersonal, national, international, and institutional. They have labored to create new systems of human relationships and a new world in which all of God's creation is respected.

They have given of themselves. Through the transforming power of nonviolence, they have changed themselves and their communities for the better. We too, as people of hope, must do the same and sow the seeds for a better tomorrow, even if we don't see the results. In our personal habits, in our daily lives, in our relationships with others, in the ways we choose to live in the world and the policies we support, we can begin to take small steps of nonviolence. The nonviolent struggle, which needs all of our voices, hands, and ideas, will not always—or even often—be easy. We do not know where this journey will lead us, but we know that we are called. Let us begin.

Let it be remembered by us,
By any who read
The pilgrim chronicle of our time,
That those who joined hands
For the journey in Christ
Sang their way through darkness
And found it pierced by light...

—Apocalypse and Hope,
Pastoral Letter
Episcopal Bishops
of the United States

World Peace Prayer

–Song by Marty Haugen

Lead us from death to life,
from falsehood to truth,
from despair to hope,
from fear to trust.
Lead us from hate to love,
from war to peace;
let peace fill our hearts,
let peace fill our world,
let peace fill our universe.

Verse 1:
So many lonely hearts,
so many broken lives,
longing for love to break
into their darkness.
Come, teach us love,
come, teach us peace,
come and teach us your way of compassion.

Verse 2:
Let justice ever roll,
let mercy fill the earth,
let us begin to grow into your people.
We can be love,
we can bring peace,
we can still be your way of compassion.

Dona Nobis Pacem

Grant Us Your Peace.

Closing Prayer

Reader 1: God of mystery, beauty, and awe,
God of love beyond all our understanding,
thank you for the gift of this day,
for the chance to see your love for us reflected
in the eyes of another person, in a flower,
in the song of a bird, in the gently falling rain.
Thank you for sending your child to us,
for the wisdom Jesus brought,
for his example of the ways of your peace.

Reader 2: We know that you are with us
as we begin and continue
the struggle to be a nonviolent people.
Help us to bring our many and diverse gifts
to the work for creation-wide justice.
In the words of Zechariah,
guide our feet into the way of peace. (Luke 1:79)
Guide also our hands to build your peace,
our mouths to speak your peace,
our ears to hear your peace spoken by countless others in many ways,
and our lives to reflect your peace.
Amen.

Reader 1: And so we pray together,

All: O Holy Mystery, Creator God, pour into me your Sanctifying Spirit, that I may water the world with the love and example of Jesus.

Help me to strive for peace within, and to make peace in my life this day.

Strengthen me to accept suffering rather than inflict it. In the face of provocation and violence, be my calm.

Preserve me in nonviolence of tongue and heart. Quench my inner violence with your life-giving Word.

Help me drink deeply of the small joys of life. Sustain me in a simple life, so others may simply live.

Energize me to work against injustice and to actively resist evil. Empower me to overcome the sins of racism, sexism, and materialism.

Stream through me to abolish war from my own heart and from the face of the earth. Equip me to build the reign of justice and peace.

O Holy Mystery, Creator God, I trust in your sustaining love and power. I believe that just as you gave me the desire to offer this prayer, so you will also bestow abundant grace to fulfill it.

Amen.

(Second prayer adapted by Kathy Schmitt from *The Vow of Nonviolence* by Pax Christi USA)

To Tomorrow's Child

Part Ten: Reflections

1. Maguire writes that our real enemies are "injustice, war, starvation and poverty." Do you agree or disagree? Would you add anything? Subtract anything?

2. How can we live in ways that "give justice and respect" to every person's right to life?

3. The Seville Statement on Violence says, "Just as 'wars begin in the minds of [people]', peace also begins in our minds. The same species who invented war is capable of inventing peace. The responsibility lies with each of us." What steps can you and your communities take to build a nonviolent world? In what ways do you need to think and act differently?

4. If you have not done so, consider taking the PCUSA vow of nonviolence (in Appendix F). If you have, how have you attempted to live out this vow?

5. How are you opening up to the grace of God? How can you, "in the obedience of faith" (Merton's words), allow yourself to be used by God's love?

6. Where do you feel God might be calling you?

Suggestions for Action

- Write your own letter to the future.
- If you have been working on this book with a group, continue as a discussion group, an action group, or a support group. If you have been working alone, see if there are others with whom you can share.
- Work on building relationships–write some letters, share time, let someone know that you care.
- Find out more: use some of the resources in this book; get involved with at least one of the organizations.
- Use what you have learned: reject violence in all its forms and work to uproot it from your own heart and life.
- Trust in God and in God's overwhelming love. Pray. Celebrate.

Next steps:
A Sampling of Resources for Further Reading and Reflection

Organizations:
American Friends Service Committee. 1501 Cherry Street; Philadelphia, PA 19102; phone: 215/241-7000; e-mail: afscinfo@afsc.org; http://www.afsc.org

Center for Campus Organizing: 165 Friend Street, #1; Boston, MA 02114-2025; phone: 617/725-2886; e-mail: cco@igc.org; http://www.cco.org

Fellowship of Reconciliation. PO Box 271; Nyack, NY 10960; phone: 845/358-4601; e-mail: for@forusa.org; http://www.forusa.org (For Fellowship magazine, e-mail: fellowship@forusa.org)

Nonviolence International: http://www.nviusa.org

Peace Action. 1819 H Street NW, #420; Washington, DC 20006; phone: 202/862-9740; http://www.peace-action.org

War Resisters League. 339 Lafayette Street; New York, NY 10012; phone: 212/228-0450; e-mail: wrl@igc.org; http://www.nonviolence.org/wrl

Periodicals:
National Catholic Reporter. Box 419281; Kansas City, MO 64141; phone: 816/531-0538 or subscriptions 800/333-7373; http://www.natcath.org

The Other Side magazine. 300 W. Apsley Street; Philadelphia, PA 19144; phone: 215/849-2178 or 800/700-9280; http://www.theotherside.org

Sojourners magazine and ministry. 2401 15ᵗʰ Street NW; Washington, DC 20009; phone 202/328-8842 or 800/714-7474; e-mail: sojourners@sojo.net; http://www.sojourners.com

Books, manuals, etc.:

Bouchen, Christine M., ed. *Thomas Merton: Essential Writings.* Maryknoll, NY: Orbis Books, 2000.

Butigan, Ken with Patricia Bruno. *From Violence to Wholeness: A Ten Part Program in the Spirituality and Practice of Active Nonviolence.* Las Vegas: Pace e Bene Franciscan Nonviolence Center, 1999.

Called to be Peace at Home: Rituals and Resources for Peacemaking in Family Life–Under the guidance of Dr. James and Kathy McGinnis of the Parenting for Peace and Justice Network, this resource packet is designed to help families explore, articulate and witness to Christian nonviolence. The packet includes a reflection booklet with rituals for throughout the year, the Family Pledge of Nonviolence, prayer cards and more. Pax Christi USA, 532 W.8th St., Erie, PA 16502; phone: 814-453-4955 ext. 231; e-mail: sales@paxchristiusa.org; http://www.paxchristiusa.org

Dellinger, David. *From Yale to Jail: The Life Story of a Moral Dissenter.* New York: Pantheon Books, 1993.

Erie Benedictines for Peace, ed. *A New Moment: An Invitation to Nonviolence.* Erie, PA: Pax Christi USA, 1986.

If Only Today You Knew the Things that Make for Peace: High School–Peacemaking Activities in Response to Violence, Terrorism and War for Christian High Schools & Youth Groups by Dr. James McGinnis and Kevin LaNave–Resource for teachers and youth ministers on peacemaking. Divided into two sections–Images of Peace and the Pledge of Nonviolence and Responding to the Violence of Terrorism & War–these insightful units provide reflection and activities on the themes of: The Peacemaking Vision of Jesus, Visions of Peace from Other Faith Traditions, Patriotism and the Christian, the U.S. War on Terrorism and Iraq, the United Nations Decade for a Culture of Peace and Nonviolence and many more. Pax Christi USA, 532 W.8th St., Erie, PA 16502; phone: 814-453-4955 ext. 231; e-mail: sales@paxchristiusa.org; http://www.paxchristiusa.org

If Only Today You Knew the Things that Make for Peace: K-8 Peacemaking Activities in Response to Violence, Terrorism and War for Christian Education and Elementary Schools, K-8 by Dr. James McGinnis and Kevin LaNave–Resource for religious educators on peacemaking–challenges students to put the Gospel call to peace into practice at a critical moment in history. Pax Christi USA, 532 W.8th St., Erie, PA 16502; phone: 814-453-4955 ext. 231; e-mail: sales@paxchristiusa.org; http://www.paxchristiusa.org

Pax Christi USA. *Words of Peace series.* Erie, PA.

Plowshares movement (pictures, statements, court documents, etc.): http://www.plowsharesactions.org

Shannon, William H., ed. *The Hidden Ground of Love: The Letters of Thomas Merton on Religious Experience and Social Concerns.* New York: Farrar, Straus, Giroux, 1985.

Zinn, Howard. *A People's History of the United States: 1492 to the Present. (20ᵗʰ anniversary edition.)* New York: HarperCollins, 1999.

Credits

Maguire letter reprinted with permission of the author.

About the Original Authors

GERARD A. VANDERHAAR is Professor Emeritus of Religion and Peace Studies at Christian Brothers University in Memphis, Tennessee, where he taught for 28 years. He has served on the National Council of Pax Christi USA and is a Pax Christi USA Ambassador of Peace. He helped found the Mid-South Peace and Justice Center and the M.K. Gandhi Institute for the Study of Nonviolence. Vanderhaar lectures widely on nonviolence and has authored numerous articles and books, including Christians and Nonviolence in the Nuclear Age, Enemies and How to Love Them, Nonviolence in Christian Tradition, and Nonviolence: Theory and Practice. In 1998 he received the Pax Christi USA book award for Beyond Violence: In the Spirit of the Nonviolent Christ.

MARY LOU KOWNACKI, OSB, a member of the Benedictine Sisters of Erie, is the former National Coordinator of Pax Christi USA. She is the founder of Pax Center, a Christian community for nonviolence, and Benedictines for Peace. She is the author of A Race to Nowhere: An Arms Race Primer for Catholics and Peace Is Our Calling: Contemporary Monasticism and the Peace Movement. Her articles have appeared in a wide range of publications.

About the Current Author/Editor

SHANNON McMANIMON has worked with the American Friends Service Committee's National Youth and Militarism Program (which deals with the impact of war, militarism, and recruiting on young people). She has been involved with the Catholic Worker Movement and has been a member of Pax Christi USA's Youth and Young Adult Forum and the Pax Christi USA National Council. She is currently a staff member at Pax Christi USA.

Artists

SISTER HELEN DAVID BRANCATO, IHM
>   Sojourner Truth - p. 15
>   Gandhi - p. 17
>   Peace Dove - p. 40
>   Mother and child - p. 41
>   Daniel Berrigan - p. 50
>   Dom Helder Camara - p. 83
>   Thomas Merton - p. 84
>   Oscar Romero - p. 84
>   Peter Maurin and Dorothy Day - p. 117
>   Oscar Romero - p. 138

JUDY SPEER
>   Community - p. 54

ROSSI
>   Gandhi - p. 67

REBECCA VENN
>   Protecting the Environment - p. 137

ARTIST UNKNOWN
>   Farm worker - p. 47
>   Farm workers - p. 118

(Every effort has been taken to properly credit the works used in this publication.)

Glossary of Terms

affinity groups: Affinity groups are used in non-violent actions or campaigns. They are generally groups of 5 to 20 people who agree to support each other by making decisions and acting together. Affinity groups are self-sufficient; often, people in the group have different roles, such as providing medical help, risking arrest, providing support, etc. Affinity groups have been used very effectively in mass actions as a way of decentralizing power and allowing each person to have input, support, and a role.

apartheid: Apartheid most often refers to a South African governmental policy of discrimination and segregation based on race. Started in 1948, it institutionalized racism. It impacted every aspect of South African social and economic life, for instance, prohibiting interracial marriages, requiring Blacks always to carry "passes" for identification, and leading to brutal human rights violations. By the 1960s, apartheid physically separated Blacks and whites and subjected the majority Black population to police repression. Blacks were confined to "homelands," small portions of South Africa's least fertile land. In 1990-91, most of the social legislation that provided the basis for apartheid was repealed. However, racial segregation, so deeply rooted, continued. In 1993 all races were given the right to vote, and elections in 1994 brought a coalition government with a Black majority.

arbitration: Arbitration is a way to settle differences among people or groups. They meet with an arbitrator, a person chosen to settle the differences. Each side presents their opinions or stands and then the arbitrator makes a decision. It is an alternative to the legal system (such as suing in a courtroom).

BCE and CE: abbreviations for "before common era" and "common era." They are used in place of BC and AD, which refer to Christ's life.

campesino: Campesino is a Spanish word, meaning a small farmer or rural person. In English, we might translate it as "peasant."

civil disobedience: Civil disobedience is a refusal to obey a law, policy, or practice that a person considers unjust. The law is disobeyed in an attempt to call attention to its injustice and to bring about change. People who commit civil disobedience do so openly and accept the consequences of their actions. Often, people who do civil disobedience are motivated by a higher law (such as God's commandments or a belief in the dignity of all humans).

conscientious objector: Usually, the term "conscientious objector" refers to a person who finds war unjust for reasons of conscience and thus refuses to participate in the military-war system. Conscientious objection (the act) occurs both during times of war and times of "peace." During the latter, people may refuse to register for the draft. The term can also refer to refusing to participate in other systems for reasons of conscience.

consensus: Consensus is a cooperative group process for decision-making that allows each person's voice to be heard and valued. The process often works something like this: discussion of the perspectives and ideas, noting the agreements and disagreements, combining the ideas into one, evaluating, restating the idea, looking for support. In consensus decision-making, everyone discusses the issue or decision and comes to agreement, combining ideas from the group as a whole. Once everyone agrees with the plan or idea, the group is in consensus. (A person does not have to be in total agreement, however, but can decide that his or her objections are not strong enough to block the process from moving forward. On the other hand, sometimes one or several people will not agree to the idea and then there is no consensus.) Unlike voting, in which there are "winners" and "losers," in consensus decision-making, everyone agrees to the plan of action or the idea. It often takes a long time and requires patience, creativity, and flexibility.

consumerism: Consumerism is a desire for more and more material goods. Consumerism is when people buy and buy, without paying attention to whether they truly need something, if it will last, where and how it was made, and how their purchase impacts the earth. Rather than working for healthy relationships and communities, a society based on consumerism focuses on the desire and search for more things. Consumerism is harmful to the earth, as people throw things away to buy new ones or buy disposable products. Consumerism also implies that a person's worth is based on how much he or she has. People themselves become commodities–to be "valuable," consumerism says you must look a certain way, drive a certain vehicle, wear certain clothes. Consumerism is driven by huge amounts of money spent on advertising, trying to create a desire for things.

direct action: Direct action is an attempt to change a situation or policy directly. In a direct action, people take action on their issue of concern, for instance, squatting in an abandoned house to provide housing for the homeless.

the disappeared: This term is often used in reference to Central and South America. During the brutal wars there (especially in the 1980s) and in other parts of the world, many people–community activists, students, religious workers, union leaders–disappeared without a trace. Since there was no news of their whereabouts, they were called the disappeared. Most were kidnapped, tortured, and killed by the militaries and para-militaries. To this day, it is not known where most of these people are, although in some cases, their bodies have been recovered.

draft: The draft is the process by which countries call up young men (women are usually exempt) for war. In countries such as the United States and Chile, all young men are required to register for the draft. If war was declared and the country needed more troops, a lottery system would be started to select people from the draft lists. This is what happened, for instance, in the late 1960s and early 1970s when the United States was fighting a war in Vietnam. The draft is part of the overall military system; it is the way that militaries mobilize enough people to fight in major wars. Around the world, young people have refused to take part in this system.

freedom rides: Freedom rides challenged the segregation of interstate busses and trains. Groups of whites and Blacks rode together on busses or trains going to the South. Along the way, they used the same facilities (such as water fountains and rest rooms) or used facilities designated for the opposite race (whites using those marked "colored" and vice versa), even though Jim Crow laws said this was illegal. Free-dom Riders faced violent hostility and were often arrested. They revealed the injustices of the system, in which people of different races were treated very differently. The first Freedom Ride was in 1947; a campaign of freedom rides was held in 1961. These actions forced the U.S. administration to take a stand on the integration of travel.

genocide: Genocide is a deliberate attempt to wipe out a group of people of a certain racial, political, or cultural background. For instance, the Nazis during World War II attempted to commit genocide against the Jews.

GNP (Gross National Product): A GNP is the total value of the output produced in a certain country during a certain period of time. It is figured out by taking the market value (monetary worth) of all goods, services, and products produced in that period of time (usually yearly).

IMF (International Monetary Fund): The IMF is an institution that was created in 1944, at the Bretton Woods Conference. The IMF tries to maintain a balance of international trade and payments. It does this by examining countries' economies and making loans to those countries that are having financial difficulties. Along with the World Bank, the IMF determines whether developing countries can get aid and how that money will be spent. Often, in order to get money, countries have to reform their economies in ways that harm people, such as cutting government spending on health care and education, privatizing state-run enterprises, and opening to foreign trade. (These programs are called structural adjustment programs.) This system has led to massive debt that countries are unable to pay off. Voting at the IMF and World Bank is determined by the contributions of member states. Therefore, wealthy countries such as the United States make decisions. The unfair and harmful practices of these institutions have been greatly criticized; many people have participated in protesting them.

indigenous people: "Indigenous" means what is grown, produced, or lives naturally in a certain region. Indigenous peoples are those people who originally occupied the land, before colonization and displacement occurred.

intentional community: In our society, the typical family pattern is nuclear: parent(s) and children. Intentional communities are created when (usually non-related) people choose to live together. They can take many forms. Sometimes, the members share everything: food, finances, decision-making, child-rearing, spirituality, etc. Other intentional communities may have separate finances but share a vehicle, meals, etc. Intentional communities allow people to support each other more intimately in both daily decision-making and long-term decisions. Living in community is very countercultural: it goes against strongly-held ideas of individualism. Often, people living in community choose to make other countercultural choices, such as engaging in resistance work. Catholic Worker houses and religious communities are examples of intentional communities.

just war theory: Just war theory is an attempt to set rules and limits for the conduct and means of war. It has both religious and secular roots. St. Augustine, for instance, said that a just war was one fought for the right reasons (meaning the desire for peace) and waged under rightful authority. Expanding on this thought, St. Thomas Aquinas stated that just wars had to be declared by a lawful authority who had the power to wage war and carried out with just cause and right intention (to achieve some good or to avoid some evil). He outlined the justification for wars as well as the kinds of activities permissible in war. Just war theory states that war must be declared only as a last resort (when other efforts have failed) and if there is a reasonable expectation for success. Noncombatants should be protected, captives treated humanely, and certain types of weapons avoided (especially those which cannot discriminate between combatants and civilians). Just war theory has been hotly debated within the Catholic Church. While social teaching allows for just wars, many people say that the nature of warfare today (such as nuclear, biological, and chemical weapons) rules out the possibility of war ever being just. Thus, many people–some who would call themselves nonviolent and some who wouldn't–disagree with this theory.

kindom: "Kindom" is often used in place of the word "kingdom," meaning God's reign. Kin-dom stresses the family of God, that all people are brothers and sisters, children of God. It also does away with language of "kings," a system based on wealth and power in which people were not equal.

LGBT: An abbreviation for lesbians, gay men, bisexuals, and transgendered people.

liberation theology: Liberation theology arose out of the experiences of Christians in South and Central America. Groups of Christians–often called base Christian communities–gathered together to reflect on the Bible. They realized that such reflections change according to the place (social, cultural, political, etc.) of the people studying the Word. Liberation theology recognizes the importance of the context–especially social–in which the Bible is read; it analyzes society and structures and how faith and theology relate. In liberation theology, the Bible is a powerful tool that helps people to understand both their oppression and the liberation and justice that God desires. It sees the Gospels and Jesus as bringing a message of freedom and as tools for liberation. Because it emphasizes struggling for justice here and now, it has inspired action and organizing and also led to repression from governments. Liberation theology has been an important means of study and action for oppressed people around the world struggling to end military and economic oppression.

mediation: Mediation is a way of resolving conflict in which people together work out their problems. Someone who is not involved in the conflict listens to both sides and helps them to dialogue and work toward a solution. Mediation is used as an alternative to the legal system.

pacifism: Pacifism is usually defined as opposition to war or violence as a means of settling disputes. Some people do not like this term because it sounds like "passivism"–being submissive or inactive. Many people prefer to emphasize that it is not enough just to oppose violence: we must be actively engaged in stopping it and in bringing about new means of resolving conflict.

Plowshares: The term "Plowshares" comes from Isaiah 2:4 and Micah 4:3 which state, "they shall beat their swords into plowshares, and their spears into pruning hooks; nation shall not lift up sword against nation; neither shall they learn war any more." The first Plowshares action took place in September 1980; eight people entered a General Electric plant outside of Philadelphia and hammered on nose cones for nuclear warheads and poured blood on documents. In the past twenty years, on over five dozen occasions, groups (and occasionally individuals) have entered military bases and weapons facilities and in such a way symbolically disarmed nuclear weapons and other weapons of mass destruction. The main tools are household hammers and blood (calling attention to and naming the bloodshed caused by the weapons). Such disarmament actions are called Plowshares. People (parents, grandparents, Catholic Workers, students, artists, religious community members, and many others) who do these actions go through a long period of intense spiritual preparation, nonviolence training, and community formation. After their action, Plowshares activists stay at the site, attempting to explain why they acted and taking responsibility for their actions. As a result, many people have spent years in prison for their action. In some places, such as Scotland, juries have found Plowshares activists not guilty, especially after a 1996 World Court decision declared that nuclear weapons are illegal and that all citizens have responsibilities for disarmament. Veteran Plowshares activist Art Laffin writes, "the basic hope of the plowshares actions. . .is to communicate. . .an underlying faith that the power of nonviolent love can overcome the forces of violence; a reverence for the sacredness of all life and creation; a plea for justice for the victims of poverty and the arms race; an acceptance of personal responsibility for the dismantling and the physical conversion of weapons; and a spiritual conversion of the heart to the way of justice and reconciliation." (*Swords Into Plowshares*)

preferential option for the poor: In 1979, the Catholic bishops of Latin America met in Mexico and created a document in which they spoke of the "preferential option for the poor." This term means a serious willingness to address poverty and to place first the needs of those who are most poor. In the Christian and Jewish scriptures, God shows a special love for those who are most poor and outcast and instructs the people of God to do the same: to care for orphans and widows, to redistribute land, to be friends with those "on the outside" of society. The preferential option for the poor means that we must be directly involved with people who are poor, that we ask questions about why people are poor, that we work with people to relieve poverty, and that we examine our own lifestyles and consumption. It also means that people of privilege should give away or surrender that privilege, especially in order to serve others. It means acting out of faith, with love.

satyagraha: Mohandas Gandhi coined this term while living in South Africa in the early twentieth century. He offered a small prize to the person who could use a single word to describe the principles of truth and love in the process of social change. He made a variation on the winning entry and came up with *satyagraha*, which literally means holding on or grasping to truth or searching for truth. *Satyagraha* came to identify the nonviolent struggle for truth and justice–nonviolent direct action. It relates to all aspects of life and involves dedication, commitment, and a willingness to suffer for the truth. People who engaged in *satyagraha* are called *satyagrahis*.

segregation: Segregation is keeping groups separate and isolated. In the U.S., segregation often refers to a system that had different facilities, laws, and treatments for Black and white people (mainly in the South). The facilities (such as schools) for Black people were much worse, laws denied people basic civil and human rights, and Blacks were subjected to torture and humiliation at the hands of whites. The 1960s Civil Rights Movement was an attempt to undo segregation based on racism. See Part 8.

sit-ins: A sit-in is when people sit somewhere, such as an office or a store, in an attempt to get people in power to either dialogue about an issue or to change an unfair or harmful policy or procedure. For instance, students used sit-ins in the 1960s to desegregate dining facilities. Other people have done sit-ins at the offices of elected representatives to draw attention to important issues; other have done sit-ins at corporations to protest policies or ways of doing business that harm the earth or people.

street theater: Street theater is a creative way of engaging people in learning about social injustice. Using puppets, dance, song, musical instruments, costumes, and other props, activists tell stories about the world and our place in it. Street theater is a visually and audibly attractive way of communicating a message. Street theater groups are usually highly mobile and flexible, which allows them to do their work in a wide variety of settings.

war tax resistance: War tax resistance (wtr) is refusing to pay taxes which support war and the military. Like conscientious objection to war, it is a way to take personal responsibility and to refuse to cooperate with a violent, unjust system. War tax resisters argue that just as they would physically not participate in war, they cannot in conscience allow their tax dollars to be used for killing (tax dollars are drafted just like people are). Currently, about half of all discretionary funds (money that Congress decides how to spend) goes to pay for war and war preparations. War tax resisters state that this huge amount of money could go to support the needs of people, communities, and the environment. There are different forms and ways of doing war tax resistance. Some people choose to live below the poverty line and thus do not owe taxes. Others pay their taxes to groups or organizations that support communities rather than paying them to the government. This last method is illegal and can have significant consequences for the resister.

World Bank: The World Bank was formed in 1944 at the Bretton Woods Conference. It is composed of five agencies that make loans or guarantee credit to its member countries. Loans are for large projects such as roads and dams. The World Bank aims to reduce poverty. However, it has increasingly been protested as undemocratic and its policies as harming people (especially those who are poor) and the environment. See the entry "International Monetary Fund" for more information.

Appendix A: A Declaration of Life

I, the undersigned, being of sound and disposing mind and memory, do hereby in the presence of witnesses make this Declaration of Life,

I believe that the killing of one human being by another is morally wrong.

I believe it is morally wrong for any state or other governmental entity to take the life of a human being for any reason.

I believe that capital punishment is not a deterrent to crime and serves only the purpose of revenge.

THEREFORE, I hereby declare that should I die as a result of a violent crime, I request that the person or persons found guilty of homicide for my killing not be subject to or put in jeopardy of the death penalty under any circumstances, no matter how heinous their crime or how much I may have suffered. The death penalty would only increase my suffering.

I request that the Prosecutor or District Attorney having the jurisdiction of the person or persons alleged to have committed my homicide not file or prosecute an action for capital punishment as a result of my homicide.

I request that this Declaration be made admissible in any trial of any person charged with my homicide, and read and delivered to the jury. I also request the Court to allow this Declaration to be admissible as a statement of the victim at the sentencing of the person or persons charged and convicted of my homicide; and, to pass sentence in accordance with my wishes.

I request that the Governor or other executive officer(s) grant pardon, clemency or take whatever action is necessary to stay and prohibit the carrying out of the execution of any person or persons found guilty of my homicide.

This Declaration is not meant to be, and should not be taken as, a statement that the person or persons who have committed my homicide should go unpunished.

I request that my family and friends take whatever actions are necessary to carry out the intent and purpose of this Declaration; and, I further request them to take no action contrary to this Declaration.

I request that, should I die under the circumstances as set forth in the Declaration and the death penalty is requested, my family, friends and personal representative deliver copies of this Declaration as follows: to the Prosecutor or District Attorney having jurisdiction over the person or persons charged with my homicide; to the Attorney representing the person or persons charged with my homicide; to the judge presiding over the case involving my homicide; for recording, to the Recorder of the County in which my homicide took place and to the recorder of the County in which the person or persons charged with my homicide are to be tried; to all newspapers, radio and television stations of general circulation in the County in which my homicide took place and the County in which the person or persons charged with my homicide are to be tried; and, to any other person, persons or entities my family, friends or personal representative deem appropriate in order to carry out my wishes as set forth herein.

I affirm under the pains and penalties for perjury that the above Declaration of Life is true.

WITNESS

_____

_____ printed name

DECLARANT

_____

_____ printed name

_____
Social Security Number

STATE OF _____

COUNTY OF _____

Before me, a Notary Public in and for said county and state, personally appeared the Declarant and acknowledged the execution of the foregoing instrument this_____day of _____ 20___.

WITNESS my hand and notarial seal.

_____
NOTARY PUBLIC

_____
Printed Name

My commission expires: _____

County of Residence:_____

Please send a copy of this notarized form to:
Cherish Life Circle, Convent of Mercy
273 Willoughby Avenue,
Brooklyn, NY 11205.

Appendix B: More Statistics on Violence

WAR
- From the mid-1980s to the mid-1990s wars killed 2 million children and seriously injured or permanently disabled 6 million more. *The Impact of Armed Conflict on Children*, UN, 1995
- Civilians now account for over 90% of all war deaths. UN, 1995
- In the 1990s, civil wars killed five million people worldwide. United Nations Development Program, *Human Development Report*, 2000
- War and internal conflicts in the 1990s forced 50 million people to flee their homes. United Nations Development Program, *Human Development Report*, 2000

MILITARY SPENDING
- The U.S. share of global military spending was 36% in fiscal year 1999. Center for Defense Information, 2001
- The U.S. military budget is more than 19 times as large as the combined spending of the seven countries traditionally identified by the Pentagon as the U.S.'s most likely adversaries–Cuba, Iran, Iraq, Libya, North Korea, Sudan, and Syria–which together spend just over $15 billion annually. Center for Defense Information, 1999
- The U.S. and its close allies account for approximately two-thirds of world military spending. Together they spend more than 37 times more than the seven rogue states. Center for Defense Information, 2001
- The seven rogue nations, along with Russia and China, together spend $116 billion, less than one-half (36%) of the U.S. military budget. Center for Defense Information, 2001
- Every jet fighter sold by a developed country to a developing country costs the schooling of three million children. Jeff Gates, May 2000 (Shared Capitalism Institute)
- The cost of a submarine denies safe drinking water to 60 million people. Jeff Gates, May 2000 (Shared Capitalism Institute)
- Half of the world's governments spend more to guard their citizens against military attack than to protect them against all the enemies of good health. World Military and Social Expenditures 1996
- 12% of the $125 billion spent by developing countries on their militaries could provide health care for all of their citizens, including immunization of all children, elimination of severe malnutrition, reduction of moderate malnutrition by half, and provision of safe drinking water for all. United Nations Development Program, *Human Development Report*, 1994
- Despite a decline in the past five years, world military expenditures in 1995 amounted to more than $1.4 million per minute. World Military and Social Expenditures 1995
- Global military spending, even after a decline, equals the combined incomes of half of humanity each year. United Nations Development Program, *Human Development Report*, 1994
- While global spending declined between 1987 and 1994, there was no clear link between reduced military spending and enhanced expenditure on human development. United Nations Development Program, *Human Development Report*, 1994
- Since 1960, low-income countries have increased their military spending twice as quickly as the average per capita income. The military budgets of these countries are now seven times as large as they were in 1960. Center for Defense Information 1991; UNICEF 1990
- 86% of the current arms supplies originates from the 5 permanent members of the UN Security Council. United Nations Development Program, *Human Development Report*, 1994
- From 1989 to 1996 the U.S. sold more than $117 billion of arms, about 45% of the world's total. U.S. State Department and Department of Defense, report to Congress, September 1997
- The U.S. dominates the global arms market. Between 1994 and 1996, it exported $67.3 billion worth of armaments–55% of global arms exports and quadruple the share of the closest competitor. World Military Expenditures and Arms Transfers, 1997
- Military budgets, 2000: U.S. $324.8 billion, Russia (1999) $56 billion, Japan $45.6 billion, China (1999) $39.5 billion, UK $34.5 billion. Center for Defense Information
- The U.S. spends $4.5 billion per year on nuclear weapons research, up from an average $3.7 billion per year during the Cold War (both in 1998 dollars). U.S. Department of Energy, 1998
- From 1940-1996, U.S. expenditures for nuclear weapons ($5.5 trillion–$5,500,000,000,000–1996 dollars) exceeded combined total federal spending on education, training, employment and social services, agriculture, natural resources and the environment, general sciences and space research,

community and regional development, law enforcement, and energy production and regulation. Brookings Institute 1998

• The cost of nuclear weapons and dismantling surplus weapons from 1940-1996 was $5.8 trillion. If you put this much money into a stack of dollar bills, it would reach from the Earth to the moon and nearly back again. 459,000+ miles. Brookings Institute 1998

• The top three expenses for the U.S. government, 1940-1996: Department of Defense (less nuclear weapons), Social Security, nuclear weapons. Brookings Institute 1998

• 60% of all federal research funding for universities is military related.
Center for Defense Information 1998

• Two-thirds of all U.S. scientists and engineers work for defense contractors or on defense contracts in industry or universities. Nowhere else in the world is this true. Center for Defense Information 1998

CORPORATIONS

• Every year, the U.S. federal government provides an estimated $150 billion in direct federal subsidies and tax breaks to corporations. *Boston Globe*, July 7, 1996

• Thirty years ago, U.S. corporations paid about the same share of taxes as individuals; now, they pay about one-quarter. U.S. Office of Budget and Management, 1996

• Giant corporations are responsible for much pollution. Just 122 corporations account for 80% of the world's carbon dioxide emissions. Corporation Watch, 2001

• Corporate crime costs the U.S. more than all street crime combined. For example, the FBI reports that in 1995 all burglary and robbery cost the United States about $4 billion. Professor W. Steve Albrecht of Brigham Young University estimates that white-collar fraud (usually committed by lawyers, doctors, accountants, and businesspeople) costs 50 times as much–about $200 billion per year (not counting injuries or pollution). Global Exchange, website, 2001

CONSUMERISM

• "Never forget that your country has 4 percent of the world's people and 22 percent of its wealth. We've got to sell something to the other 96 percent if we want to hold on to our standard of living."
Bill Clinton speech, October 13, 1999

• A conservative estimate of global advertising spending is $435 billion per year.
United Nations Development Program, *Human Development Report*, 1998

• In the U.S., we spend more on advertising than on all our public institutions of higher education.
U.S. Bureau of the Census, Abstract of the United States, 1995

• Studies of U.S. households found that the income needed to fulfill consumption aspirations doubled between 1986 and 1994. United Nations Development Program, *Human Development Report*, 1998

• North Americans consume twice as much energy as those in Japan and Switzerland, 25 times those in Brazil, 60 times those in India, 191 times those in Nigeria, 351 times those in Ethiopia.
Rich Christians in An Age of Hunger: Moving from Affluence to Generosity by Ronald J. Sider, 1997.

• During the 40 years following the mid-1990s, the U.S. will add approximately 50 million people to the world, but this will have about the same global impact in terms of resource consumption as 2 billion more people in India. Sider, 1997

• Developed countries have 20% of the world's population, 85% of the income, 70% of the energy consumption, and produce 66% of the world's greenhouse gases.
Bread for the World International, *Hunger 1995*

•

	The fifth of the world's people in the highest income countries	The fifth of the world's people in the lowest income countries
total private consumption expenditures	86%	1.3%
consumption all meat and fish	45%	5 %
consumption total energy	58%	> 4 %
consumption total paper	84%	1.1%
ownership of vehicles	87%	>1 %
CO2 emissions	53%	3 %

United Nations Development Program, *Human Development Report*, 1998

• A child born in the industrial world adds more to consumption and pollution in her or his lifetime than 30-50 children in developing countries.
United Nations Development Program, *Human Development Report*, 1998

WEALTH DISTRIBUTION

• The richest 10% in the United States have 73.2% of the total wealth; the richest 1% have 35%.
The Progressive, January 2000, vol. 64, no. 1

• Income disparity in the US is rising. In 1998, the richest one-fifth of households received 49.2% of all national before-tax income. The poorest one-fifth failed to increase between 1989 and 1998 while the top one-fifth grew 23%. Center on Budget and Policy Priorities, 10/99

• The richest 1% of Americans (2.7 million) are projected to have as much as the lowest 38% (100 million). Center on Budget and Policy Priorities, 9/99

• In 1989, the U.S. had 66 billionaires and 31.5 million people below the poverty line. In 1999, there were 268 billionaires and 34.5 million below the poverty line. The top 1% has more wealth than the bottom 45%. United for a Fair Economy, 12/99

• In both income and wealth, the United States ranks as the most unequal of any industrial country: in 1994 the poorest fifth had less than 3.6% of the total U.S. income, while the richest fifth had 49.1%, the highest disparity on record. World Military and Social Expenditures 1996

• CEO compensation skyrocketed 535% in the 1990s, while worker pay increased 32% (not adjusted for inflation). United For a Fair Economy and the Institute for Policy Studies, 8/00

• If the pay of the average production worker had risen at the CEO rate of the 1990s, the average production worker would have been paid $114,035 in 1999 (instead of $23,753) and the minimum wage would be $24.13 an hour (instead of $5.15).
United for a Fair Economy and the Institute for Policy Studies, 8/00

• International CEOs make between 4 and 27% the salary of the average U.S. CEO. In Japan, the average CEO makes 20 times the average worker and in Great Britain 35 times.
United for a Fair Economy, 4/99

• The poorest tenth of U.S. citizens has an average income higher than two-thirds of the world. *Left Business Observer*, 2/00

• The one-fifth of the world's people who live in the highest income countries has 86% of the world's GDP and 74% of the phone lines. The bottom one-fifth has 1% and 1.5% of these, respectively. United Nations Development Program, *Human Development Report*, 1999

• The income gap between the richest one-fifth of the world's people and the poorest one-fifth (measured by the average national income) increased from 30:1 in 1960 to 74:1 in 1997.
United Nations Development Program, *Human Development Report*, 1999

• The 200 richest people in the world doubled their net worth from the mid-90s to $1 trillion. Their assets are worth more than the total income of 41% of the world's people. A 1% tax on the wealth of these people could fund primary education for all the world's children who lack access to schooling.
United Nations Development Program, *Human Development Report*, 1999

•More than $1.5 trillion is exchanged daily in the world's currency markets.
United Nations Development Program, *Human Development Report*, 1999

POVERTY

World
• 3 billion people live on less than $2 per day. Bread for the World International, *Hunger 1997*, released 1996
• One-fifth of the world's population, 1.2 billion people–half of whom are children–lives in "conditions of almost unimaginable suffering and want." UNICEF 2000
• Three-fourths of the world's poorest people live in rural areas.
United Nations Development Program, *Human Development Report*, 1997
• Human poverty refers not just to income poverty but to a short life, lack of basic education, etc.
United Nations Development Program, *Human Development Report*, 1997
• Eradicating world poverty would cost about 1% of global income and no more than 3% of the national income in all but the poorest countries.
United Nations Development Program, *Human Development Report*, 1997
• "Global poverty is one of the greatest threats to the sustainability of the physical environment and to the sustainability of human life." United Nations Development Program, *Human Development Report*, 1994
• In industrial countries, more than 100 million people live below the income poverty line; 37 million are jobless. United Nations Development Program, *Human Development Report*, 1997
• "The progress in reducing poverty over the 20th century is remarkable and unfrequented." Over the past 50 years, poverty fell more than in the past 500 years.
United Nations Development Program, *Human Development Report*, 1997

United States

- The U.S. minimum wage used to bring a family of three with one full-time worker above the poverty line. Now, it doesn't bring one worker with one child above the poverty line. United for a Fair Economy, 12/99

- Although the number of poor children in the U.S. has gone down by 3.6 million since its peak in 1993, progress in reducing child poverty has slowed a lot since 1955. Children who remain poor have become poorer in the late 1990s, meaning that the average amount that their families fell below the poverty line rose. Center on Budget and Policy Priorities, 12/1999 and 10/2000

- In 1998 in the U.S., one of the richest countries in the world, 12.7% of the people (34.5 million) lived in poverty–a rate lower than previous years. For the first time since 1980, the poverty rate for children dipped below 19%–to 18.9% (13.5 million). More than one-third of Black and Latino/a children were poor. 55% of children under six living in female-headed households were poor, including 60% of those in Black families and 67% of those in Latino/a families. U.S. Census Bureau, 1998 figures, published 1999

- The number of children living in U.S. families with incomes below one-half of the poverty line rose to 2.7 million in 1997, up by 426,000 from the previous year. Much of this was directly linked to the weakening protective role of cash assistance and especially food stamps. Children's Defense Fund, 8/99

- The percentage of poor children whose families received cash assistance benefits fell from 62% in 1994 to 43% in 1998. Center for Budget and Policy Priorities, 10/99

- Food stamp rolls fell five times faster than poverty between 1995 and 1997. Center on Budget and Policy Priorities

- In 1998, 13.5 million children in the U.S. lived in poverty–one in five. U.S. children are nearly twice as likely as adults to be poor. Children's Defense Fund, website (3/00)

- More than three out of four poor children (78%) live with a family member who worked at least part of the year, up from 61% just six years ago. Children's Defense Fund, 2001

- One out of three poor children (3.8 million) lives in a household where someone is employed full-time. Children's Defense Fund, 2001

- The number of families with children who were poor despite being headed by a full-time, year-round worker in 1999 is the highest in the 25 years for which data exist. Children's Defense Fund, 2001

- From 1997 to 1998, the number of full-time, year-round workers with incomes below the poverty line rose by 459,000. Center on Budget and Policy Priorities, 10/99

* Children make up 38% of the poor but only 26% of the total population. Their poverty rate is higher than that of any other age group. U.S. Census Bureau, 2000

- The base for the federal poverty line was established nearly 50 years ago, based on a government estimate of a minimal food budget and multiplied by three (on the assumption that households spend an average of one-third of their income for food). The level is then adjusted for inflation. The poverty line has continued to decline as a percentage of median income: 43% in 1959, 33% in 1982, 28% in 1998. Were poverty defined more reasonably, like, say, half the median income, a common measure among academic researchers, U.S. poverty rates would be half again to twice as high as they are. US Census Bureau, 1999

- The average poverty threshold for a family of 4: $16,600, for a family of three: $13,003. 25.6% of Hispanics live in poverty, 8.2% of whites, 26.1% of African-Americans, and 12.5% of Asian Pacific Islanders. US Census Bureau, 1999, 1998 figures

- The percentage of people in extreme poverty (less than half of the federal poverty level) in the U.S. rose in 1998 to 5.1%. United for a Fair Economy, 12/99

LACK OF BASICS

- Every day, 30,500 children under age 5 die of mainly preventable causes. UNICEF 2000
- Nearly one billion people are illiterate; over one billion lack access to safe water. United Nations Development Program, *Human Development Report*, 1997
- 23% of the population of Ireland is functionally illiterate. United Nations Development Program, *Human Development Report*, 1999
- From 1975-1997, the life expectancy in developing countries increased from 53 to 62 years and adult literacy rose from 48% to 76%. Under-5 mortality declined from 149 per 1000 live births to 85. United Nations Development Program, *Human Development Report*, 1999
- Since 1960, malnutrition rates have declined by almost one-third and the share of rural families with access to safe water has risen from one-tenth to three-fourths. United Nations Development Program, *Human Development Report*, 1997

- 2.2 million people die each year from indoor pollution, such as burning dung for fuel.
United Nations Development Program, *Human Development Report*, 1998
- About two billion people in developing countries lack access to electricity.
United Nations Development Program, *Human Development Report*, 1998
- In 1999, 15.5% of those in the U.S. (42.6 million) did not have health insurance (a decline from previous years). U.S. Census Bureau, 9/00
- Nearly one-third of the people in the least developed countries–mostly in sub-Saharan Africa –are not expected to survive to age 40. United Nations Development Program, *Human Development Report*, 1997
- The United Nations Development Program estimates that the basic health and nutrition needs of the world's poorest people could be met for an additional $13 billion per year–less than people in the U.S. and Europe spend on pet food. Bread for the World website

Hunger

- If the world's food were fairly distributed, there would be enough available to give everyone 2500 calories per day (200 calories more than minimally necessary).
United Nations Development Program, *Human Development Report*, 1994
- Worldwide, nearly 50% of the deaths of children under age 5 are due to malnutrition.
World Health Organization, 1998
- More than six million children in developing countries die each year, mostly from hunger-related causes. Bread for the World website
- More than 800 million people worldwide are hungry. Bread for the World website, 5/01
- In the U.S., 12 million children live in households where people have to skip meals or eat less to make ends meet. One-tenth of households lives with or is at risk of hunger. Bread for the World website
- The U.S. is the only industrialized country with widespread hunger–31 million people are at risk.
Bread for the World International, *A Program to End Hunger: Hunger 2000*
- 39% of emergency food recipient households (at soup kitchens and food pantries) have at least one adult working. Of these, 49% are employed at least full-time. Second Harvest Food Banks, website
- In 1999, 67% of those who requested emergency food aid in 26 major U.S. cities were employed.
U.S. Conference of Mayors

Homelessness

- At least 2.3 million (and possibly closer to 3.5 million) adults and children (nearly 1% of the U.S. population) are likely to experience homelessness at least once during a year. If you consider only the people living in poverty, the percentage increases to 6.3%. There is high seasonal variety.
Urban Institute, website
- 44% of the nation's homeless have some sort of job. (U.S. Department of Housing and Urban Development 1999) Those who work with the homeless say that this is a growing trend.
- In 30 US cities, children accounted for 25% of the homeless population and unaccompanied minors accounted for 3% of the urban homeless population. U.S. Conference of Mayors, 1998

Women

- At least one-third of the women in the world have been beaten, coerced into sex, or abused.
John Hopkins School of Public Health, Center for Health and Gender Equity, January 2000
- There may be as many as 60 million "missing" women because of gender discrimination.
UNICEF 2000
- Women make up half the world but hold less than 5% of positions of power in determining global economic policy and own only an estimated 1% of global property. Global Exchange, website, 2001
- A woman in the U.S. makes 73.5 cents for every dollar a man makes.
Institute for Women's Policy Research, 1/01

Racism

- The median U.S. Black household income is 60% that of whites; the median Hispanic household income is 67% of white income. United for a Fair Economy, 10/99
- Black men in the U.S. have a 29% chance of serving prison time in their lives; Hispanic men have a 16% chance; white men have a 4% chance. The Sentencing Project, April 2000
- According to a government study, Native Americans are victims of violent crime at a rate that is twice the national average. Unlike crimes committed against other racial groups, 70% of those committing violent crimes against Indians are of a different race. Whites commit 60% of these

crimes. *ColorLines* magazine, Summer 1999
- Public schools became more segregated in the 1990s, undermining the educational prospects of Blacks and Lintino/Latinas. New York Times, July 2001
- In LosAngeles 71% of Blacks and 50% of Latinos/Latinas live in areas with the most polluted air, as opposed to 34% of whites. National Urban League, 1992

ENVIRONMENT

- The burning of fossil fuels has almost quintupled since 1950.
United Nations Development Program, *Human Development Report*, 1998
- The rapid use of fossil fuels released 160 billion tons of carbon into the atmosphere between 1970 and 2000. In comparison, 110 billion tons were released between 1751 and 1970.
Worldwatch Institute, Earth Day Report Card 2000
- Waste generation per capita in industrial countries has increased almost threefold in the past 20 years. United Nations Development Program, *Human Development Report*, 1998
- One-sixth of the world's land area has been degraded as a result of overgrazing and poor farming practices. United Nations Development Program, *Human Development Report*, 1998
- Some 20% of the world's susceptible drylands are affected by human-induced soil degradation, putting the livelihoods of more than one billion people at risk. UN Environmental Program, 2000
- The world's forests, which bind soil, prevent erosion, regulate the water supply, and govern climate, are shrinking. Since 1970, the wooded area per 1000 inhabitants has gone from 7.3 km squared to 1.4 km squared. United Nations Development Program, *Human Development Report*, 1998
- One-fourth of the world's vertebrate species (birds, mammals, reptiles, amphibians, fish) is on the verge of extinction or is now extinct. Worldwatch Institute, Earth Day Report Card 2000
- The world's armed forces are responsible for two-thirds of the gases that have depleted the ozone layer. When a suggestion was put forth that the Earth Summit in Brazil in 1992 consider the effects of the military on environmental degradation, the U.S. delegation objected and the suggestion was defeated. June 1992 Earth Summit environmental conference, Brazil

Appendix C:
Michael Nagler's Steps of Nonviolence
(Effective Peacemaking Action)

1. Awakening nonviolent power

2. Knowing your conflict (development)

3. Choosing clear goals (Distinguish between goals [principles] and strategies [techniques]. Compromise on the latter but never on the former.)

4. Using right means

5. Clinging to the truth

6. Coping with success

7. Building peace: through peace education, reconciliation and healing, constructive programs (Nagler, like Gandhi, stresses constructive programs along with a resistance campaign.)

From Nagler, Michael. "The Steps of Nonviolence." Nyack, NY: Fellowship of Reconciliation, 1999

Appendix D:
Martin Luther King, Jr.'s
Philosophy and Practice of Nonviolence

1. Resists evil and oppression

2. Does not seek to humiliate or defeat but to win friendship and understanding

3. Is an attack on forces of evil rather than the person doing evil

4. Is willing to accept suffering without retaliation

5. Avoids external physical and internal spiritual violence (has an ethic of real love)

6. Maintains a deep faith in the future: the forces of the universe are on the side of justice

Appendix

Appendix E:
Building Blocks of Catholic Social Teaching

1. *The Principle of Human Dignity:*
"Every human being is created in the image of God and redeemed by Jesus Christ, and therefore is invaluable and worthy of respect as a member of the human family."

2. *The Principle of Respect for Human Life:*
"Every person, from the moment of conception to natural death, has inherent dignity and a right to life consistent with that dignity."

3. *The Principle of Association:*
"Our tradition proclaims that the person is not only sacred but also social. How we organize our society–in economics and policies, in law and practice–directly affects human dignity and the capacity of individuals to grow in community."

4. *The Principle of Participation:*
"We believe people have a right and a duty to participate in society, seeking together the common good and well-being of all, especially the poor and vulnerable."

5. *The Principle of Preferential Protection for the Poor and Vulnerable:*
"In a society marred by deepening divisions between the rich and the poor, our tradition recalls the story of the last judgement (Mt. 25:31-46) and instructs us to put the needs of the poor and vulnerable first."

6. *The Principle of Solidarity:*
"Catholic social teaching proclaims that we are our brothers' and sisters' keepers, wherever they live. We are one human family. . .Learning to practice the virtue of solidarity means learning that 'loving our neighbor' has global dimensions in an interdependent world."

7. *The Principle of Stewardship:*
"The Catholic tradition insists that we show our respect for the Creator by our stewardship of creation."

8. *The Principle of Subsidiarity:*
The principle deals chiefly with "the responsibilities and limits of government, and the essential roles of voluntary associations."

9. *The Principle of Human Equality:*
"Equality of all persons comes from their essential dignity. . . While differences in talents are a part of God's plan, social and cultural discrimination in fundamental rights. . .are not compatible with God's design."

10. *The Principle of the Common Good:*
"The common good is understood as the social conditions that allow people to reach their full human potential and to realize their human dignity."

Source: *Building Blocks of Catholic Social Teaching* by William J. Byron, *America*, October 31, 1998.

Appendix F:
Pax Christi USA Vow of Nonviolence

Recognizing the violence in my own heart, yet trusting in the goodness and mercy of God, I vow for one year to practice the nonviolence of Jesus who taught us in the Sermon on the Mount: Blessed are the peacemakers, for they shall be called the sons and daughters of God. . .You have heard how it was said, "You must love your neighbor and hate your enemy," but I say to you, "Love your enemies, and pray for those who persecute you. In this way, you will be daughters and sons of your Creator in heaven."

Before God the Creator and the Sanctifying Spirit, I vow to carry out in my life the love and example of Jesus
• by striving for peace within myself and seeking to be a peacemaker in my daily life;
• by accepting suffering rather than inflicting it;
• by refusing to retaliate in the face of provocation and violence;
• by persevering in nonviolence of tongue and heart;
• by living conscientiously and simply so that I do not deprive others of the means to live;
• by actively resisting evil and working nonviolently to abolish war and the causes of war from my own heart and from the face of the earth.

God, I trust in your sustaining love and believe that just as you gave me the grace and desire to offer this, so you will also bestow abundant grace to fulfill it.

Prayer for a Nonviolent Heart

O Holy Mystery, Creator God, pour into me your Sanctifying Spirit, that I may water the world with the love and example of Jesus.

Help me to strive for peace within, and to make peace in my life this day.

Strengthen me to accept suffering rather than inflict it. In the face of provocation and violence, be my calm.

Preserve me in nonviolence of tongue and heart. Quench my inner violence with your life-giving Word.

Help me drink deeply of the small joys of life. Sustain me in a simple life, so others may simply live.

Energize me to work against injustice and to actively resist evil. Empower me to overcome the sins of racism, sexism, and materialism.

Stream through me to abolish war from my own heart and from the face of the earth. Equip me to build the reign of justice and peace.

O Holy Mystery, Creator God, I trust in your sustaining love and power. I believe that just as you gave me the desire to offer this prayer, so you will also bestow abundant grace to fulfill it.

Amen.

—Adapted by Kathy Schmitt from *The Vow*